Learning to Flourish

Learning to Flourish

A Philosophical Exploration of Liberal Education

DANIEL R. DeNICOLA

continuum

Continuum International Publishing Group
A Bloomsbury company
80 Maiden Lane, Suite 704, New York, NY 10038
50 Bedford Square, London WC1B 3DP

www.continuumbooks.com

© Daniel R. DeNicola, 2012

ISBN: HB: 978-1-4411-5106-3
ISBN: PB: 978-1-4411-1163-0

Library of Congress Cataloging-in-Publication Data
A catalog record for this title is available from the Library of Congress.

Typeset by Fakenham Prepress Solutions, Fakenham, Norfolk NR21 8NN
Printed and bound in the United States of America

CONTENTS

PREFACE AND ACKNOWLEDGMENTS

Sometimes, a book reflects the preoccupation of a lifetime. This is such a book. Liberal education has not only defined the environment in which I have worked, but has also been the focus of much of that work. From one perspective, my experience in liberal education has been deep and broad: as an undergraduate, graduate student, full-time professor, and visiting scholar, my field has been philosophy, especially the philosophy of education; as an alumnus, dean, college vice president, provost, trustee, workshop facilitator, and consultant, I have served in the practical contexts of decision-making and institution-building to articulate a vision of the liberal arts and to enhance programs of liberal education. From another angle, however, my experience is narrow: I have always worked in higher education, never at the pre-college level; my academic appointments have been only in the United States; I have served mostly small, independent, liberal arts colleges, primarily with "traditional" undergraduate students (though I have also had the pleasure of teaching adult undergraduates, graduate students in professional programs, returning adults students in a Masters of Liberal Studies program, and senior academic administrators in professional development programs); and I am privileged to work in a place where the liberal arts thrive.

I present this biographical brief for several reasons. The first is to acknowledge that readers are likely to find both the strengths and (despite my best efforts) the limitations of my experience reflected in this book. It seems better, in the spirit of transparency, to disclose these facts at the outset. Second, I want to affirm that the call to write this book and the ideas it contains have been gestating for many years. Moreover, although it is a philosophical work, a work of educational theory, it also draws upon decades of administrative experience and the labors of educational practice.

The third reason is, frankly, an attempt to gain credibility with those who have a peremptorily negative response to any tract of educational philosophy. "With all the problems facing education today, and especially with the immediate threats to the very survival of the liberal arts," they would say, "why do we need to spend time on airy philosophical ideas?" My answer is that my experience has shown me that philosophy matters, not only in elucidating an institutional or programmatic vision, but even in day-to-day decision-making. "Is it good education?" is an excellent test of every institutional decision. I am not so much suggesting that educators all need to be guided by a pellucid ideal; rather, I am commending the habit of individual and collective philosophical reflection on practice—the clarification of aims and assumptions, the rearticulation of values and commitments, the sharpening of differences, the learning from dialogue, and the opening of a space for innovative possibilities. In that sense, despite the experience distilled here, such a book is finally and inevitably a work in progress, awaiting the distilled experience and critique of others.

This is a work in four parts. Following an Introduction, the two chapters of Part I discuss the confusion of contemporary discourse about liberal education and present a concept of liberal education as a vital tradition of theory and practice. The account is, I hope, sufficiently definitive yet "thin" enough to accommodate many different historical conceptions. Part II consists of five chapters, each of which develops one of the strands or "paradigms" that represent polarities of theory and practice, and that interact to produce much of the dynamism of the tradition. In Part III, I survey some of the core concepts, values, and moral implications of liberal education. Part IV considers both perennial obstacles and contemporary threats to the liberal arts, and then closes with a chapter on the place and prospect of liberal education in the contemporary world. Throughout, I have situated the discussion within the broad realm of ideas created by educators and philosophers and institutions, ranging from Plato to the public, contemporary pronouncements of colleges and universities.

Words of caution: this book is a philosophical exploration. Its purpose is not to prescribe a curriculum, pedagogical methods, or specific forms of institutional practice. And there are, of course, many other things this book is not: a history of education, a polemic on educational policy, a guide for teachers, an administrators' handbook, a diatribe about the current state of education, or a personal memoir. Those looking for such tracts will be disappointed. My approach, however, requires that any adequate educational theory should address educational practice holistically, including the institutional setting, the community of learners, the co-curriculum, and other elements as well as the formal curricular content and methods of instruction. Moreover, I have often taken the perspective of the learner, not only that of the educator.

The first appearance of some of the central ideas and arguments of this book occurred in two recent articles. I have drawn heavily on these pieces; though their formulations have sometimes altered significantly with expansion, a few sentences are repeated verbatim or nearly so. The first is "Liberal Education and Moral Education," which appeared in *Character and Moral Education*, edited by Joseph DeVitis and Tianlong Yu (Peter Lang 2011), 179–92. I am grateful to Joseph DeVitis for the invitation to write the article and to Peter Lang Publishing for permission to draw from that article and to reprint portions of it herein. The second article is "Friends, Foes, and Nel Noddings on Liberal Education." It was delivered to a general session of the Philosophy of Education Society in April 2011, where I benefited greatly from the gracious response of Nel Noddings. That article is forthcoming, along with Noddings' response, in *Philosophy of Education 2011*, edited by Rob Kunzman (Carbondale, IL: PES, 2012).

Intellectual debts accumulate and can never be fully discharged—but they are gifts that can be gratefully acknowledged. In this case, they are imposing indeed, and I am delighted with the opportunity to express publicly my gratitude. To undergraduate mentors Troy Organ, Stanley Grean, and many others at Ohio University; to graduate mentors Israel Scheffler, John Rawls, Roderick Firth, Jane Roland Martin, and many others at Harvard University; to my tolerant and brilliant colleagues in philosophy at Rollins College and Gettysburg College; to the astute professionals with whom I have served in the administration of those colleges; to Thaddeus Seymour (Rollins) and Gordon Haaland (Gettysburg), presidential mentors who gave me both encouragement and scope to do my work; to the many philosophers and friends who must be nameless here, but whose happy crossings of my path I have not forgotten—I express my continuing gratitude and admiration. I thank Gettysburg College, which has supported this work through the Provost's Professional Papers Fund and Faculty Research grants. I also wish to thank my editor, David Barker, and others at the Continuum International Publishing Group, for an incredibly smooth and professional publishing process. My wife, Sunni, to whom I owe everything, takes credit for little and is responsible for so much—including help with the final stages of the text. No one, however, is responsible for any errors, misstatements, and flaws in what follows, except me.

Finally, to my teachers who remained learners, and to my students who have taught me much, I dedicate this book. Surely, one of the powerful continuities of human history is its long, unbroken succession of teachers and students.

Introduction

Education, in its largest sense, is one of the most inexhaustible of all topics ... Education, moreover, is one of the subjects which most essentially require to be considered by various minds, and from a variety of points of view. For, of all many-sided subjects, it is the one which has the greatest number of sides.

JOHN STUART MILL, *INAUGURAL ADDRESS AT ST. ANDREWS*

Thinking philosophically about education is a challenging task. In the first place, there is the daunting issue of theoretical complexity: any philosophical account of education rests on a theory of human nature and points toward interconnected theories of ethics and politics. It is therefore difficult to keep one's thoughts and their exposition clear and focused, as the lines of justification and implication inevitably exert their pull into deeper and broader considerations. Yet those considerations cannot responsibly be ignored. Attempting a thorough-going, house-cleaning foundation-alism—boring down to metaphysical bedrock in order eventually to construct, stone by stone, a grand edifice of systematic educational thought—is neither fashionable nor feasible, at least for me.

Second, the concept of education is now widely agreed to be "essentially contested."[1] This means that "education" is one of those normative, qualitative abstractions like "justice" or "beauty" for which divergent and competing interpretations are continually advanced. While we seem to share a sense of the concept, a core idea, sufficient for its meaningful use in everyday contexts, we disagree ceaselessly about the full-fledged and proper account of the concept, about its "essential" qualities (especially when we try to be philosophically precise). To claim to have the final and definitive account of an essentially contested concept is worse than presumption; it is a logical mistake. Instead, we must recognize that the concept is a notional screen onto which we necessarily project our cultural and personal values and experience. The idea of "education" has a normative gravity; as we try to delineate its features, we are inexorably drawn toward our sense of "education proper," or "an education worthy of the name," and the resultant interpretation is forever open to discussion and debate. The long, distinguished history of such interpretations is always vitally present, a moraine of ideas and images.

This is true *a fortiori* for "liberal education." The concept has disputed origins and a history of freighted interpretations as a distinctive type of education, but sometimes advocacy seems to have stretched the term to mean simply "a *good* education"—an example of what the philosopher Kwame Anthony Appiah has called "conceptual mission creep"[2] inflated by aggressive marketing. Moreover, there is the inherent and subtle connection of the concept with others like "liberalism" and "liberty"—which are also essentially contested in vast literatures of their own.

Third, philosophizing about education *at this time* offers additional challenges. One historian of liberal education has characterized our contemporary intellectual outlook as "named by prefixes: post-, meta-, neo-, anti-, and de-." He continues, "These prefixes and the associated adjective 'critical' signify that these movements are defined in terms of some other view, beyond, after, away, against which they claim to stand. In this way, the current movements define themselves in terms of some other viewpoint from which they seek to break away."[3] It is as though we are now living through a kind of intellectual post-traumatic stress syndrome after colonialism and the horrific violence of the twentieth century. Among the casualties are many of the ideas that long have been essential to influential thinking about education. Reason, objectivity, and indeed truth itself seem now to be deflated or tainted ideas; we grasp instead for the resurgent ideas of will, subjectivity, and narrative interpretations. Universality is a futile standard, because there is no "human nature." The freed and heroic individual, a center of autonomy and responsibility, has been dissected and revealed to be a creature of biology, culture, and group identity. Indeed, these concepts, all fundamental to most historic theories of education, are deconstructed as so much intellectual hypocrisy, veiled attempts at hegemony, stained with racism, sexism, classism—a colonialism of the mind. What can one expect to weave from such tatters? What can one hope to construct when we are left, as it were, with only poisoned wells, broken tools, and dirty hands?

Yet another source of challenge is the fact that education is a complicated and cooperative human enterprise, dominated by its bureaucratized forms (schools), dispersed among various roles (teachers, students, administrators, counselors, etc.), stratified by academic levels, partitioned into modules (lessons, courses, and degrees), and influenced by a variety of stakeholders (parents, policy-makers, employers, etc.). Furthermore, there is great diversity in the pattern of these elements among the nations, and remarkably so within the United States. Educational thinking and writing has tended to follow suit: it is stratified by academic level, each with its distinctive vocabulary and concerns; it is written from a single perspective, such as teacher or student or taxpayer; and it frequently sacrifices theoretical concerns in favor, ironically, of complaints, demands for accountability, and calls for reform. This is by no means all there is, of course: there is a fine body of technical, philosophical writing about education that gains little public notice; there are many vivid, inspirational narratives of teaching and learning; there is exciting and illuminating research on the neurological bases and styles of learning; there are engaging and helpful discussions of alternative teaching methods—but the vitality, impact, and incandescence all seem to fade as soon as we struggle for a more comprehensive, synoptic viewpoint. In short, it is difficult to integrate the insights of abstract, "top-down" thinking with the vivid particulars of "bottom-up" thinking when dealing with so complex a human enterprise.

Obviously, it is not my intent to abandon the adventure, nor do I intend to add to the discouragement, because of this challenging context. If the concept of education is theoretically complex and essentially contested, then it is also intellectually arable and culturally significant. As to the postmodern critiques, many are instructive if not edifying, and they must be addressed; but many strands of postmodernism have—to this point, at least—deconstructed more than they have created, and some are perilously close to undermining themselves, their proponents arguing themselves into a lonely corner in which they are bereft of all motive for utterance, and we of any reason to listen. Harassed into that corner, left only to grotesquerie, the concept of education dies. In any event, our postmodern fever may have broken—there are signs of restlessness and frustration with the most self-undermining of the critiques—and the possibility for moving on or even for genuine advancement is in the air. But whatever the situation (and we shall return to these issues later), it seems important to think deeply about education. We have only what we have to work with; so we must pick up our tools, duly mindful of their defects, and begin.

Education is, after all, a human endeavor that is built on hope. Oriented to the future and enabled by the sense of individual potential, education requires and enhances a sense of bright possibility. It is what Jonathan Lear has called (in a different context) "a radical hope": "What makes this hope *radical* is that it is directed toward a future goodness that transcends the current ability to understand what it is. Radical hope anticipates a good for which those who have the hope as yet lack the appropriate concepts with which to understand it." It arises within ignorance, but it is not *of* ignorance—otherwise, such a hope would simply be a form of wishful thinking. It is *of* our moral imagination.[4]

And we pin our hopes on that hope: it is, indeed, our first and final hope, the hope of shining promise and the hope of last resort. Beginning anew in unfamiliar lands, settlers, immigrants, and colonists quickly turn to the building of schools or the provision for instruction, planting their flag in the future. But when the all-too-familiar social and political scene leaves us in despair, better education may be our one remaining hope for social redemption— as it was for Plato, when he despaired for Athens and turned to the work of his Academy in the hope that he could inspire wisdom in some of the young who might eventually have power. In a secular age, education supplants religion as the path to salvation. Yet there are many ways to snuff out hope and asphyxiate education: not only the usual sources of cynicism and disillusionment, of which there are all too many, but also having excessive expectations. Our American propensity to burden our public schools with providing a direct solution to social problems—poverty, hunger, familial dysfunction, parental abdication, and so on—whether it actually reflects excessive expectation or irresponsible deflections from other social institutions, has continued despite rising public concern about educational quality. In higher education, the expansion of expectations has led inexorably to expanded facilities, enhanced services, and higher costs—consequential institutional alterations.

As we begin, it will be helpful to distinguish some key terms, the broadest of which is "learning." "Learning" is a generic term that, in its unreconstructed and most generous usage, designates the various processes by which an individual acquires knowledge, skills, affects, attitudes, dispositions, and behavior, along with the resulting cognitive and evaluative structures that may emerge. Learning may be intentional or unintentional, conscious or unconscious, formal or informal.[5] "Education," as I use the term, refers to a structured and multi-purpose program of learning, designed and presented intentionally, though we should be attentive to the inevitable unintended learning that results in consequence of such a program. (In a later chapter, I will reflect on the value of a wider use of the term, as well as its distinction from "training.") "Schooling" refers to institutionalized education, and especially to those formal and sequenced programs of learning offered through schools of various kinds. It is possible for one to learn outside schooling, which is, in fact, a universal experience; it is also possible to engage in education outside schooling, though that is a much rarer experience. John Stuart Mill, for example, whose address upon being elected Rector of St. Andrew's University is quoted as the epigraph of this Introduction, was a person of dazzling learning whose remarkable education was achieved without any schooling whatsoever; although he was never a student in any classroom, his "home schooling" under the guidance of his father is the stuff of legend.[6] All three may refer either to a process or to its product: for example, "education" may refer to a process one pursues or undergoes, or to the education one "has." The qualifier "liberal" or "liberal arts" may be applied to all three of these terms and, putatively, indicates a distinctive type of learning, education, or schooling. (I will use "liberal education" and "liberal arts education" interchangeably unless and until differences in nuance become relevant.) Consider these terminological stipulations to be provisional, because their implications will resurface at later points.

The focus of this work is liberal education, so it will be important to identify its distinctiveness from other types of education; nevertheless, our discussion is bound to proceed within the context of education *tout court*. Our topic is not educational institutions, but we shall need to be alert to the ways in which schools may embody or distort educational ideals. Whether institutionalized or not, however, education as defined here links the intentions and plans of educators with the activities of students. (Let us ignore, for the moment, the question of whether an autodidact cannot only learn by teaching himself, but can plan and successfully undergo his own education.) This means that all education, liberal education included, involves the emplacement—the imposition, if you prefer—of the plans of purportedly qualified or authorized agents upon the time and efforts of others. Education is, however, a paternalism that aims at its own undoing, beginning with compulsory or at least unchosen educational experiences and moving to milder forms that blend the voluntary (academic tracks, course selection, institutional choice, etc.) with the required (course and degree requirements, mandatory credentialing, etc.). Any valid account of education must honor this intersection of interests and intentions, an intersection that can become congruence, harmony, or collision; it must acknowledge its risks as well as its imperatives. Education is, in short, an asymmetrical interaction between human beings, but an interaction of an odd sort, because it works to undo the otherwise lasting causes of its asymmetry.

These, then, are but some aspects of the context within which we must work: contested and complex concepts; the challenges of postmodernism; the multifaceted, layered, and diverse forms of institutionalization; the unique, fading nature of its paternalism; its essential hopefulness. We will discover more along the way, including the way in which education itself responds to—and reshapes—its context. Education is, as Mill states, a "many-sided" subject, requiring "to be considered by various minds, and from a variety of points of view." To that end, I will draw upon ancient and contemporary sources, and many in between. But in our exploration of liberal education, there is a sort of extreme argument that I will summarily reject—as soon as it is detected. In general, these are arguments that drive us to dead-ends, philosophical culs-de-sac from which any relevant constructive claim becomes impossible. For example, the argument that no one is entitled to impose an educational agenda on anyone else, to presume to decide what it is best that someone else learn, when advanced in an extreme version, not only rules out typical educational programming but undercuts adult, especially parental, responsibilities for children. That sort of argument is a non-starter if our aim is to understand liberal education. The same is the case for arguments that support a nihilist position in which no valid normative comparison of claims can be made, in which no assertion is importantly better than any other—plus here we should also note the implosion that its self-reference would cause. Finally, we should keep in mind that there is a gap between arguments *against* forms of education, anguish about negative effects, critiques of practice, however thorough-going, and arguments *for* ignorance. While there is much to be said for ignorance, this will not be the place to say it. My presumption here will be that the burden of argument is on claims for willful ignorance, claims to restrict or prevent education, and not on the claim that education—in some form(s) yet to be specified—is generally a good thing. We now turn to the form that is our focus: liberal education.

Notes

1 The term was introduced by Walter Bryce Gallie in "Essentially Contested Concepts," *Proceedings of the Aristotelian Society* 56 (1956): 167–98. The debate among different interpretations in these "essentially contested" cases cannot be settled by empirical research, by logical analysis, or by reference to patterns of ordinary language usage. I should acknowledge that there is now an extensive literature derived from Gallie's term, and the term is in danger of being self-referential.

2 Kwame Anthony Appiah, *The Ethics of Identity* (Princeton, NJ: Princeton University Press, 2005), 38. Appiah introduces the metaphor in his discussion of autonomy—a topic to be taken up in chapter 8.

3 Bruce Kimball continues prophetically: "This definitional strategy reveals what will someday be seen as the adolescence of recent thinking—the fierce desire to break away and become independent, coupled with a limited capacity to do so." He alerts us that we should beware the integrity of such thinking, since "the blatant desire to

move beyond, after, away, or against something is bound to skew the account of that thing ..." Quoted from Kimball's homonymously titled opening essay in *The Condition of American Liberal Education: Pragmatism and a Changing Tradition,* ed. Robert Orrill (New York: The College Board, 1995), 49–50.

4 Jonathan Lear, *Radical Hope: Ethics in the Face of Cultural Devastation* (Cambridge, MA: Harvard University Press, 2008), 103.

5 For a richer discussion of learning, see Peter Jarvis, *Towards a Comprehensive Theory of Human Learning* (London: Routledge, 2006).

6 See John Stuart Mill, *Autobiography* (1873), in *The Collected Works of John Stuart Mill, Vol. 1,* ed. John M. Robson and Jack Stillinger (Toronto: University of Toronto Press, 1967).

PART I

Toward a Theory of Liberal Education

1

Mixed Messages
and False Starts

*You cannot go anywhere without hearing a buzz of more
or less confused and contradictory talk on this subject
[liberal education].*

T. H. HUXLEY, "A LIBERAL EDUCATION AND WHERE TO FIND IT"

*What is a liberal arts education? How does it differ from other
forms of learning? What are its place, its value, and its prospects in
the contemporary world?*

Anyone who entertains such questions today—and they are
our questions at hand—encounters mixed messages and receives
conflicting responses. There are, of course, many eloquent articula-
tions of the ideal of liberal education, and there is ample positive,
celebratory rhetoric of achievement and prestige promulgated by
its advocates. But they coexist with a negative discourse: the jibes
of popular culture, dire warnings of degradation and demise, and
sophisticated scholarly critiques. The Association of American
Colleges and Universities proclaims that "The spirit and value
of liberal learning are equally relevant to all forms of higher
education and to all students," and "liberal learning is society's best
investment in our shared future."[1] In contrast, however, prominent

educational and ethical theorist, Nel Noddings, contrarily asserts "straight-out" that liberal learning is "a false ideal for universal education." It is not the best education for everyone, and moreover, "liberal education as it is now defined is not the best education for anyone."[2] Worse yet, at the low end of popular culture where once-snappy quips become clichés on T-shirts, mugs, and bumper stickers, one finds this: "I have a degree in liberal arts. Do you want fries with that?"

The situation is more a discord than a dialogue, for although all these voices seem confident in their grasp of liberal education, their conceptions are often quite divergent. The dissonance can be especially troubling to students and their parents, generating confusion and acute anguish as they confront fateful, educational choices: choosing the appropriate "track" in a secondary school curriculum, the ideal college, the best program, or the right major. And the dissonance afflicts educators as well: those who teach, advise, or administer sometimes harbor uncertainty or confusion about these questions regarding liberal education; they work at cross-purposes and may even misguide their students, however unintentionally. Occasionally, someone will conclude that "liberal arts education" has become such a freighted term that we should abandon it altogether.

What are we to make of this discord? Can the fundamental questions about liberal education be answered or even addressed clearly? Might a philosophical approach to the issues be of help? For some—not those most likely to be readers of this book—the value of a philosophical approach is dubious, for we live in a world that is increasingly impatient with theory. I can, however, offer three reasons for thinking that taking such an approach might be useful, even necessary. First, whenever discourse is so discordant, it is likely that a contributing factor is conceptual confusion or incongruence, and it is a basic aim of philosophy to clarify concepts—a task for which it has forged many helpful tools. Second, liberal education is broadly understood to embody a "philosophy of education," so explicating it carefully will inevitably require philosophical work. Third, philosophers themselves have contributed to the dissonance, and indeed many of the deeper issues and genuine disagreements behind the mixed messages are philosophical in character.

What I propose, therefore, is to undertake a philosophical exploration of liberal education. Rather than simply plumping for "the correct view," I want to develop a way to explain and clarify the differences in viewpoint, or at least a way to organize the conflicting claims. I hope, within this frame, to explicate the distinctiveness of liberal education, its dynamism, and its diversity; to examine and evaluate major lines of criticism; and to elucidate its vulnerability and its promise. Ultimately, I will offer a contemporary synthesis of the nature and value of liberal education. These are, I admit, embarrassingly ambitious goals, yet in this situation (as in most others), it seems wise to begin humbly: first, we need to listen more closely to the din, discerning patterns of disagreement in contemporary discourse.

The Champions of Liberal Education

The positive view is very positive indeed: liberal education seems to be the gold standard, the most valuable form of education. At the level of theory, it has a long line of distinguished and articulate champions: such thinkers as John Henry Newman, Mortimer Adler, Michael Oakeshott, Charles Bailey, and Martha Nussbaum, have written influential, visionary tracts that defend and commend liberal education.[3] Its perceived worth is reflected in the ever-greater inclusivity advocated and established, both in the movement to extend liberal education to all and in the desire to include all within the greater scope and diversity of its content. As a practice, it is widely institutionalized in several forms in the various strata of schooling, being most prominent (and often required) in late secondary and undergraduate programs. An exemplary form, an institution developed in the United States, is the free-standing liberal arts college. Today, elite liberal arts colleges thrive across the land, admitting only a fraction of applicants, balancing hefty tuition fees with generous scholarships, concentrating on enriched undergraduate programs in the liberal arts, and projecting prestige and privilege. They describe themselves in mission statements, websites, admissions brochures, and public ceremonies, as offering a venerable but contemporary, intellectually challenging, skill-enhancing, character-building, life-altering, educational experience. "The most versatile, the most durable, in an ultimate sense, the most practical knowledge and intellectual resources that we can offer students are the openness, creativity, flexibility, and power of education in the liberal arts"[4]—so declares Williams College in a statement that exemplifies this group. These colleges evince and extol the success of their alumni—and they have indeed produced a disproportionately large share of successful scientists, writers, academics, and CEOs.[5] Liberal education is, professedly, the commanding concern of these small colleges, which number in the hundreds in America, though many, especially the less elite among them, struggle to retain their liberal arts focus. Judging them simply as businesses, however, these colleges are, in general, remarkably successful enterprises, typically surviving for over a century already.[6] (Gettysburg College, for example, where I now teach, was founded in 1832, has had only one name change—from "Pennsylvania College"—and has not had a deficit year within memory, perhaps ever. Few business corporations can claim such a record.)

But excellent liberal education is not confined to those distinctive liberal arts colleges. Historic European universities all developed from and within a liberal arts heritage. In the United States, major research universities—some of which grew up around historic liberal arts colleges (Harvard University, for example), and others which were founded as universities with several educational purposes (such as land-grant universities)—offer degrees in the liberal arts (both under-graduate and graduate) and often work to retain or embody attractive aspects of the small liberal arts colleges despite their difference in scale. Many states have designated one or more institutions as "public liberal arts universities"; they offer at least an emphasis on liberal arts programming and some have fully taken on the character of liberal arts colleges, but are subject to state budgeting and governance. Moreover, most contemporary universities endorse the essential worth of liberal learning by requiring every undergraduate student, regardless of area of study, to have some "exposure" to the liberal arts (truncated, of course, within a "university college" or in components of the degree known collectively as "general education"). No doubt, the level of genuine commitment to liberal learning varies among universities, but it is probably a safe generalization to say that the more influential and prestigious the university, the stronger the liberal arts ethos on its campus.[7] And it is revealing that nearly all such institutions feel the need to display at least some pretense of the endorsement of liberal education.

Immediately after the collapse of the Soviet Union, there was a surge of interest in liberal education within former Soviet-bloc nations. Study in the liberal arts was identified with the apparent triumph of Western democracies. It seemed to empower individuals, to value critical thinking, self-expression, and debate; it was associated with freedom. It was the antithesis of the Soviet-era education, which was didactic, authoritarian, utilitarian, and technical. Reformers seemed undaunted by the challenges of such a shift, which would require significant and difficult changes not only in curriculum, but in pedagogy, in the expectations of students, and in institutional ethos. Not only in Eastern Europe, but also in progressive locations in Asia and Africa, the desire swelled to establish education in the liberal arts.[8] (Ironically, the world seemed to be embracing liberal education just as, in the West—especially in Britain and the United States—the criticism and concern about liberal education were becoming strident.) In many places, it seemed easier to establish new institutions than to transform existing ones, and a host of aspiring liberal arts institutions—schools, colleges, universities, and programs—was launched. These fledglings have had varying fortunes in the last decade, but a particularly successful and interesting example is the European College of Liberal Arts (ECLA), located in Berlin. With substantial assistance from an American foundation, ECLA has become a state-recognized private university with an international student body, offering "a new form of liberal education" that is "dedicated to an integrated study of values."[9] Liberal education seems, in short, to reflect aspirations of free people around the globe, for themselves as individuals and for their nations.

Years before college, moreover, most pupils in developed countries hear the positive rhetoric about liberal education. Very young pupils are taught basic skills and foundational knowledge, which, in subsequent years, undergird a prescribed curriculum that likely includes mathematics, literature, social and natural sciences, and—if they survive school budget pressures—the arts. The official rationale for such requirements may invoke informed citizenship, the needs of the nation, and preparation for college—but they are most often presented as a liberal arts curriculum. "Pre-college" tracks and special honors opportunities, such as Advanced Placement courses and International Baccalaureate degrees, aim at refining and accelerating liberal learning. In short, the educational establishment, whether governmental or independent, whether at the introductory or advanced levels, seems to say that liberal education is both fundamental and preeminent. Within this positive rhetoric, however, even a sympathetic observer might notice what appear to be puzzling contradictions or inconsistencies—though perhaps they are only superficial. Is liberal education for elite intellectuals, or is it essential for every democratic citizen? Does it celebrate learning that is of intrinsic value ("knowledge for its own sake" and "learning for the sheer love of learning"), or is liberal education immensely practical, invaluable because of the powerful and transferable skills it develops (such as critical thinking and effective communication)? Is it about the life of the mind or the crafting of character—or is there in some way an academic fusion of the intellectual and the moral? Is liberal education a foundational preparation for more advanced, professional study; or is it essentially a life-long learning? Even if they do not mark outright contradictions, such questions encapsulate perplexing divergences or creative tensions among the affirmations of liberal arts advocates. They suggest an agenda for examination.

And then there are the critics.

Worried Friends, Ardent Reformers, and Radical Foes

Critics of liberal education have been a boon to publishers since at least the 1980s, issuing a barrage of books and articles that range from the scholarly and philosophical to the polemical and slogan-eering. To get some sense of this expansive literature, it is useful to make an initial partitioning by distinguishing two types: critiques of practice and critiques of theory.

I will call the first type "narratives of decline."[10] In general, these works are written by worried friends of the liberal arts, people who believe that the ideal of liberal education is sound, but we are every-where failing to live up to it. They decry performance gaps: failures, degradations, corruptions, or perversions of the ideal in current practice. The impulsive retort, of course, is to cite the fact that any complex, institutionalized, normative practice will frequently display regrettable, even shocking, gaps in performance—think of the systems of criminal justice or health care. Alas, sound theory does not ensure excellent practice! But that response is insufficient, because these critics discern *widespread* and *systemic* degradations of performance, sounding the alarm by means of jeremiads, and ultimately aiming to motivate readers to reform practice. Many do indeed write prophetically and often apocalyptically: their critiques are torn between the dramatic recital of the sins of current practice and the pleadings to return to a salvational ideal of liberal education, to which ideal we are enjoined to keep faith henceforth. Frequently, they write nostalgically, as though there were a "golden age" which once manifested their ideal of liberal education, and many trace from there the melancholy history of decline. In the end, however, these critiques are calls to repent, to mend, to correct and reform; they are not strikes against liberal education itself. One might deplore widespread failures in our criminal justice system, for example, but that would not discredit the ideal of justice—on the contrary, to decry performance gaps or to be outraged over a decline is to *endorse* or *reaffirm* the value of the ideal.

Interestingly, these despairing loyalists often disagree about the causes of the perceived decline and its symptoms; they also differ in the particular ideal of liberal education they elevate. Their diversity can be illustrated with even a small sampling of this large genre; often the title or subtitle alone conveys their asserted etiology, prognosis, or remedy—and the cumulative effect of such an admonitory list is distressing and depressing. One of the earliest (1987) and most frequently cited works in this category is *The Closing of the American Mind: How Higher Education Has Failed Democracy and Impoverished the Souls of Today's Students*, by the late philosopher and classicist, Allan Bloom. Bloom has many targets of blame, from curricular innovations to rock music, but summatively his charge seems to be a loss of educational focus and fading commitment to perennial values and high standards for learning and scholarship. Harry Lewis, former dean of Harvard College, neatly condenses his diagnosis in his critique's title: *Excellence Without a Soul: Does Liberal Education Have a Future?* He finds liberal education today both morally and intellectually incoherent. Anthony T. Kronman, professor and former dean of Yale Law School, in *Education's End: Why Our Colleges and*

Universities Have Given Up on the Meaning of Life, pinpoints the invasion and metastasis of the German scientific model of education with its research ethos as the problem. And Victor E. Ferrall, Jr., former president of Beloit College, in *Liberal Arts at the Brink*, observes that the increasing demand for career credentials has driven institutions toward vocational training, alarmingly displacing the liberal arts. What these critics share is a sense that the mission of liberal education is being perverted, displaced, or abandoned.[11] But notice that the ideal of liberal education is the touchstone for these critics, not the target. Or perhaps I should say, *an* ideal, since their particular visions of liberal education differ: the key ideas range from a study of the Great Books to character education, from critical thinking to learning for its own sake, from disciplinary depth to the integration of knowledge, from scholarship to leadership—and the possibilities abound.

Now liberal education does, indeed, confront serious threats (we will examine some of the most toxic trends in Part IV), so I do not mean to belittle these prophetic voices. Nonetheless, I find I am often reluctant to embrace such anxious friends, either because of their anxiety—I may dispute their diagnosis or the supposed scale of the problem—or because of doubts about their genuine "friendship"—I may reject the particular interpretation of the liberal education they elevate. Sometimes, they make their gloomy case only by willfully ignoring the successful exemplars of liberal education that arise around them in each year's graduating class. These critics, often with experience at distinguished institutions, must surely encounter students who are models of an education-in-process in the liberal arts. But let's not whistle in the dark: liberal education may thrive in some places and survive in others, but a wholly different enterprise of higher education has grown up around it; the portion of students who earn college degrees in the liberal arts— once, essentially everyone—has now dwindled to a modest fraction.[12]

Of greater philosophical concern, however, are the critics in the second group: they argue that it is the ideal of liberal education itself that is problematic. Some straightforwardly, often sarcastically, dismiss the liberal arts as an impractical luxury, an injudicious waste of time and money that does not lead to worldly success. (Remember the T-shirt slogan?) These critics—among them many fretful parents—focus on the indices of income, career, and useful skills; they are not moved by claims of intrinsic value and transformative experiences. Their all-too-familiar concerns seem to increase in validity with each level of learning, becoming most trenchant at the graduate level; but they are currently (and historically) a formidable force at the undergraduate level as well. This is by no means a new critique; it has echoed from the ancients. In our era, however, when the costs of education and the lingering debt that often results are very high, the concern for the literal "cash value" of liberal education increases, and arguments about its practical advantages become more acute. While it may be possible to answer these critiques (and I will try later on), there is an underlying sense that this position is more an attitude than an argument. And an attitude is more difficult to rebut. It is likely to reflect values as much as evidence. One can choose to disparage such detractors as anti-intellectual, utilitarian, shallow, or even cynical, and undoubtedly that is true for some commentators. But as a blanket assessment, that disparagement is unfair; it misses much in its insensitivity. The fact is that one's life prospects are certainly understandable, legitimate concerns; and it is true that some accounts of liberal education frankly demean any form of life outside the academy. We need to be more thoughtful about whose attitude is questionable.

There are academic critics in this second group as well. Their critiques take aim, not at performance gaps nor at impracticality, but at theory. Ironically, they are likely to be concerned that liberal education *does* have practical effects: harmful effects that are traceable to the theory itself. These thinkers work from a diversity of perspectives—postmodernism, deconstructionism, feminist theory, critical theory, among others—but they commonly employ what the philosopher Paul Ricoeur has called a "hermeneutics of suspicion," a strategy or stance of interpretation in which venerable concepts, theories or belief systems are shown to disguise dubious and disreputable origins, motives, and functions.[13] Various critics have revealed arrogant colonialism, insouciant elitism, fatuous essentialism, entrenched sexism, and other evils to be inherent in the ideal of liberal education. Provocative revelation is often where these incisive analyses end; if and when they turn to constructive proposals, however, whatever the basis and charge of their critiques, these critics advocate something very different, not a faithful recommitment to a tarnished ideal. They comprise a group of reformist and radical theorists, and their proposals form a catalogue that ranges from a prosthetic supplement to liberal arts education to its wholesale replacement with a distinctly different paradigm.

For illustrative purposes, let me highlight one constructive thread of such critiques: those grounded in feminist theory. In the early 1980s, Jane Roland Martin, a prominent philosopher of education, showed that the voices and experience of women had largely been absent from traditional conceptions of liberal education and declared that women should "reclaim the conversation" and "change the educational landscape." More specifically, noting the curiously undeveloped "ideal of the educated woman," she proposed a vision of education that is "gender-sensitive." In a series of influential works since then, she has also called for a wariness of education's potential for transformative harm as well as for good, and an awareness of its cultural (rather than merely institutional) breadth.[14] A careful study of Martin's work, along with the liberal arts visions of John Henry Newman and Mortimer Adler, recently led philosopher D. G. Mulcahy to offer "a new paradigm for liberal education": one that is recentered on "preparing students to deal with the major demands of everyday living."[15] Nel Noddings, whose negative judgment of liberal education I cited earlier, argues "that liberal education (defined as a set of traditional disciplines) is an outmoded and dangerous model of education for today's young." Implicitly addressing the secondary school environment, she explains that she is not attacking the disciplines as such, but rather her argument is directed:

> ... first, against an ideology of control that forces all students to study a particular, narrowly prescribed curriculum devoid of content they might truly care about. Second, it is an argument in favor of greater respect for a wonderful range of human capacities now largely ignored in schools. Third, it is an argument against the persistent undervaluing of skills, attitudes, and capacities traditionally associated with women.[16]

What Noddings proposes, in addition to reversing these faults, is for the curriculum to embrace the aim of happiness and to nurture the capacity to care.

A very different sort of critique and reform is offered by Carl Bereiter, educator and psychologist, in "Liberal Education in a Knowledge Society," a keynote essay published with a set of largely supportive responses.[17] The explosion of knowledge and the shape of the future are his motivating concerns. He is worried that "liberal education today is embroiled in serious controversy about *what* cultural objects, representing *whose* culture, are to figure in the curriculum." Even more, he is fearful that decisions reflecting well-intentioned multiculturalism will "exclude students from enculturation into a cosmopolitan world" of ideas, abstract concepts, and theories. Bereiter proposes a radical revision in which knowledge is taken as a form of productive work, learning is research, and the classroom becomes similar to "industrial laboratories" and "university research centers" in constructing knowledge. The objective and universalist scientific ideal of a community of inquirers can, he argues, lead us from being trapped in divisive identities.

These summaries are undoubtedly so concise that they verge on the simplistic, but they are intended to be illustrative, not definitive. Many such probative critiques are elaborated in a vast literature of articles and books that have deep theoretical underpinnings, and it is just not possible to address fully all of the various criticisms and proposals with the care they deserve—although we will address major lines of criticism in developing the ideas of later chapters. I do, however, think we can make considerable headway now by identifying some family resemblances among the critiques, a few of which are troublesome. What one may conclude about liberal education, even from the most effective of these arguments, will be at issue.

Initial Thoughts on Reformist and Radical Critiques

What follows in this section are my initial responses to the second group of critics, those who seek to reform or replace the ideal of liberal education. They are quite general, unsupported here by any careful explication of specific texts. (Examples will be discussed as the issues become relevant in later chapters.) They are intended as observations about a range of discourse, to help us come to grips with various critiques, and to point the way to a more adequate understanding of liberal education. Their point is not to reject reform or bolster the status quo; in fact, I think many among these critics have made persuasive cases, and my own account will ultimately accent the need for continual reform. Rather, these comments caution against certain fallacies of analysis and limn the justified range of the impact of certain critical arguments.

(1) I have already noted one family resemblance among current reformist and radical critiques of liberal education: they draw upon a "hermeneutics of suspicion." That is not a flaw, of course, but it does carry the implication that liberal education is only one of a set of interrelated concepts or ideals that suspicious critics are likely to question, reject, or reconstruct. Such intertwined concepts as liberalism, autonomy, authority, humanity (or human nature), democracy, the idea of a canon of great texts, objectivity, rationality—even education itself—may either become related targets or vulnerable to collateral damage. These critiques, I must again emphasize, cannot be dismissed out of hand; but despite their sophisticated analyses, perceptive insights, and iconoclastic subversion, I approach them warily. For some postmodernists, what begins as an exercise of critical thinking in search of the truth leads to apparent delight in the deconstructed ruination about them. Unmasking is all the rage, but when it threatens to leave us with no normative concepts, no authority—just power and the phenomena it may generate—it becomes a philosophical dead end. That won't do for educational theory or practice, which are inherently normative. Nonetheless, the main and modest point here is that many postmodernist critiques are ultimately directed at the intellectual underpinnings of liberal education, at the web of ideas of which liberal education is one, but only one, potent instantiation. Tugging at one strand threatens to unravel a surprisingly large portion of our intellectual fabric.

(2) Another common feature is that these critiques are premised, explicitly or implicitly, on some particular, influential conception of liberal education (like that of John Henry Newman, the cardinal whose nineteenth-century discourses on university education are classics, or Robert Hutchins, the controversial educator who founded the "Great Books Program") or on a particular historical institutionalization of liberal education (like the Victorian-era university or contemporary programs of general education). The critic has in mind and draws upon a specific thinker or model as a

foil for the critique. This natural and legitimate strategy becomes problematic when the critic takes (or mistakes) a particular conception for the concept itself,[18] and concludes expansively that the concept of liberal education has been discredited. It is as though one were to criticize the theory of justice developed by Aristotle or John Rawls and conclude briskly that the concept of justice itself is defective. (Or, to use a biological analogy, it is to mistake the phenotype for the genotype.) This fallacious move would be obvious if the targeted conception was clearly out of date—if one were to critique the medieval version of *artes liberales*, for example, and proceed to claim, therefore, that liberal education is (for all time) a misguided ideal. But the error is less overt if the critic believes, or leads us to believe, that what is targeted is in fact *the* timeless ideal of liberal education. Yes, it is ironic that some critics who charge liberal education with essentialism, assume they are targeting the essence of liberal education. One *may*, of course, mount the more ambitious argument and argue that the concept itself is flawed—by showing it to be incoherent, for example, or claiming that no workable conception is possible, or that it has inherent moral deficiencies—and in making such an argument, one might even need to adduce prominent examples or "particular conceptions" as cases in point. But any such argument would need to aim higher and have a different target, content, and structure.

(3) If it is a mistake to equate the concept of liberal education with one of its conceptions or iterations, it is also egregious to reduce it to a specific curriculum or pedagogy—or even to a theory of curriculum or pedagogy. Liberal education is more than the *trivium* and *quadrivium* of the medieval university or the Great Books Program, more than Oxbridge tutorials or the University of Chicago's Committee on Social Thought, though these are among its famous manifestations. If one equates liberal education with the Great Books model or a set of traditional disciplines (as Nel Noddings, for example, has[19]), one's conclusions, however well argued, most likely have import only for that specific curriculum and not for liberal education generally. As we shall see, there is a relationship between various curricula or pedagogies and liberal education—but it is not one of identity.

(4) Many critics, perhaps because of the conceptual reductions just described, are often led to another mistake: they restrict their view of liberal education to the classroom only—to

instruction—and ignore other aspects of the educational situation. But liberal education is always situational, shaded by place and time, and its educational impact is shaped by a community of learners, a co-curriculum, a "hidden curriculum," and an institutional context—as well as by what transpires in classrooms and laboratories. These aspects are not fixed ideals either; they, too, develop and change in response to many factors—but they are relevant, even indispensible, to a holistic understanding of liberal education. Today, a liberal education frequently involves experiential, collaborative, and service learning; the boundaries of the classroom have become increasingly porous as, enabled by technology, classes have evolved into 24/7 learning communities. Any adequate understanding of liberal education must incorporate these complements to classroom instruction, especially if we are to honor the perspective of the learner as well as the teacher. They are as salient as the globalization of the curriculum or the evolution of the canon, and they are especially relevant to the understanding of moral education within a liberal arts context.

(5) Most disturbing, I find many critiques of liberal education to be self-refuting—not in a formal, logical sense, but in an existential sense: a refutation of the self. Most critics of liberal education are drawing upon their own liberal learning—it seems undeniable—to attack the ideal of liberal education. My argument here is not *ad hominem*—at least not in the familiar sense. What I mean is that it is truly the critics' own liberal education that has enabled the substance, acuity, and eloquence of their complaints—and thereby it belies them. More than a disheartening ingratitude, more than a sophisticated self-deception, this amounts to an educated refutation of one's own education, an *alma matricide*.

Truisms, False Starts, and Promising Leads

Even this brief overview of contemporary discourse about liberal education suggests that an important advancement would be to frame the concept of liberal education as distinct from its conceptions, or perhaps a meta-theory vis-à-vis first-order theories. To return to the comparison with justice, this would be like framing the concept of justice itself, as distinct from the various conceptions, interpretations, or theories of justice, such as are offered by Aristotle or John Stuart Mill or John Rawls. But is such a partition feasible? Isn't this just where the point that "liberal education" is "an essentially contested concept" gains traction? The point (discussed in the Introduction) is that "liberal education" (like "justice" and "democracy" and "human nature") is beyond the reach of uncontested formulation. No attempts to defy this claim by resorting to a more stringent formal analysis or to the usage of ordinary language are likely to succeed in a postmodern world. We need, therefore, to acknowledge the implications of that judgment: every age must construct and debate its own interpretations, its own realizations of liberal education; and understanding how such construction occurs, what forces and motivations shape it, will be especially significant to one's understanding. Moreover, there is no final or correct account; our allegiance to a particular interpretation cannot rest firmly on its truth or accuracy.

Unfortunately, this caustic revelation gives us little help in our current task: we still need to have some grasp of what concept it is the various conceptions are contesting! Newman and Nussbaum offer different theories of liberal education—but what makes them theories of liberal education and not, say, theories of vocational education or even theories of justice?

We ask again: *What is liberal education?* To answer that question by reference to specific curricular content is, as I intimated earlier, a false start—although it is quite a common approach: Bloom, Hutchins, and Adler (as advocates) and Noddings (as critic) all seem to have made this equation. They take liberal education to be defined by the study "the canon"—that list of great texts, including art and music, which have shaped culture (especially Western culture). These are the "masterpieces," the "classics," the works of quality that matter. Other critics think of the canon as a set of authors, great thinkers and writers rather than great texts.[20] The problem with this formulation at this juncture is not the issue of judgmental arrogance, nor the probable exclusion of many voices, nor the marginalization of other perspectives that results (though these issues arise later). Rather, as philosopher John Searle, puts it, the problem is that "there never was, in fact, a fixed 'canon'; there was rather a certain set of tentative judgments about what had importance and quality. Such judgments are always subject to revision, and in fact they were constantly being revised."[21]

The same objection applies if we replace the canon with specific "essentials of cultural literacy." As E. D. Hirsch himself, the author of this phrase,[22] ultimately acknowledges, any list of enshrined "essentials" (and he lists over 5,000 "essential" facts) are items of cultural currency and therefore relative to one's time, place, subculture, and intent. Take Shakespeare, for example— certainly a "canonic" writer with works on most lists of great texts, basic knowledge of which might be considered essential. Ignoring the fact that liberal education was pursued for centuries before Shakespeare wrote a word, and setting aside the implicit reference to Anglophone cultures, thinkers who take this approach may declare that any liberal education worth the name necessarily involves the study of great English literature, to wit, Shakespeare; they may bemoan the disappearance of such study among the lists of graduation requirements as evidence of educational decay. What they conveniently forget is that study of English literature was not deemed worthy of academic credit by colleges and universities until well into the nineteenth century—hundreds of years after the Bard's genius flowered.[23] Reading the literature of one's own language (here presumed to be English)—even Shakespeare—was something one was expected to do on one's own time, outside of class; it was simply part of genteel culture (though novels, of course, were initially morally suspect). The canon had included only "classic" works in Latin and Greek or, occasionally, translations drawn from that literature. If one takes the long view, Shakespeare, indeed all British authors, are comparatively recent additions to the curriculum—American literature, even more recent; and Canadian and Australian literature, a very recent and still sparse presence. As a matter of historical fact, curricular content changes over time; claims of the universality of masterpieces and fundamental facts are balanced against the need for continual reformation in response to cultural changes. A particular syllabus will never serve to define liberal education, at least not with the range of applicability we need to understand the discourse.

An obvious move is simply to broaden the defining content: rather than cite specific subject matter, texts, facts, or authors, might we not identify liberal education as the study of certain disciplines? We can then capture liberal education as the study of philosophy, history, economics, sociology, and so on. Such a move seems plausible by its fidelity to the term "liberal arts." After all, both the original Latin term, *artes liberales*, and the earlier Greek term, *eleutheriai technai*, suggest a set of arts, methods, or disciplines. An option is to take a step further, to argue that these disciplines or clusters of them (or practices akin to them) display patterns of inquiry or "ways of knowing," and it is such patterns that form the content of liberal education. This is the approach taken, for example, by philosopher Philip Phenix in the 1960s, though he preferred the term "realms of meaning."[24] Or one might go still further and claim that the disciplines reflect *a priori* epistemological structures; one might thereby claim to ground liberal education in the very structure of knowledge. This is the position developed by P. H. Hirst, who sought to distinguish his account from that of Phenix.[25] As promising as these ideas are, it is difficult to keep faith with educational history if one unfolds that idea as a set of disciplines, methods, or forms of inquiry, or universal epistemological structures.

Disciplines change. Compare these historical snapshots:

(1) Medieval universities famously divided requisite knowledge into the seven liberal arts: the three foundational studies of the *trivium* (grammar, logic, and rhetoric) and the four substantive studies of the *quadrivium* (arithmetic, geometry, music, and astronomy); these prepared the student for the advanced studies of philosophy and theology. This curriculum, rooted in Plato's *Republic*, was also shaped by an elaborate but hugely influential allegory written in the fifth century CE: *De nuptiis de Philologiae et Mercurii* (*The Wedding of Philology and Mercury*), by Martianus Capella.[26]

(2) American colleges in the 1830s typically offered "degrees in course"—that is, all students enrolled in the same set of courses—though some offered optional, additional courses. Under the leadership of President Josiah Quincy III, Harvard College began tentatively to experiment with "elective" courses. Required study included these disciplines: languages (usually Latin, Greek, French, and perhaps German and Hebrew); rhetoric and literature (of classical Greece and Rome only); natural philosophy (studies in today's natural sciences, limited maybe to botany and mineralogy); mathematics (sometimes with applications to surveying, navigation, or other tasks), and—as a capstone—moral philosophy, a course usually taught by the College president. While we can easily trace a line from the medieval university to the nineteenth-century

college, their required disciplines are not at all the same, nor are
they approached with the same methods, even when they have the
same label. What the medieval schoolmen meant by "music," for
example, was drawn from the Greek *mousikē* (which referred to
those fields of humanities and arts inspired by the Muses), was
narrower than its classical, original meaning, and broader than
later usage.

(3) Finally, let us turn to the development of contemporary
liberal education. The study of English literature, and later,
American literature, became worthy of credit—though initially as
a source of rhetorical examples and only later as a field of intrinsic
interest. The social science fields that were spawned by philosophy
in the nineteenth century have become venerable disciplines, their
professors seeming to today's students to have always occupied
their faculty chairs: anthropology, economics, political science,
sociology. The rest of the world that was missing from the purview
of our new republic's Eurocentric curriculum has come bursting
in: the most common non-English language study is now Spanish,
and other languages are featured as well; materials related to Latin
America, Eastern Europe, Asia, Africa, Australia/New Zealand,
are commonly included; the arts in all their splendor—not only
history, theory, and criticism, but performance, too—adorn the
curriculum. And, of course, there are interdisciplinary studies, like
Environmental or Religious Studies; area studies, like East Asian or
Latin American Studies; and cultural studies, like Native American
or Islamic Studies. This profusion of fields has not only transformed the roster of disciplines available, but has challenged the
very paradigm of the discipline as the organization of knowledge.
Unless we arbitrarily identify the concept of liberal education with
one such historical snapshot, dismissing all others, trying to anchor
the concept of liberal education in a specific set of disciplines or
forms of inquiry will not work.

We are trying to isolate a concept of liberal education that
transcends the particular interpretations of different educational
epochs, and to this point it seems that knowledge itself will not be
key—neither specific information, nor specific works and authors,
nor any other knowledge content, nor the structures that organize
our knowledge. They all come and go with time and circumstance.
Perhaps a more promising approach would be to turn attention
to human capacities, to stipulate skills rather than aspects of

knowledge: skills of communication, critical thinking, quantitative reasoning, scholarly and scientific research techniques. Might not these be among the "arts" that perennially define a liberal education? (Interpreting "arts" as "skills or artful techniques" is certainly etymologically sound.) Skills like these are applicable to learning across a wide range of ever-changing subject matter and fields of inquiry. Besides, an interpretation based on skills would be especially attractive in offering a response to those who seek practical outcomes from all forms of learning. But this approach is subject to the same issues as the earlier formulations. Even if one could establish a list of such skills that applied nicely throughout educational history (which seems unlikely), our understanding of these skills, what they involve, changes over time as well—though perhaps more slowly than content. For example, "critical thinking," as that term is championed today, is significantly different from (though traceable to) the art of dialectic, which was the culmination of Platonic education. What evolved from the classical skill of rhetoric as taught, for example, by Isocrates, the famous rhetor and schoolmaster in ancient Athens, is remarkably rich; the legacy evolved to include not only the rhetoric of the medieval *trivium*, but also the oratory or declamation skills of the nineteenth century, and the techniques of PowerPoint presentations today. "Information literacy," a cluster of skills of contemporary importance, could not have developed except in response to the recent explosion of information and the technology to store, compute, and communicate it. One would have to blanch the term of nearly all content to make it applicable to earlier eras.

Despite these arguments, it seems intuitively correct (and surely it is frequently asserted) that great texts and essential knowledge, disciplines, and skills have important relevance to liberal education. But we need to formulate of the concept of liberal education that comprehends the shifts in subject matter, the evolution of disciplines, and the changing construals of salient skills; an account that accommodates such diverse figures as Isocrates and Newman, Hutchins and Martin, Oakeshott and Nussbaum—or that at least illuminates their differences. Can we not reach beyond or behind these models, these iterations, to grasp the ideal of liberal education itself? Can we not distill an essence of liberal education?

It is wise, I think, to abandon the search for a resplendent Platonic ideal that defines a timeless essence of liberal education. In any event, I shall take a different tack. My approach is to develop a "thin theory" of liberal education, by which I mean one that is genuinely informative (not empty), that successfully distinguishes liberal education from other types of education (and from education *tout court*), and that is historically defensible—yet which yields various paradigms and accommodates innumerable "thick theories" that are developed by theorists in response to the fluid circumstances of history. The thin theory articulates the concept; the thicker theories present various conceptions.[27] The next several chapters are devoted to the development of this account. Chapter 2 will present the thin theory, my explication of the concept of liberal education; the theory will then be elaborated in the chapters of Part II, which position the divergent conceptions under five "paradigms," a scheme that facilitates contrast and comparison. The first step in constructing the thin theory is, I propose, to understand liberal education as a *tradition*.

Notes

1 Association of American Colleges and Universities (AAC&U), "Statement on Liberal Learning," adopted by the Board of Directors, October 1998, http://www.aacu.org/about/statements/liberal_learning.cfm (accessed March 2011).

2 Nel Noddings, *The Challenge to Care in Schools: An Alternative Approach to Education*, 2nd edn (New York: Teachers College Press, 2005), 28 and 43.

3 Mortimer J. Adler, *The Paideia Proposal: An Educational Manifesto* (New York: Macmillan, 1982); Michael J. Oakeshott, *The Voice of Liberal Learning: Michael Oakeshott on Education*, ed. Timothy Fuller (New Haven, CT: Yale University Press, 1989); Charles Bailey, *Beyond the Present and Particular* (London: Routledge & Kegan Paul, 1984; repr., London: Routledge, 2010); Martha C. Nussbaum, *Cultivating Humanity: A Classical Defense of Reform in Liberal Education* (Cambridge, MA: Harvard University Press, 1997).

4 Williams College, "Mission and Purposes," approved by the Board of Trustees, April 14, 2007, http://archives.williams.edu/mission-and-purposes-2007.php (accessed March 2011).

5 The Annapolis Group, a coalition of over 100 American liberal arts colleges, quotes on its *College News* website the report of "a

1998 study" which found that although only 3 percent of American
college graduates were educated at a residential liberal arts college,
alumni of these colleges accounted for:

- 8 percent of Forbes magazine's listing of the nation's wealthiest
  CEOs in 1998
- 8 percent of former Peace Corps volunteers
- 19 percent of U.S. presidents
- 23 percent of Pulitzer Prize winners in drama, 19 percent of the
  winners in history, 18 percent in poetry, 8 percent in biography,
  and 6 percent in fiction from 1960 to 1998
- 9 percent of all Fulbright scholarship recipients and 24 percent
  of all Mellon fellowships in the humanities
- 20 percent of Phi Beta Kappa inductions made between 1995
  and 1997

On a per capita basis, liberal arts colleges produce nearly twice as
many students who earn a Ph.D. in science as other institutions.
Liberal arts graduates also are disproportionately represented in
the leadership of the nation's scientific community. In a recent
two-year period, nearly 20 percent of the scientists elected to
the prestigious National Academy of Sciences received their
undergraduate education at a liberal arts college.

A few of the statistics are misleading: for example, the comparison
is seemingly made between the then-current percentage of liberal
arts college graduates and all U. S. Presidents throughout history—a
period of significant change in the demographics of higher education.
At the very least, the period for which the first percentage applies
is not made explicit. Nonetheless, the record of alumni success is
indeed favorable. "About Liberal Arts Colleges," http://collegenews.
org/about-liberal-arts-colleges (accessed August 2011).

6 For essays on the history, character, and impact of these institutions,
   see: Stephen Graubard and Steven Koblik, eds, *Distinctively
   American: The Residential Liberal Arts Colleges* (New Brunswick,
   NJ: Transaction Publishers, 2000). For a pensive consideration of
   their future, see: Samuel Shuman, *Small Colleges in Twenty-First
   Century America* (Baltimore: Johns Hopkins University Press, 2008).

7 Universities and institutes that have a less comprehensive,
   technological focus are exceptions. But even at such institutions,
   students may be advantaged for having, if not expected to have, a
   liberal arts background in their undergraduate work for admission
   to graduate study. In the United States, there are also distinctive

smaller institutions that combine features of colleges and universities; see my attempt to define these schools in DeNicola, "The Emergence of the New American College," *Perspectives: The Journal of the Association for General and Liberal Studies* 24, nos. 1–2 (Spring–Fall, 1994): 63–78.

8 For an account of this phenomenon, see Susan Gillespie, "Opening Minds: The International Liberal Education Movement," *World Policy Journal* (Winter 2001–2): 79–89.

9 A full presentation of ECLA's history, philosophy, and program is available on its website: http://www.ecla.de/ (accessed August 2011). Philanthropic support and nurturance for ECLA have been provided by the Christian A. Johnson Endeavor Foundation of New York. As I was finishing this book, the Foundation announced that ECLA has become a subsidiary of Bard College (New York) with commitment to continue its mission.

10 The phrase is attributed to Francis Oakley, president *emeritus* of Williams College. For his analysis of such narratives, see Oakley, "Against Nostalgia: Reflections on Our Present Discontents in American Higher Education," in *The Politics of Liberal Education*, ed. Darryl J. Gless and Barbara Herrnstein Smith, (Durham, NC: Duke University Press, 1992), 267–89.

11 Allan Bloom, *The Closing of the American Mind: How Higher Education Has Failed Democracy and Impoverished the Souls of Today's Students* (New York: Simon & Schuster, 1987); Harry R. Lewis, *Excellence Without a Soul* (New York: Public Affairs, 2006); A. T. Kronman, *Education's End: Why Our Colleges and Universities Have Given Up on the Meaning of Life* (New Haven, CT: Yale University Press, 2007); Victor E. Ferrall, Jr., *Liberal Arts at the Brink* (Cambridge, MA: Harvard University Press, 2011). There is an even wider circle of writers whose target is higher education in general, largely with the same overarching complaint: distortion of mission. Examples of this genre are: Derek Bok, *Universities in the Marketplace: The Commercialization of Higher Education* (Princeton, NJ: Princeton University Press, 2003); Frank Donoghue, *The Last Professors: The Corporate University and the Fate of the Humanities,* 3rd edn (New York: Fordham University Press, 2008). There is also a plethora of books that fault higher education for its intransigence, inefficiency, and adherence to allegedly obsolete practices. Examples of these are: Mark C. Taylor, *Crisis on Campus: A Bold Plan for Reforming Our Colleges and Universities* (New York: Knopf, 2010); and Louis Menand, *The Marketplace of Ideas: Resistance and Reform in the American University* (New York: W. W. Norton, 2010).

12 The data are notoriously malleable and imprecise, but the trend
    is clear. Much depends on what fields are included within "liberal
    arts," and published statistics often aggregate liberal studies with
    other programs. The National Center for Education Statistics
    (NCES) collects such data, but there is a lag time for analysis and
    publication. At this writing, the most recent information I find on
    the fields of baccalaureate degrees awarded (2008–09) states that
    over half of all degrees were concentrated in five fields: business
    (21.7 percent), social sciences and history (10.5 percent), health
    professions and related clinical sciences (7.5 percent), education (6.4
    percent), and psychology (5.9 percent)—all categories that include
    pre-professional degrees, though at least two of those also include
    traditional liberal arts disciplines; degrees in the humanities totaled
    about 6.4 percent. Source: NCES, http://nces.ed.gov/programs/coe/
    tables/table-fsu-1.asp (accessed December 2011).

13 My definition is paraphrased from Thomas Mautner, *The Penguin
    Dictionary of Philosophy*, 2nd edn (London: Penguin Books, 2005),
    s.vv. "hermeneutics of suspicion."

14 Jane Roland Martin's major works move from critique to
    educational vision and include: *Reclaiming a Conversation: The Ideal
    of the Educated Woman* (New Haven, CT: Yale University Press,
    1985); *Changing the Educational Landscape: Philosophy, Women,
    and Curriculum* (New York: Routledge, 1994); *Coming of Age in
    Academe: Rekindling Women's Hopes and Reforming the Academy*
    (New York, Routledge, 2000); *Cultural Miseducation: In Search of
    a Democratic Solution* (New York: Teachers College Press, 2002);
    *Educational Metamorphoses: Philosophical Reflections on Identity
    and Culture* (Lanham, MD: Rowman and Littlefield, 2007); and
    Education Reconfigured: Culture, Encounter, and Change (New
    York: Routledge, 2011).

15 D. G. Mulcahy, *The Educated Person: Toward a New Paradigm
    for Liberal Education* (Lanham, MD: Rowman and Littlefield,
    2008). Mulcahy immediately points out in the passage quoted (from
    page 191) that this need not "rule out an important role for liberal
    education in its traditional sense."

16 Nel Noddings, *Educating Moral People: a Caring Alternative to
    Character Education* (New York: Teachers College Press, 2002),
    94. For elaborations of these and related claims, see n. 2 above
    and Noddings, *Happiness and Education* (Cambridge: Cambridge
    University Press, 2004).

17 Carl Bereiter, "Liberal Education in a Knowledge Society," in *Liberal
    Education in a Knowledge Society*, ed. Barry Smith (Chicago: Open

Court, 2002). The quotations that follow are from pages 30–1 (italics original).

18 This distinction between "concept" and "conception" gained traction, I believe, when used by John Rawls in *A Theory of Justice* (Cambridge, MA: Harvard University Press, 1971) to distinguish the idea of justice from the various competing theories of justice. He modestly claimed to have borrowed it from H. L. A. Hart's *The Concept of Law* (Oxford: Oxford University Press, 1961). While Hart does explicate "law" in a similar way, he does not use the contrasting terms "concept" and "conception."

19 For the "Great Books" definition, see Noddings, *Educating Moral People*, 123ff; for the "a set of traditional disciplines" definition, see Noddings, *The Challenge to Care*, 28.

20 For example, literary critic Harold Bloom in *The Western Canon: The Books and School of the Ages* (New York: Riverhead Books, 1995).

21 John R. Searle, "The Storm Over the University," *The New York Review of Books,* December 6, 1990, http://www.nybooks.com/articles/archives/1990/dec/06/ (accessed April 2011).

22 E. D. Hirsch, Jr., *Cultural Literacy: What Every American Needs to Know* (New York: Vintage Books, 1988).

23 Gerald Graff, *Professing Literature: An Institutional History*, 20th anniv. edn (Chicago: University of Chicago Press, 2007).

24 Philip H. Phenix, *Realms of Meaning: A Philosophy of the Curriculum for General Education* (New York: McGraw-Hill, 1964).

25 This account was initially presented in P. H. Hirst, "Liberal Education and Nature of Knowledge," in *Philosophical Analysis and Education*, ed. Reginald Archambault (London: Routledge & Kegan Paul, 1965). It was elaborated in P. H. Hirst, *Knowledge and the Curriculum* (London: Routledge & Kegan Paul, 1974).

26 See the two-volume study and translation of *De nuptiis Philologiae et Mercurii* (c. 420 CE): Martianus Capella, William Harris Stahl, Richard Johnson, and E. L. Burge, *Martianus Capella and the Seven Liberal Arts*, 2 vols, Records of Civilization: Sources and Studies, no. 84 (New York: Columbia University Press, 1971–7).

27 I have not adopted the distinction between "meta-theoretical" and "first-order" theories here, a usage that connotes logically distinct domains of discourse and levels of meaning; whereas, as we shall see, the concept of liberal education enables a cascade of theories

of increasing specificity, from its supreme aims down to specific curricular and pedagogical programs. The more levels of this cascade that a theory contains, the "thicker" it is. Thus, conceptions of liberal education may be more or less thick (replete or specific).

2

Liberal Education and Human Flourishing

The tradition of liberal education is not uniform and continuous but full of variety, discontinuity and innovation. It has been and is a conflicted tradition.

BRUCE A. KIMBALL, "A HISTORICAL PERSPECTIVE"

Liberal education is a perdurable tradition of educational theory and practice traceable in the West to the classical cultures of Greece and Rome. It is a living tradition, one that is deeply connected to its ever-changing cultural context. During its long evolution, it has adapted to emergent social, intellectual, and technological developments—and has, in turn, shaped them, being a fecund, ever-flowing well-spring of culture and academic life. It has spawned many diverse conceptions and institutionalized forms, along with numerous theories of curriculum and pedagogy. But each of these iterations is derivative, and no single such conception can capture or characterize its richness as a tradition; rather, we should first understand the tradition as a tradition. I prefer to characterize it in the Aristotelian manner: by its *aims*. Liberal education is supremely aimed at *the good life*: it pursues the articulation of a compelling vision of a good life, along with the preparation for and the cultivation of such a life. It is, in short, *structured learning that aims at human flourishing*. The "breadth" so often associated with liberal education is not, in the first instance, breadth of content (*that* is derivative); rather, it is the breadth of its normative concern: the activity of living as a human being and the view of one's life as a whole. It is, therefore, both descriptively and in its aspirations, fundamentally a moral education. Insofar as the pursuit of a liberal education is an intentional action, its purpose is transformative; that is, it involves sustained efforts intended to improve the agent *as an agent*.

This concise statement represents what I take to be the core of the concept of liberal education. There is, of course, much more to be said, even for an adequate "thin theory." But this brief statement itself is dense and needs to be unpacked carefully. That is the work of this chapter. In the sections that follow, I will explain and annotate, elaborate and refine, the ideas and implications of this core statement—and attempt to forestall some misunderstandings and objections.

Liberal Education as a Tradition

The term "tradition" sometimes connotes hoary rituals or ideologies that are received with a dusty but heavy obligation to be repeated or preserved without alteration. That is not at all what is meant here. To conceive of liberal education as a tradition (rather than as an ideal) is to place its various conceptions or interpretations as episodes in a history; to describe it as a living tradition suggests its open texture as a concept and its continuing vitality and evolution as a practice. Alasdair MacIntyre's explication of the idea is particularly apt: "A living tradition then is an historically extended, socially embodied argument, and an argument precisely in part about the goods which constitute that tradition."[1] Continuous dialogue, conflict, responsiveness, and innovation mark a vital tradition. Conceiving liberal education as a tradition, therefore, allows us to honor its historicity, its internal dynamism and tensions, its continuing openness to reform, and the diverse and particular ways in which its practice is situated. Its scope includes not only theory, such as the theories of curriculum and pedagogy it generates, but also practice, incorporating not only the classroom, but forms of institutionalization and educationally relevant out-of-classroom elements, such as the co-curriculum, "hidden curriculum" (what is typically learned or reinforced without the intention of educators), and patterns of relationships between teachers and learners, and among learners themselves. Framing liberal education as a tradition will allow us to understand a good deal of the mixed messages and discord about liberal education as disputes internal to the tradition.

That there actually is such a tradition should not be in doubt, though it will not be my purpose here to present its history. That task has been well accomplished by others, especially by educational historian Bruce Kimball, who has interpreted the deepest tensions in the tradition as deriving from the original opposition of classical orators and philosophers, and their preferred arts of rhetoric and dialectic. Kimball has shown that we can indeed trace an educational narrative that runs from Plato, Isocrates, and Aristotle, through Cicero and Quintilian, through the instaurations of medieval schoolmen, on to Renaissance humanism, and thence to the Enlightenment and subsequent modern theorists of liberal education. (One could write a parallel institutional history, focusing on the succession of schools that have embodied the practice of liberal education.) While he credits the Greeks with the invention of the forms of inquiry of the seven traditional liberal arts, Kimball believes that a "normative program" of instruction worthy of the term "liberal arts education" was not codified until Roman times, as reflected in the writings of Cicero.[2] My own judgment is that prominent Greeks clearly identified the relationship of a type of learning to the cultivation a good life and that, along with the invention of relevant subject matter, is sufficient to mark the beginning of this tradition. Although identified with Western (European) culture, elements of liberal education may also be found in parallel traditions of Eastern educational theory and practice as well, especially in the heritage of Confucianism[3]— though that too is an argument that must be left to others.

My brief core statement on liberal education identifies three drivers of its evolution: intellectual, social/political, and technological change. Noteworthy examples, cited from a process now nearly two and a half millennia long, may be helpful. The emergence of the social sciences in the late nineteenth century is an obvious instance of an intellectual development that forever altered the curricular landscape of the liberal arts and also offered new methods for analyzing classrooms and schools. Colonialism, the rise of democracies, and the establishment of public education are examples of social and political changes that have had enormous impact on educational theory and practice. And, of course, the printing press, computers, and the Internet are landmarks of information technology that not only altered instructional possibilities, but also changed our understanding of knowledge itself. At times, all three factors combine with dramatic impact: for example, the field of classical studies has, in the last two decades, been reshaped and revitalized as a result of the intellectual developments of feminist theory and queer theory, the social changes regarding sex and gender issues, and the employment of an array of technology making classical texts, images, visualizations, and interactive programs freely available and searchable. The classical studies of today are, as a result, astoundingly different from those that dominated liberal education in the nineteenth century—or even in the mid-twentieth century. But these processes work both ways: liberal education in turn has shaped developments in these spheres—in much the same way that, while environmental changes affect natural selection, the activities of animals also alter their environment. Liberally educated persons, their decisions, and their creative products, affect not only the world of ideas, but social and political events and institutions, and technological innovation and dispersal. It should not be surprising to point out that liberal education is both a human enterprise subject to human conditions, and also, like all education, one that seeks to shape and improve those conditions. Nevertheless, it is important to affirm the significance of this dynamic, because it is all too easy for philosophers to abstract a shining ideal of education as the object of inquiry, washed clean of the messy interactions that are implicated *in situ*.

What is distinctive about this tradition, I have proposed, is its aim: human flourishing. Being guided by this aim is what distinguishes liberal education from other forms of education, such as vocational, professional, religious, or military education—and therefore from education in general. An education that aims at preparation for a trade or profession, at the inculcation of a creed, or at the acquisition of the skills and ethos of a particular role, has quite different aims; differences in curricula and pedagogy will follow naturally. The proposed thin theory, therefore, is neither empty nor so thin that one cannot distinguish its concept from other varieties of education. Of course, institutions and practices driven by intentions may fail to achieve their goal for many reasons; so all of these forms of education are subject to better and worse efforts, and to success and failure in the outcome. "A liberal education" is therefore not synonymous with "a good education"—nor is any other type of education.

The remainder of this chapter is devoted to explicating the two elements of the thin account: the concept of an educational aim and the idea of the good life, or flourishing. Each explication is followed by a brief defense against important objections to these elements.

The Notion of an Educational Aim

Among the most famous sentences in Aristotle's writings is the opening sentence of the *Nicomachean Ethics*: "Every art and every inquiry, and similarly every action and choice, is thought to aim at some good; and for this reason the good has rightly been declared to be that at which all things aim."[4] From this observation, Aristotle proceeds to unfold a profound and nuanced relationship among three concepts: an art or skill (*technē*), an aim or purpose (*telos*), and the good (*agathos*). An art like medicine (one of Aristotle's favorite examples) has an aim or a purpose: health, its promotion and, when necessary, its restoration. Health is taken as a good; excellence in the practice of medicine is whatever optimally nurtures health. *Technai* are intentional activities, whether arts, crafts, skills, methods, practices, or processes; they serve ends outside themselves; they accomplish things; they are not pastimes or experiences sought for their own sake. Moreover, such tripartite relationships are nested within a hierarchy of aims. Medical diagnosis is itself an art, the aim of which is to correctly identify the cause of illness or affliction; it may be done poorly, which means misdiagnoses will be likely, or with excellence, which means it will fulfill its purpose. But diagnosis is an art that is subsidiary to medicine as a whole; correct and timely diagnoses are important because they ultimately facilitate good health. The more comprehensive the aim, the "higher" or more "governing" it is; I use the term "supreme" for the highest, relevant, governing aim. So, if a technique were developed that greatly improved the accuracy of medical diagnoses but which also produced a serious health problem, it would likely be abandoned—after all, the *supreme* aim in medicine is health, not correct diagnoses. Though Aristotle considers all sorts of crafts and skills, he finds the most comprehensive, the most governing of all, to be the arts that aim at a good life (ethics, or *ethikē*) and at a good community (politics, or *politikē*). And at the intersection of these is the art of education (*paideia*).

While learning may often be incidental, accidental, or even unconscious, education is purposeful, it has a telic normativity. I have chosen to identify liberal education by its aim because of the governing role an aim plays. The *telos* or aim of an activity "governs" in several related ways: (1) it reflects a value, a particular notion of the good, which serves to justify the effort; (2) it concentrates attention on sharpening our understanding of contributive goals and on identifying possible techniques or means for achieving them; (3) it establishes relations of salience, structures effort and activities, and orders subsidiary arts; (4) it establishes criteria of success and failure, excellence and shoddiness; (5) it calls forth virtues, or qualities which conduce to its achievement, and commits to the rejection of vices, or qualities which inhibit its achievement; (6) it develops roles that contribute in complementary ways to its achievement; (7) it generates, over time, an interplay between inclusive theory and reflective practice; and (8) it reflects both the exertion of will and competence, and the limits of human control over events, oneself and other beings, and the materials of the world. To have a *telos* thus brings coherence, value, and direction to activity. It elicits and focuses our care. An aim is a powerful, definitive thing.

A distinctive educational aim may be attributed to a type of theory, a form of practice, a type of institution, whole systems that combine these—or to a tradition that comprehends all of them. It will be adopted, at least implicitly, by individual educators who work within the tradition. For those agents and agencies that adopt a distinctive aim, it is the way in which they conceive of what they do. In all those manifestations, it is an aim that is directed toward others: liberal arts educators strive for their *students* to flourish. But it may, as understanding awakens, certainly come to be owned by students *for themselves*; it may become a motivating aim that governs their own efforts.

To avoid misinterpretation, I must re-emphasize the nested character of such aims. Education is a complex pursuit with many subsidiary activities. If we take liberal education to be aimed supremely at the articulation of a conception of the good life and at the preparation for and cultivation of such a life, as I propose, this does not mean that it is the operative aim of every moment and activity within the educational process—but it governs (or should) nonetheless. Turn again to the parallel with medicine: preventive medicine may require such subsidiary activities as mammograms and colonoscopies, in which diagnosis is the operative aim, but— as we say—the larger aim of health still governs, if only indirectly and at some distance. So, liberal education may require such subsidiary activities as the study of geometry or memorization of French verb forms, but the larger, supreme aim of the good life should still govern, even if it seems out of sight at the moment; that, or else practice should be reformed so as to better honor the ultimate goal. Unfortunately, practices may sometimes become rigid, their subsidiary activities ritualized, their derivative aims elevated to the governing position, and an effective connection to the original, supreme aim lost and forgotten. When this happens, whether in education or medicine or any other important activity, the obsessive result is tragic. The precise link between means and ends, between subsidiary activities and ultimate goods, is often a complicated matter involving issues that are, in principle, empirical and approaches that can be tested and adjusted over time; but also conceptual matters, which are consequently the subject of philosophical debate; and matters that reflect the intellectual, social, or technological developments of the time.

Although I have spoken of the "achievement" of an aim, not all aims are subject to such finality. Those that are, I will call *terminal aims*, or simply, *objectives*—for example, learning the Greek alphabet or making the Olympic team. They direct us toward an accomplishment, an end-state, or an acquisition. When we do succeed in accomplishing our objectives, their governance is relinquished, and we move on to other purposes. But there is a different sort of aim: one's aim may be to attain a normative quality in an ongoing activity or process. Such aims are dynamic, because sustaining the desired quality requires unceasing attention, feedback, and redirected effort, for as long as one engages in the activity or process. These are *continuous aims*; they direct us to the endless tuning of the relevant activity or process in according with some sense of excellence. Health, for example, is a continuous aim, and so, as Robert Pirsig famously portrayed, is the maintenance of a motorcycle.[5] The aim of liberal education is also such a continuous pursuit. Though one may achieve with finality the terminal aim of completing one's schooling, or earning a liberal arts degree, the aim of flourishing, of cultivating a good life, requires lifelong attention. "Success" in achieving such a goal is never fully or finally secured, but failure is clearly possible—and one may also abandon or pervert the aim as well.

It is a striking and problematic aspect of the current milieu of schooling that attention is fixated on educational objectives. There is downright impatience with discussion of the continuous aims of education, and such talk is either foregone or foreclosed by relegation to insipid boilerplate statements. Nel Noddings calls "aims-talk" the "missing dimension" in education today; she charges: "At the beginning of the twenty-first century, educational discussion is dominated by talk of standards, and the reason given for this emphasis is almost always economic."[6] It is true that political and economic concerns about the effective use of resources have narrowed the span of attention, effort, and interest in education. Within such an environment, focusing on aims seems to have little pay-off: the aims of education have been debated since Plato without resolution—what benefit is there for getting pulled into a never-ending, philosophical debate? The trouble with this attitude is that our efforts then lose the governance of our supreme aim, the reason we engage in the activity in the first place. We forego all of the functions of an aim listed above; our objectives become disconnected from their purposes; moreover, they become vulnerable to selection and interpretation by the divergent aims of others. We doggedly try to achieve our received objectives without ever asking, "Is it good education?" Though continuous aims naturally generate short-term objectives; the former are never reducible to the latter.

This is not to discount all assessment: there are compelling reasons for judicious evaluation. All our intentional activities and choices, including arts and skills, benefit from feedback that allows us to adjust our efforts to ongoing results in light of our goal. Continuous aims, especially, require continuous monitoring, constant adjustment. If the aim of liberal education is continuous in this way, some form of attunement will be lifelong, a responsibility not just of educators, but of students themselves.

There is still more to be said about the special sort of *telos* that is the aim of liberal education. In an essay on the relation between truth and democracy, the American philosopher Richard Rorty, wrote: "The grounding premise of my argument is that you cannot aim at something, cannot work to get it, unless you can recognize it once you have got it."[7] This seeming truism is, however, misleading or false when it comes to a certain sort of aim (like that which defines liberal education) if Rorty means that we must be able to recognize it from the moment we aim at it.[8] In liberal education and in certain other sorts of pursuits as well, we do not and cannot fully understand or recognize what our goal is at the outset; it is only by undertaking the activity that we come to clarify our aim. I will refer to this as an *emergent aim*.[9] (Notice that I am now speaking from the perspective of the student, for whom the aim is emergent.) What may mislead us on this point are the connotations of the words "aim" and "aiming": namely, the worlds of hunting, warfare, and sport. When one "takes aim" at something, it becomes a target; and in archery, for example, one must see the target and recognize what it would mean to hit it—or else one is not "aiming." When one doesn't aim, can't identify a target, one shoots blindly, or at random, into the air. These implications may, however, be misleading when applied to contexts in which "to aim" means "to have as one's purpose or goal," "to intend" or "to display a *telos*." And within such contexts there are activities, like liberal education, in which the goal is continually clarified and more fully comprehended only through its pursuit. A child might want to become a master chess-player, but it is only through learning to play chess well that she can come to understand what "mastery" means. Similarly, a first-grader can't fully understand what it is to be educated, but the further learning proceeds, the clearer becomes his understanding of what being educated involves. Our education begins "through a glass darkly"; we don't really know what we're in for. The practice of education, unlike that of medicine, cannot, strictly speaking, employ the principle of informed consent—at least not from the beginning.

Let us summarize the characteristics of the type of aim that defines the tradition of liberal education.[10] The aim of "learning to flourish" has four defining characteristics. (1) It is a continuous aim which involves the attainment of a normative dynamic quality rather than the accomplishment of an objective. It is, as the old saw about happiness has it, a mode of travel, not a destination—or better, it is a quality of the activity of traveling. (2) It is an emergent aim for the student, more fully comprehended only through pursuing the goal with excellence, for it can only be grasped dimly and simplistically at the outset. (3) One may pursue this sort of aim, but success is contingent; it is impossible to assure attainment or continuance, because our best efforts may be thwarted by factors beyond human control. (4) Such an aim governs and orients many aspects of experience, and in so doing it shapes our life and identity. These are the qualities that characterize not only the supreme aim of liberal education—to understand and prepare for human flourishing—but also, as we shall see, the activity of flourishing itself.

The discussion in this section has been centered on my rationale for employing an aims-based definition of the liberal education tradition, along with points about the nature and function of an aim, and the type of aim we have before us. I have done this at some length because there are influential arguments against the use of aims-talk to define education. Before we can examine substantively the particular aim of flourishing, we must consider four such arguments.

Objections to Educational Aims

The British philosopher, R. S. Peters, authored a provocative article titled "Must an Educator Have an Aim?"[11] in which he distinguished between aims and "principles of procedure." He argued that "aims" suggests an all-too-specific end-in-view that can, when pressed, lead to abuses; whereas complying with "principles of procedure" offers a way of attaining expectations of excellence and ethics without the enforced specificity of aims. Peters illustrates his point by contrasting the goal of political equality as a "general aim" with the use of equal treatment as a procedural test of proposed actions. The source of Peters' concern is the way in which the normative aspect of "education" is extracted as a goal external to the educational process; this distorts, he believes, the normative aspect which is inherent in the general concept of education. Nonetheless, Peters does allow that we raise questions of aims when the purpose of an activity is debatable, unclear, contested, yet important. I must note that this is precisely the situation of the contemporary discourse about liberal education (see chapter 1)!

While I agree that principles of procedure are important to educational endeavors, by themselves they provide no motivation, no guidance, for what even Peters acknowledges is an intentional activity. Putting his argument in slightly (but significantly) different terms and applying it to liberal education, however, I can find agreement with Peters: it is both distorting and risky to think of the aim of liberal education as a terminal aim, or to replace the thin theory with a thick one, that is, with a particular conception. I believe that we can capture the openness Peters seeks, as well as the need for procedural principles, through the use of a thin theory and the concept of a tradition.

Another attack on aims-language is mounted in a recent book by Tasos Kazepides, a philosopher of education. "Since education is neither a person nor an activity or institution ... [it] therefore cannot logically be said to have aims." He argues that grand formulations of the aims of education are merely tautologies, selective emphases, or disguised programmatic proposals—but in any case, only vacuous or nebulous slogans. Attacking the "mistaken view that aims, goals, and objectives ought to be understood hierarchically, from the most general to the specific," Kazepides claims that "Appeals to the aims of education are idle and illusory ways of avoiding the complex tasks of selecting the educationally worthwhile subjects, skills, rules, values, and habits and the most appropriate manner of teaching them to the young." In short, to try to think through overall purposes is simply to dodge issues of curriculum and pedagogy. But even when we turn to curricular issues, he argues, the exercise of specifying curricular aims is harmful in its reductionism. "We should put an end to this entire talk about 'aims of education,'" he concludes.[12]

This is quite a broadside! In these claims, Kazepides is discussing education *tout court*, not liberal education; I am confident he would apply these claims to liberal education, nonetheless. In any event, it seems to me that he omitted the most obvious possibility: education is a *practice*. And practices are purposeful; they do have aims or purposes. It is odd that our only options in formulating aims are to be empty of content or covertly (and illegitimately?) programmatic. (I believe that such formulations might be definitional, if they are "thin" and accommodate a wide range of divergent programmatic interpretations.) It is also odd that we could not—even if we were diligent and not "idle"—select our curriculum or pedagogy in light of our larger educational purposes; but we cannot, according to Kazepides, because there is no hierarchy of aims, no cascade of specificity, in which larger purposes govern and guide occasional efforts. No wonder the selection of curriculum is a complex task! I share his concern with the reductionist tendencies of a fixation on learning objectives; but I believe this concern only emerges when we compare such objectives with the larger aims of liberal education.

There is, however, a broader challenge to educational aims in another recent book. Jane Roland Martin has provocatively characterized the standard view of education as narrow and false in its implications, because it restricts educational agency to teachers in schools, and construes education as "a consciously intentional, volitional, rational, and morally acceptable activity."[13] The result is a correspondingly deficient view of the processes of learning, which she theorizes as cultural encounters in which individual capacities are yoked to items of "cultural stock." The received view misguides our practices and skews our educational values, she says, causing us to elevate the public, the intellectual, the traditionally male spheres, over the rest of life. She argues that, in reality, our education is typically achieved in many ways and through multiple agents that do not appear in the standard model. Her dramatic proposal is to expand the boundaries of the educational realm so as to incorporate the learning received from all sources in our culture—from parents and other family members, friends and peers, television and other media, events and experiences, animals and the natural world, as well as, yes, teachers, books, and school environments. And the census of learners should be retaken, for even animals may gain an education, she affirms.

The full complexity of these provocative ideas can neither be explained nor critiqued here, but some response is called for because our core statement of liberal education seems, at least initially, to exemplify the standard view she has targeted. First, let us note that Martin is presenting a general theory of education (or a theory of education *tout court*), not an account of liberal education. She does indeed allow (though not very enthusiastically, I admit) that "those who wish to focus exclusively on education in the ... narrow sense of the term are free to cultivate that small patch of the educational terrain."[14] Second, she uses the term "education" descriptively to refer to the totality of what one has learned—both good and bad, consequential and trivial. John Stuart Mill began his Inaugural Address with a similarly inclusive definition of education:

> Not only does it include whatever we do for ourselves, and whatever is done for us by others, for the express purpose of bringing us somewhat nearer to the perfection of our nature; it does more: in its largest acceptation, it comprehends even the indirect effects produced on character and on the human faculties, by things of which the direct purposes are quite different; by laws, by forms of government, by the industrial arts, by modes of social life; nay even by physical facts not dependent on human will; by climate, soil, and local position. Whatever helps to shape the human being; to make the individual what he is, or hinders him from being what he is not—is part of his education.[15]

Such a broad usage is certainly not wrong; it is commonplace: think of the expression "he received his education from the school of hard knocks"; or think of the truism that parents are the first educators of their children; or think of the continual fretting over how television and video games may be educating our children. Though this is a very broad and descriptive usage, it is chosen by Martin (and, I suspect, Mill) strategically to awaken us to all the various agents that affect and effect learning, to reaffirm aspects of life and personal qualities that are typically ignored or undervalued in school settings.

But "education" also has an inherently normative usage, and when we turn to the normative questions, our interest changes: of the myriad things one can learn, which of them should be learned?

How should they be learned? On this broad view, education happens, whether intended by official educational authorities or not. But this gives no special place to the effort the student makes, to learning as an achievement that draws on skills and virtues. Moreover, while it is prudent to be alert to all the educational forces in a culture, whether competing or complementary, education is undertaken in the hope that learning can be normative through selection and sequence: normative in the value of what is learned, in the interconnectedness and mutual reinforcement of what is learned, and in the efficiency with which it is learned. Undertaking an education, engaging in education in this normative sense, is intentional and volitional and requires "moral acceptability," and its selection of means subjects it to rational constraints. It is purpose-driven learning. It is still useful to distinguish education as "a structured program of learning" from the idiosyncratic totality of what someone has learned. It is not surprising that Mill, in the Address cited, immediately focuses on "education in the narrower sense," which he defines as intentional: "the culture which each generation *purposely* gives to those who are to be its successors."[16] Martin is correct, of course, in the observation that one should not simply identify education with schooling (which is reflected in the definitions I offer in the Introduction), and she is wise in leading us to re-examine formal education so as to compensate, counteract, or complement all the other sources we learn from.

The fourth objection to aims-talk may be found in the writings of the postmodernist philosophers who reject intentionality or rational purpose as the pivotal concept for analysis of institutions and replace it with *power*. Michel Foucault, does this, for example, in his analyses of penal and other institutions.[17] Similarly, one might argue that we should not try to understand education or liberal education in terms of its purposes or aims, but rather work to expose the power relationships in schooling. It is fair to say that approach has proved to be illuminating, offering surprising insights, sensitizing readers to the manifold power relations in society, stimulating new questions. A problem, however, is that the understanding of power relationships does not take us anywhere *educationally*. This is because all grounds of normativity for the institution are removed; the result is descriptive: power relationships "are what they are."

This is not especially troubling to some postmodernists, however. Another French philosopher, Jean-François Lyotard, describes any statement of the supreme purposes of education (or any other major cultural institution) to be a "metanarrative," a grand story that undergirds the authority of educators and schools. He advocates the abandoning of all such modernist metanarratives in favor of a recognition that human enterprises are more pluralistic, less coherent, less rational than such stories suggest.[18] Exposing metanarratives has become a philosophical sport for some, and these unveilings are often perceptive and chastening. Nonetheless, narratives give our actions shape and meaning; we can construct them, treat them as hypotheses, debate them, modify them—in sum, we can employ them valuably without being hopelessly and permanently in their thrall. There are many ways to recognize pluralism and the limits of rationality without abandoning all attempts at cohesive meaning—and I hope to illustrate that for liberal education through this and the following chapters.

All attempts to structure a program of learning are normative, but the tradition of liberal education is also substantively normative in aiming at the *good* life. The next section is devoted to a portrayal of the distinctive aim of liberal education: flourishing.

Flourishing and the Good Life

In the opening paragraph of this chapter, I described the normative concern of liberal education as "the activity of living as a human being and one's life as a whole," and I noted the breadth of such concern. It is broad in the sense that it is not directed toward aspects of one's life—one's career, finances, health, romances, or family—but rather toward the integrated or primordial whole of one's life. In his monumental work of 1927, *Sein und Zeit (Being and Time)*, Martin Heidegger observed that being human necessarily and distinctively involves asking the question of what it is to be human, as part of the deeper ontological questioning of Being itself.[19] I share Heidegger's view that to be concerned about living as a human being, to address one's life as a whole, is a peculiarly human enterprise; it grows from profound, existential questions: *What does it mean to live "humanly" or humanely? What is our relationship to the world and to those with whom we share it? How does the knowledge that we will we die shape our life? What, in the face of it all, are our possibilities—and is there one which is our "ownmost"?* These are the deep, philosophic springs from which flows the fundamental question of liberal education: *What is a good life, and how might we live it?* So described, liberal education is as much about persistent questions as it is about comforting answers. Indeed, the interplay of question and answer is not only the structure of an internal, individual dialogue; it is also the rhythm of liberal learning.

There are, I have claimed, two parts to the supreme aim of liberal education: (1) to pursue the articulation of a compelling vision of the good life, and (2) to prepare for and cultivate such a life. The substantive term in this dual aim is, of course, "the good life." What does it mean? The question is simple, but answering it is tricky because we must think strategically: here again, we need to delineate a clear but thin meaning that is open to multiple interpretations. After all, this aim has, I have said, defined a tradition in which theorists and practitioners have described, justified, promoted, and institutionalized many different visions of the good life and varying means by which students may pursue it. Moreover, attaining a thick and robust meaning, what I have called "a compelling vision of the good life," is part of the aim itself.

Predictably, we may trace the concept to the Greeks. Both Plato and Aristotle developed rich conceptions of the good life, and although achieving a good life has occasionally been seen as a lonely quest for individuals, they took the view that virtuous individuals and good communities entail each other—and that both are required for the good life. Aristotle characterized the good life as a life of *eudaimonia*. It is a complex term, not easily translated. Its etymology suggests the having of a good fate: *eu-* ("good") + *daimon* ("guardian spirit or fate"). The most frequent English translation is "happiness," which has a parallel etymology: the root *hap* ("luck" or "fate") gives us words like *happen* and *perhaps*, and of course *happy*, which originally meant "lucky." But translators, alert to our contemporary usage, quickly qualify the term for clarity: what Aristotle meant by happiness was not a state of mind, still less an upbeat feeling, but rather a continuous activity of self-actualization drawing upon and exhibiting excellences or virtues. It is thriving or well-being—what I call "flourishing."

This cluster of ideas has generated a dauntingly vast literature— or, rather, literatures that overlap and intersect in ways that reflect language. There is a literature on the concept of *eudaimonia*, largely exegetical and analytical, centered on Aristotle's writings, but often with contemporary applications. The concept of happiness has an independent history[20] as a subject of writing and reflection in every age; the topic is especially popular at the moment; its burgeoning literature is not only philosophical, but also psychological—therapeutic and self-help tracts, works of positive psychology, and empirical studies abound. There is also a smaller but interesting genre of works that question or critique the connection of happiness and a good life.[21] Human welfare or well-being is, of course, the focus of the field of welfare economics, and the literature examining the concept of welfare and linking it to notions of the good life has been strong since nineteenth century Utilitarians. Very recently, the term "flourishing" has been invoked, and there is a growing philosophical literature that gives it center stage. All of this may be subsumed in works that attend more broadly to "the good life."[22] Within all these literatures, we may distinguish three minimal tasks regarding their focal concepts: definition, component analysis, and consideration of means. Take "happiness," for example; the tasks are: (1) to define it cleanly or offer a thin characterization of the concept; (2) to elucidate the components of happiness, the qualities or elements it contains; and (3) to identify the means to achieve happiness, the ways to become happy. In other words, for each concept, we want to know what it is, what it involves, and how it is attained.

What I have in mind, however, is not reducible to some of the traditional interpretations of "happiness." It is not, for example, simply a matter of experiencing pleasure or luxuriating in a pleasurable existence; nor is it to be understood as routinely having one's desires satisfied. These interpretations, among other problems, miss the normativity and scope of the idea of flourishing, basing everything on a positive feeling. A better thought is that the key idea is satisfaction with one's life as a whole and its prospects. This expands to a global scope (at least in terms of one's own life) and implies a normative, if subjective, judgment—not just a feeling. But we are still trapped into a judgment that is made purely in terms of subjective marks. "Flourishing" and "the good life"—if not "happiness"—imply objective indicators as well, something that points to how well one is doing in the world, whoever is making the judgment. Harry Brighouse, a philosopher who has espoused the view that "education should aim at enabling people to lead flourishing lives," has argued succinctly that this involves two elements: (1) "For somebody actually to flourish, they have to identify with the life they are leading. They have to live it from the inside, as it were." This is the subjective marker. (2) The life they live must be "truly worthwhile, it must contain objective goods." This position doesn't preclude controversies over any given list of objective goods nor does it remove the need to reassess one's sense of what is truly valuable.[23] I would add to these two components (3) a quality of functioning in the world with excellence and effectiveness. To combine these three ideas leads us to eudaimonistic conceptions—to flourishing.[24]

Aristotle's masterful account of *eudaimonia* resounds through the educational, ethical, and political theories of the West; it is a fertile term that has much philosophical baggage. I need to be precise at this point about how much of that baggage I mean to carry. In the *Nicomachean Ethics, Eudemian Ethics, Politics,* and other treatises, Aristotle analyzed the components of *eudaimonia*; its motivational force; its activities, techniques and particular excellences; methods for developing its contributing virtues; obstacles and limits to such a life—both internal and external; and its intrinsic and extrinsic rewards. I do not want to claim or imply any of those specifics, though they remain both venerable and provocative. Rather, for the discussion at hand, what I take from Aristotle is the simple view that we naturally desire a good life, a life in which we thrive. This claim has several components: fundamentally, it assumes our lives have genuine possibilities, which we may affect if not control; second, it recognizes that we judge life's possibilities normatively, in the basic sense that we would find some better than others; third, that paths of possibilities define ways of living—and some would be better than others; and finally, that in one or more of these ways of living, we might flourish as a human being. Aristotle also observes that *eudaimonia* has intrinsic worth, not in the sense that it has no practical benefit, but rather that it is the ultimate good for humans, that it is the *summum bonum*, the good toward which all other human endeavors and choices aim. Ultimately, all of life's efforts, though they may fail because of others or chance events or our own self-defeating faults, are undertaken to attain a happy, thriving—flourishing—life. This claim has an intuitive appeal, but only at a level of generality; as specific differences surface in the matter of what comprises such a life, the disagreements begin and intuitions are tested. I will carry forward only the most general claim here.

In addition, Aristotle claims that this normative possibility, this eudaimonistic life, may be derived from human nature itself. This view, commonly called *perfectionism*, asserts that the fulfillment or actualization of aspects of human nature is essential to the theory and practice of ethics and education (and sometimes of politics). The next natural step, of course, is to identify those aspects of human nature and the means of their actualization. The lurking problem, however, is that this way of thinking tends to assume a single and universal human nature from which one projects a single and universal conception of perfected life. I do not wish to carry that load. While I do believe that there are aspects of human nature and also human culture that are universal, I also believe there are individual qualities and contextual particulars that are salient to the vision of a good life.[25] I will therefore carry forward only the unrefined but still meaningful notion that liberal education, like all education, is clearly perfectionist in actualizing, developing, or at least being guided by, among other things, some aspects of human nature's better possibilities.

My preference is to encapsulate these ideas in the term *flourishing*. Originally a metaphor from the botanical realm (as its etymology reveals), it suggests that humans, like plants, can "bloom." We can grow well and be healthy; we can shine and realize our best prospects; and such a quality of life may perhaps continue throughout our lives. Or not: the implicit contrast is with possible conditions of debilitation, impairment, weakness, stagnation, and unrealized potential or impact. As Thomas Gray elegized, "Full many a flow'r is born to blush unseen/And waste its sweetness on the desert air." (I accept the term "thriving" as synonymous with "flourishing," but the two have different connotations. "Flourishing" is related to "flowering" and suggests an actualization generated from within; "thriving" is related to "thrift" and connotes a grasping or gathering of needed resources from without. Both dynamics are involved in education, as we shall see in chapter 4.) Flourishing is itself a continuous and emergent aim, so we should understand it not as a momentary state—like an unpredictable moment when, under moonlight, a rare orchid opens its bloom—but rather as a sustained quality of our living that requires ongoing concern; it becomes more fully comprehensible through its pursuit, remains vulnerable to chance and luck, and yet orders our life and individuates our identity.

"Flourishing" is not one of those terms that philosophers label with "task/achievement" ambiguity. Flourishing is a success term; it is not a task we engage in. If someone asks, "What were you doing at 4:00 today?" one would not say—except for flip humor—"I was flourishing." Just as "learning" designates the success we attain when we study, and "winning" is the reward for playing well, so "flourishing" is a term of success.[26] We strive or seek to flourish, but we don't *engage* in flourishing. Flourishing is the luster from, the precious by-product of, the reflective judgment upon, our normative engagement in component activities. This nice linguistic point is significant because it reminds us that the title of this book, *Learning to Flourish*, is elliptical: parallel with such elliptical expressions as "learning to succeed" and "learning to win," it means learning *in order* to flourish. One learns what one learns, lives as one has learned—and flourishing happens. Or such is our hopeful purpose in liberal learning.

In this section, I have been occupied with characterizing the bipartite aim of liberal education. But I am aware that to stake the tradition of liberal education on the notion of the good life is to face numerous and vigorous objections. I hope that anticipating and responding to likely objections and misunderstandings, even in a general way, will add meaning and resilience to the foregoing account, and show that even in my thin characterization, there is much at stake.

Objections to "the Good Life"

It is, perhaps surprisingly, not difficult to locate objections to the good life. Those who would find fault with the good life as the aim of liberal education are less likely to be concerned about whether that ascription is accurate (many would say it is), and more likely to reject the notion itself: "Yes," they might say, "that's indeed what liberal education pursues—and that is the problem!" They might argue that "the good life" is a term that connotes an elitist, aristocratic life. It has been identified with the leisured life and values of those free men who defined and pursued it in classical antiquity. Contemplating the good life presupposes a position of privilege, as though one has no need to worry about what life requires, but is free to pursue what life has to offer. Furthermore, they might argue, it is presented as *the* good life—one prescriptive, hegemonic, and likely sexist vision of what life should be. That reveals an arrogant universalism, "the haughtiness of those who think their knowledge is Knowledge."[27] It presumes both the moral authority of educators and the righteousness of their lessons and methods. And finally, many images of the good life throughout history have conjured a life of arid, rational theorizing, lacking passion or caring relationships.

So: another bouquet of thorns and thistles from the hermeneutics of suspicion? No, these criticisms cannot so easily be brushed away, and to do so—at least without serious engagement—would display the very sort of arrogance at issue. The fact is that these critiques are valid—at least for some versions of liberal education, and a few iterations are no doubt susceptible to all of them: cultural institutions and most theories of them historically reflect the outlook of their day. These critiques are pointed at such specific conceptions of education, at particular but influential iterations; they do not, I believe, pierce to the profound concerns that inspire the tradition of liberal education. They do, however, demand that I make a more careful articulation of some of the key elements in my opening statement of the concept of liberal education.

First, let us be clear that the aim to "pursue the articulation of a compelling vision of the good life" need not imply the apprehension of a pre-existing ideal. Part of the process of liberal education is the student's struggle to develop such a vision, a dialectical process in which one's sense of the good life is both found and formed. Moreover, this task does not terminate with the completion of a course or a degree: it is life-long, generated and sustained by a self-conscious concern for the good life and one's life as a whole. It is an emergent aim. Advocates of liberal education may stand humbly with Socrates rather than proudly with Plato and disavow the arrogance of those who would claim their knowledge is Knowledge.

Second, the telic phrase, "the good life," need not designate a singular, universal vision; the struggle might lead to highly diverse, even contrasting, visions of a good life that converse with each other. Nothing in the thin theory logically demands a single conception of the good life. We are free to develop conceptions of liberal education that are democratic rather than aristocratic; that require the cultivation of emotions and relationships as well as intellect; that include experiential learning and encourage practical engagement; that are gender sensitive and culturally pluralistic, alert to issues of race and class; and that avoid indoctrination. Indeed, these possibilities are precisely those that are ascendant among contemporary trends in the practice of liberal education. That ascendancy is found at the level of theory as well: for example, the philosopher and public intellectual, Martha C. Nussbaum, in her visionary work, *Cultivating Humanity*,[28] supported the conception of liberal education as seeking engaged lives of cosmopolitan allegiances, with a sensitive and informed sense of manifold humanity. She thus astutely argues for a link between multiple, situated conceptions of a good life and a common sense of human flourishing. What the thin theory does require, of course, is that *some* notion of flourishing, albeit provisional, be in play for liberal learning.

Third, it is a serious mistake to believe that the ultimate concerns of liberal education are confined to situations of privilege and comfort—or even to the classroom. Concern for one's life and its best prospects may arise in reflective solitude, amidst poverty, in despair, when resplendent ideals of the good life have been shattered—even after great horror.[29] It is true that the study of the liberal arts, like every other form of education, presupposes enabling conditions—such as an environment of relative peace rather than disruptive violence or threat. Beyond the requisite conditions are qualities that enhance it—such as advanced and abundant institutional resources—but some version of these also apply to education in any form. But the questions that motivate liberal education are broadly planted and deeply rooted in human experience; reflection on these questions is certainly not confined to people of privilege. If privilege plays a part, it is in regard to access and educational opportunity, not in regard to concern for a good life and for the hope of flourishing as a human being.

Fourth, liberal education is a moral education (a claim that will be explored further in chapter 10). The notion of a good life entails a moral life; there are, however, more goods than moral goods within a good life. Flourishing involves more than being morally virtuous and living in an ethically unexceptional way. At the very least, the thin theory of liberal education must be open to such a possibility, for there is no *a priori* reason to restrict the notion of a good life to the moral domain.

Paradigms: The Theory Thickens

To distill and reaffirm the major points of the account so far: liberal education is best understood as a tradition of educational theory and practice defined by the supreme, dual aim of preparing students to live flourishing lives, based on their considered understanding of what a good life entails. Individuals are different, and they may reach and come to revise quite different yet appropriate interpretations of the good life; however, "flourishing" implies living a life that is worthwhile, identifying with that life and affirming it as one's own, and functioning with excellence and effectiveness in the world. The hope of flourishing and the concern for one's life as a whole are not restricted by social class or individual circumstance; rather, they arise from deep aspects of human existence.

Taking seriously the hope of flourishing implies engagement with the questions of what sort of life is good and how best to prepare for and cultivate such a life. Grappling with those issues naturally leads to other questions, such as: *What is the human condition— what prospects for human life does the world offer? Who am I really—and what might I become? What is my relationship to others—and what may I learn from their experience? What should I know—and do?* The natural pathways of such self-reflection fan out in many directions, criss-crossing each other in a network of thought. Vantage points within this network may serve to provide a perspective on the issues, and from the earliest days of the tradition of liberal education, different vantage points were adopted as the most significant. All paths lead back to the primary concern, of course, to the supreme aim of liberal education, but the different vantage points represent various ways of approaching the search for the good life; they generate strands of thought, distinct approaches to liberal education that add specificity through interpretation. They remain at such a fundamental level, however, that they are sometimes mistaken for liberal education in its entirety. Because of their comprehensiveness, I will refer to them as *paradigms*.

Thus, what I have termed "the thin theory of liberal education" includes, in addition to the elements summarized above, provision for the generation of increasingly thick theories that may be developed under the vision of these overarching paradigms. Once we begin to flesh out various paradigms, however, we add a next layer and take the initial step toward more robust theories. As T. M. Scanlon has written, "Well-being becomes much more determinate only once our central aims are chosen."[30]

There are five paradigms to be explicated in Part II, along with the main lines of received criticism of their vision; exploring their interrelationships, implications, and common values is the task of Part III. While I do not claim this list of paradigms is exhaustive or that they represent *a priori* structures of thought, I do claim they have been dominant within the tradition. Each paradigm offers, in effect, a distinctive reply to the question of how a good life is to be found and sustained through liberal education. The five I have in mind may be stated in terms of purposes:

1 *Liberal education is for the transmission of cultural inheritance across generations.*

2 *Liberal education is for self-actualization, leading to a normative individuality.*

3 *Liberal education is for understanding the world and the forces that shape one's life.*

4 *Liberal education is for engagement with and action in the world.*

5 *Liberal education is for the acquisition of the skills of learning.*

Each of these addresses the supreme aim of liberal education through a different, interpretive, instrumental, but comprehensive secondary aim; each represents a theoretical framework that is initially quite expansive, but which lets loose a cascade of increasingly specific conceptions and ideas reaching from refined goals to curriculum and pedagogy; and each paradigm embodies a distinctive vision of liberal education and ideal of the educated person, which nevertheless accommodates clusters of variant conceptions and institutionalizations. As contrasting paradigms, they establish polarities in the philosophy of education, create forms of educational discourse, and establish alternative perspectives from which constructive theory and critique, as well as model practices, may be pursued. In fact, their purview is so capacious that it is easy to forget their subsidiary connection to the cultivation of a good life. But we should keep in mind that the phrase *"in order to live a flourishing life"* is implicitly part of each of the declared positions.

While these paradigms are quite different and may conflict, they derive from strands of thought that are intertwined in the tradition. Unlike the scientific paradigms defined by T. S. Kuhn, they do not form a historical sequence in which one paradigm is replaced in an educational revolution by a new and incommensurate paradigm.[31] In fact, all five are detectable simultaneously in most robust conceptions of liberal education (and, incidentally, in most mission statements of institutions devoted to liberal education), but it is the variation in the weaving of these strands that gives such conceptions (and institutions) their particular distinctiveness. Indeed, a great deal of the dynamics of liberal education's history may be ascribed largely to the shifting relationship, balance, and blend of these strands.

Notes

1 Alasdair MacIntyre, *After Virtue: A Study in Moral Theory*, 2nd edn (Notre Dame, IN: Notre Dame University Press, 1984), 222.

2 Bruce A. Kimball, *Orators & Philosophers: A History of the Idea of Liberal Education* (New York: Teachers College Press, 1986), 24–42.

3 For example, see John Israel, "The Idea of Liberal Education in China," in *The Limits of Reform in China*, ed. R. A. Morse (Boulder, CO: Westview Press, 1983).

4 Aristotle, *Nicomachean Ethics*, 1094a, in *The Complete Works of Aristotle*, 2 vols, ed. Jonathan Barnes (Princeton, NJ: Princeton University Press, 1984). Subsequent references to Aristotle's works are from this edition.

5 Robert M. Pirsig, *Zen and the Art of Motorcycle Maintenance: An Inquiry into Values* (New York: William Morrow, 1974).

6 Noddings, *Happiness and Education*, 84.

7   Richard Rorty, "Universality and Truth," in *Rorty and His Critics*, ed. Robert B. Brandom (Cambridge: Blackwell, 2001), 2.

8   I believe this must be Rorty's meaning; otherwise he would apparently be making knowledge obtainable only *after* an action that is requisite for undertaking the action itself. Compare this, however, with the discussion of emergent aims that follows here.

9   Every English adjective has its limitations in capturing the nuances of this idea. I have settled on "emergent," but it should not suggest that the aim reveals itself without the effort of human pursuit; nor do I mean to connect this usage with the ontological position of emergentism.

10 There is a considerable literature, especially in analytic philosophy, on the nature of educational aims. For a fuller discussion with some parallel points of analysis, see R. S. Peters, "Aims of Education—A Conceptual Inquiry," in *The Philosophy of Education*, ed. R. S. Peters (Oxford: Oxford University Press, 1973), 11–29, with commentaries by others. The most comprehensive account is by John White, *The Aims of Education Restated* (London: Routledge & Kegan Paul, 1982).

11 "Must an Educator Have an Aim?" in *Authority, Responsibility and Education*, ed. R. S. Peters, 2nd edn (London: George Allen & Unwin, 1963), 83–95.

12 Tasos Kazepides, *Education as Dialogue: Its Prerequisites and Its Enemies* (Montreal-Kingston, QC: McGill-Queen's University Press, 2010); this argument is developed in chapter 3, "Can Education Have Aims?", 48–64; in the order I have presented them, the quotations are found on 54, 59, 57, and 55.

13 Martin, *Education Reconfigured*, 67.

14 Ibid., 70.

15 John Stuart Mill, *Inaugural Address at St. Andrews* (London: Longmans, Green, Reader, and Dyer, 1867), 4. This passage immediately follows the comment that appears as the epigraph for my Introduction.

16 Ibid., 5. Italics added.

17 Michel Foucault, *Discipline and Punish: The Birth of the Prison*, trans. Alan Sheridan, 2nd edn (New York: Vintage Books, 1995).

18 Jean-François Lyotard, *The Postmodern Condition: A Report on Knowledge*, trans. Geoff Bennington and Brian Massumi (Minneapolis, MN: University of Minnesota Press, 1984).

19 Martin Heidegger, *Being and Time (Sein und Zeit)*, trans. John Macquarrie and Edward Robinson (New York: Harper & Bros., 1962).

20 Two recent histories of the idea of happiness are: Darrin M. McMahon, *Happiness: A History* (New York: Grove Press, 2006); and Nicholas White, *A Brief History of Happiness* (Malden, MA: Wiley-Blackwell, 2006).

21 For example: Eric G. Wilson, *Against Happiness: In Praise of Melancholy* (New York: Farrar, Straus, and Giroux, 2008); Sara Ahmed, *The Promise of Happiness* (Durham, NC: Duke University Press, 2010); and Pascal Bruckner, *Perpetual Euphoria: On the Duty to Be Happy* (Princeton, NJ: Princeton University Press, 2010).

22 A sampler of one excellent item in each genre: Richard Kraut, *Aristotle on the Human Good* (Princeton, NJ: Princeton University Press, 1989); Sissela Bok, *Exploring Happiness: From Aristotle to Brain Science* (New Haven, CT: Yale University Press, 2010); James Griffin, *Well-Being: Its Meaning, Measurement, and Moral Importance* (Oxford: Clarendon Press, 1986); and Ellen Frankel Paul, Fred D. Miller, Jr., and Jeffrey Paul, eds, *Human Flourishing* (Cambridge: Cambridge University Press, 1999). A psychological work that proclaims the overlap in these concepts in its title is: Martin E. P. Seligman, *Flourish: A Visionary New Understanding of Happiness and Well-being* (New York: Simon & Schuster, 2011).

23 Harry Brighouse, *On Education* (London: Routledge, 2006), 15–16. I should acknowledge that Brighouse refers to education *tout court*, not to liberal education. Yet his account does not apply directly to all varieties of education (vocational or military, for example), and it is only liberal education that makes these elements a recognized aim and object of inquiry.

24 I am indebted to the excellent presentation of these issues in Julia Annas, *Intelligent Virtue* (Oxford: Oxford University Press, 2011), esp. chapter 8, "Living Happily."

25 The philosophical term for such essential individuality is *haeccity*, in contrast to *quiddity*, which refers to defining characteristics of humanity (or other entities as members of a class). For a well-researched list of hundreds of human universals, see Donald E. Brown, *Human Universals* (Philadelphia: Temple University Press, 1991).

26 We use the abbreviation "fl." (*floruit*, "flourishing") with a date when a person's birth and death dates are unknown. It indicates the person's productive years or the year of a landmark accomplishment. Note that it is a judgment made by others and in retrospect, not by the person themselves.

27 Noddings, *Educating Moral People*, 123.

28 Nussbaum, *Cultivating Humanity*.

29 Compare Theodor W. Adorno's essay, "Education After Auschwitz," in *Critical Models: Interventions and Catchwords*, trans. Henry W. Pickford (New York: Columbia University Press, 1998), 191–204.

30 T. M. Scanlon, *What We Owe Each Other* (Cambridge, MA: Harvard University Press, 1998), 131.

31 The classic treatment of paradigms is Thomas S. Kuhn, *The Structure of Scientific Revolutions* (Chicago: University of Chicago Press, 1971). I do not intend that the "cascade of specificity" be interpreted as a chronological sequence, but rather as a rational reconstruction of the conceptual relationships involved.

PART II

Paradigms of Liberal Education

3

Transmission of Culture

The dead bequeathed them life.

SIEGFRIED SASSOON, "THE GRANDEUR OF GHOSTS"

The possibility of a good life, indeed of any sort of life beyond a feral existence, depends upon enculturation. But culture will evaporate with human mortality unless it is transmitted to a new generation. We humans are beings born into helplessness and ignorance; parents cannot convey through their genes what they have learned in their lives. Learning is imperative for survival, but every generation must start to learn *ab initio*. Both the survival of culture and our individual flourishing thus depend on learning.

Fortunately, our ancestors produced two innovations that transformed the possibilities for learning: the development of complex symbol systems in which to encode experience, and techniques of preserving these codes in durable artifacts. We are thereby able to articulate, accumulate, and preserve the human experience, creating a legacy of learning that grows with each generation and can be passed along to the next. It is the urgent educational imperative to conserve and bequeath this cultural treasure, our intellectual heritage: sophisticated languages, whole disciplines of knowledge, a profusion of great texts and works of art, historical narratives, and unsolved but intriguing problems—along with the keys to understanding them. *Liberal education is for the transmission of cultural inheritance across generations—that they may live a flourishing life.* These ideas are expressed, for example, in a passage from Pier Paolo Vergerio, penned in about 1402. In a treatise of educational advice, *The Character and Studies Befitting a Free-born Youth*, written for Ubertino da Cararra, a young member of the ruling family of Padua, Vergerio observes:

> For although written records are very valuable indeed for other purposes, they are especially valuable for preserving the memory of the past, as they contain the deeds of mankind, the unhoped-for turns of fortune, the unusual works of nature, and (more important than all these things) the guiding principles of historical periods. For human memory and objects passed from hand to hand gradually decay and scarcely survive the lifetime of one person, but what has been skillfully entrusted to books endures forever.[1]

Under this paradigm, liberal education is directed toward the appreciation and assimilation of that legacy, which are averred to be indispensible to the supreme aim of discerning and living a good life. There is no greater resource for the exploration of what it means to live as a human being and to consider one's life as a whole than the archives of human experience through history reposited in libraries, galleries, and museums. The substance of liberal education is, therefore, texts (understood broadly to include works of art, music architecture, films, etc.) and the symbol systems (languages) in which they are preserved. This is an education in the humanities in the widest sense of that term (defined so as to include landmark texts in the sciences and mathematics). It privileges the skills of reading and writing (and intelligent listening and viewing); it implies that the educated person is one who is literate, who is versed in languages and knows masterworks or a body of literature—who is, in short, a scholar. The emphasis is on the intellect, the life of the mind: liberal education furnishes the mind and expands the imagination, and its pursuit enlivens the intellect. There is, moreover, a sense that the enriched life of the mind is related, in ways yet to be unpacked, to the cultivation a good life.

The Canon

Given the vastness of the resources and the brevity of a human life, some principle of selection of texts is required both for cultural preservation and for any educational program. Today we can only marvel at Aristotle's unique accomplishment, a record never to be matched: he read so widely and thought so deeply that he produced a landmark treatise in every branch of knowledge known in his day and invented some new branches himself—such as logic, a field in which his texts were definitive for roughly 2,000 years before significant new discoveries replaced them! That is simply not possible now, even if one had his genius. Consider: How many books can you read in your lifetime? Well, if you read one book each day for 80 years—which seems to me a reasonable outer limit—you would have read a total of 29,220 works. In recent years, however, nearly ten times that number were published in the United States *annually*, and roughly 400,000 books were published each year around the world.[2] (And that is only the number of "traditional" books, so not including the more than 750,000 "non-traditional" format titles, and ignoring all journals, magazines, newspapers, blogs, and other printed matter.) Whether educator or student, one must make choices about the texts one reads. Even early on, a division of labor among scholars was required to retain an effective understanding of the various subjects, forms, and languages of preserved texts. Scholarship necessarily specializes quickly. But for the liberal education of an individual, how is one to choose?

The obvious reply is to *choose the best texts*. Vergerio admonishes his readers: "Nor should we spend our time dipping into just any authors; we should read the best ... For what has been sown in young minds puts down deep roots and there is no force that can afterwards pull it up again. Hence, if they become accustomed to the best, they will use and possess them always as their paramount authorities and guides."[3] But advocating "the best" is empty advice without further explication. The dilation of this idea might invoke a focus on masterworks, works judged to be richly endowed with meaning, as measured by their influence in one's culture; works of technical brilliance or innovative impact; works of universal themes and profound insight; works that elevate the mind and normatively shape character—and indeed there have been many such interpretations. As we have seen, for a long period in the West, works of such description were thought to be confined to the classical works of ancient Greece and Rome; the body of favored works, however determined, is known, of course, as "the canon." Assimilating these texts represents the acquisition of one's cultural patrimony; but it is also typically claimed, as implied in Vergerio's comments, that such study is useful in the shaping of character, either because of the content of the texts themselves or because of aspects of the activity of textual study—or both. It is the case that a significant portion of any such cultural legacy is moral in content, explicitly or implicitly: it embodies values and portrays moral exemplars that may provide inspiration for emulation. The principles of canon selection can of course require or favor such content. More subtly, moral considerations are also involved in the evaluation of this heritage, the determination of the principles of selection, and in the implications conveyed regarding the uses and value of this legacy. Commonly (and controversially, as we shall see), theorists within this paradigm also credit the engaged study of great texts with the stimulation and honing of a student's salient moral capacities, such as moral imagination or ethical judgment.

Encountering Great Works

It is clear by now that the content of the curriculum has elevated importance in the transmission of culture paradigm. What is worth transmitting to successor generations (the perspective of the educator); or what is worth learning from recorded human experience (the perspective of the learner)—these determinations refer to curricular content. For those who work within this paradigm, the most important educational questions, the juiciest debates, often revolve around the selection of the canon. The concentration on the transmission of worthy content appears to put the student in a receptive or even passive mode. The would-be scholar must, it seems, study: that is, read, listen, receive, absorb, memorize, and assimilate the words and ideas and experiences of others. Much as a medieval monk, in copying a treasured manuscript, worked under the ideal of letter-perfect fidelity to the original, so the student requires similar virtues of intellectual humility for claiming intellectually her cultural patrimony. Woeful pedagogical practices have indeed often accompanied the replete theories of curriculum that have formed under this paradigm—especially when educators are concerned not only to transmit what they believe to be culturally worthy, but also to assure that those receiving the transmission will similarly value and commit themselves to it.

There are, however, three reasons why this seeming passivity may be deceptive—or at least is not the whole picture. The first is that "simple" reading itself involves complex cognitive processing; it is not simply the passive receipt of a sensory stamp. The second is that there are more active processes often required as well. Reading (and viewing and listening) involve more cognitive processes than simple perception, because one reads texts for more than basic information: understanding a text may be a hard-won achievement. Exegesis, commentary, explication, analysis, and evaluation may be expected of the scholarly reader. This requires more than attention; it demands active and skillful engagement, imagination, and judgment. Harold Bloom, the literary theorist and critic who authored, among many other books, *The Western Canon*, says that great texts inspire and demand a personal struggle, and it is only the agonistic dimension of such encounters that leads to the enlargement of meaning. In such encounters the social purposes of transmission give way to the richness of the inner life of the reader.[4] The third reason is that readers don't simply consume texts; they frequently produce texts themselves. Each generation adds to the repository of encoded experience. Writing or speaking or producing works of art—these require articulation, organization of ideas, the making of cognitive connections, the sorting out of one's own views, and self-expression.

Within this transmission of culture paradigm, there is room for a wide range of interpretations; one dimension along which to array them is the learner's role, ranging from the passive to the active. Passive conceptions emphasize attitudes of receptivity and submission, skills of memory and scholarly precision, and the goal of understanding and valuing canonical works. More active conceptions elevate responsiveness, the tools of critique, and the skills of hermeneutics. The most active involve finding one's own voice, expressing one's own thoughts with excellence, and engaging as a full-fledged partner in this discourse. We may also view this range as marking the journey of an individual learner, as she progresses from initial receptivity and mastery, through hermeneutics and critique, to creative contributions to scholarship and a considered, personal viewpoint. Several forms of excellence are celebrated in this paradigm: (1) those exhibited in the works themselves, that is, those qualities that are deemed to make the works worthy of preservation and selection for transmission; (2) those related to reading (also listening and viewing), including attentiveness, sensitivity, comprehension, knowledge of languages and texts; (3) those related to scholarship, including skills of translation, analysis, and evaluation; (4) those related to writing and speaking, including the rhetorical skills of articulation, expressiveness, clarity of thought, and eloquence; and (5) those targeted moral virtues that bespeak character. Theories developed under this paradigm often assert that these sorts of excellences are inherently related and mutually reinforcing: so, for example, a powerful and persuasive speech genuinely reflects deeply-held and worthy values, the projection of character; and it should be informed and graced by a familiarity with great ideas, the texts and works of our heritage. (Think of the great speeches of Americans, such as Lincoln's Gettysburg Address, Martin Luther King's "I have a dream," or Washington's Farewell Address.)

What is the claimed connection between these excellences and a good life? How does the encounter with great works conduce to a flourishing life? Put briefly (because the reply is examined more fully in a later chapter), the response of some theorists is that such an education will enlarge the mind and shape character in ways that have invaluable application throughout life; others hold the view that this educational experience and the knowledge it conveys are valuable for their own sake and are by themselves a significant part of a good life; and some theorists lay claim to both instrumental and intrinsic value without inconsistency. To absorb the best of the human legacy, or at least one's own cultural legacy, is crucial—so these theorists assert—to addressing such profound questions as *Who am I? What are my origins? What is the story into which I have entered—and how should I live my part? What have others learned and thought and felt during their lives?* And these questions are relevant to the supreme aim of determining how I might flourish, to answering the question: *What is a good life?*

Advocates and Exemplars

The abstract elements of this—indeed, of any—paradigm become more vivid when located in more specific theories that exemplify them. To that end, I will offer representative passages from noteworthy advocates of the cultural transmission model of liberal education. But first I should make a cautionary point: each of these educational theorists has written extensively on education, and all have elaborated positions that are complex and subtle. My purpose here is not to explicate or critique their individual accounts (to do that with any sort of adequacy would exceed the boundaries of this project), nor even to imply that this is the only paradigm in which they work. I do believe that the cultural transmission model outlined above is the primary orientation of their work, and I intend here only to sample their comments in that regard.

William Whewell (1794–1866) was a multifaceted figure: philosopher, historian of science, university administrator, Anglican priest, and more. In 1838, he set forth his view of liberal education with Victorian confidence:

> In nations as in men, in intellect as in social condition, true nobility consists in inheriting what is best in the possessions and character of a line of ancestry. Those who can trace the descent of their own ideas, and their own language, through the race of cultivated nations; who can show that those whom they represent, or reverence as their parents, have everywhere been foremost in the fields of thought and intellectual progress— those are the true nobility of the world of mind; the persons who have received true culture; and such it should be the business of a liberal education to make men.
>
> With these views, I cannot conceive it possible that any well-constituted system of University teaching, in any European nation, can do otherwise than make the study of the best classical authors of Greece and Rome, one of its indispensible and cardinal elements.[5]

The outlook he announced in this passage was, in fact, dominant in the European universities of the nineteenth century, especially in Britain.

About a century later, the incomparable president, and then chancellor, of the University of Chicago, Robert Maynard Hutchins (1899–1977), was a determined proponent of the "Great Books" approach—though he never really succeeded in winning broad faculty acceptance of his ideas. In *The Higher Learning in America*, Hutchins (borrowing the term "permanent studies" from Whewell) wrote:

> We have suggested that the curriculum should be composed principally of the permanent studies. We propose the permanent studies because these studies draw out the elements of our common human nature, because they connect man with man, because they connect us with the best that man has thought, because they are basic to any further study and to any understanding of the world. What are the permanent studies?
>
> They are in the first place those books which have through the centuries attained to the dimensions of classics. Many such books, I am afraid, are in the ancient and medieval period. But even these are contemporary. A classic is a book that is contemporary in every age. That is why it is a classic. The conversations of Socrates raise questions that are as urgent today as they were when Plato wrote. In fact they are more so, because the society in which Plato lived did not need to have them raised as much as we do. We have forgotten how important they are.
>
> Such books are then a part, and a large part, of the permanent studies. They are so in the first place because they are the best books we know. How can we call a man educated who has never read any of the great books in the western world? ...
>
> In the second place these books are an essential part of general education because it is impossible to understand any subject or to comprehend the contemporary world without them.[6]

Hutchins' friend and comrade-in-arms, Mortimer Adler (1902–2001), was a public intellectual and prolific author who evangelized for this form of liberal education. An American who matched elitist judgments of "greatness" with a strong streak of egalitarianism, Adler viewed the access to the cultural treasury as a universal human right—a combination neatly reflected in the title of one of his many books, *Aristotle for Everybody*. In 1952, in collaboration with Hutchins, Adler developed the "Great Books of the Western

World" program for the *Encyclopedia Britannica*—the Western canon in 54 volumes. Thirty years later, he authored *The Paideia Proposal: an Educational Manifesto*, proposing a new structure for elementary education based around the guided reading of masterworks and a Socratic pedagogy. His many works and projects redound with "greatness"—as displayed in another title, *How to Think About the Great Ideas: From the Great Books of Western Civilization*. He even founded a Center for the Study of the Great Ideas.[7]

In 1937, one of the nation's colonial-era colleges was foundering, and two academicians were appointed to save it. Stringfellow Barr (1897–1982) and Scott Buchanan (1895–1968) became, respectively, president and dean of St. John's College in Annapolis. Barr was a Rhodes Scholar and editor of the *Virginia Quarterly*; Buchanan was a philosopher who had worked unsuccessfully on curriculum reform with Hutchins in Chicago. Together they installed a curriculum based on "the great books" of the Western canon and pedagogy based on Socratic dialogue, and thereby stamped the College with a distinctive identity that continues to this day. Its publicity proclaims: "There is no other college quite like St. John's. Through sustained engagement with the works of great thinkers and through genuine discussion with peers, students at St. John's College cultivate habits of mind that will last a lifetime."[8]

Allan Bloom (1930–92), also a denizen of the University of Chicago, in his despair about contemporary higher education, admitted that "We are long past the age when a whole tradition could be stored up in all students, to be fruitfully used later by some"; nevertheless, when he finally presented his positive view on liberal education, he wrote:

> Of course, the only serious solution is the one that is almost universally rejected: the good old Great Books approach, in which a liberal education means reading certain generally recognized classic texts, just reading them, letting them dictate what the questions are and the method of approaching them—not forcing them into categories we make up, not treating them as historical products ... [W]herever the Great Books make up a central part of the curriculum, the students are excited and satisfied, feel they are doing something that is independent and

fulfilling, getting something from the university they cannot get elsewhere … A good program of liberal education feeds the student's love of truth and passion to live a good life.[9]

The final exemplar, clearly of the more active viewpoint with this paradigm, is the British intellectual, Michael Oakeshott (1901–90). He emphasized that the student was not simply to receive a cultural heritage, but to join in the dialogue (what Hutchins called "the Great Conversation") with great thinkers of the past. Among Oakeshott's many elegant essays is one of the most beautiful and oft-quoted passages describing liberal education:

> As civilized human beings, we are the inheritors, neither of an inquiry about ourselves and the world, nor of an accumulating body of information, but of a conversation, begun in the primeval forests and extended and made more articulate in the course of centuries. It is a conversation that goes on both in public and within each of ourselves … Conversation is not an enterprise designed to yield an intrinsic profit, a contest where a winner gets a prize, nor is it an activity of exegesis; it is an unrehearsed intellectual adventure…
>
> … Education, properly speaking, is an initiation into the skill and partnership of this conversation in which we learn to recognize the voices, to distinguish the proper occasions of utterance, and in which we acquire the intellectual and moral habits appropriate to conversation. And it is this conversation which, in the end, gives place and character to every human activity and utterance."[10]

Through engaging in the Immortal Conversation, we may find our own voice as well.

Critiques of the Transmission of Culture Paradigm

Critiques of various theories developed under this paradigm are plentiful. We may anticipate their spirit and substance in the sardonic portrait of "Dr Picken" given by philosopher Roger Scruton, in his delicious work, *I Drink Therefore I Am*:

Dr Picken typified the osmotic process whereby a cultural and intellectual inheritance was transmitted within college walls. Provided you approach him with a humility equal to that which he constantly displayed, you could pick up from him any amount of knowledge on any number of subjects ... and the very irrelevance to the surrounding world of everything he knew made the learning of it all the more rewarding ... He did not believe that the purpose of knowledge is to help the student. On the contrary. For Dr Picken, the purpose of the student is to help knowledge. He was throughout his life the willing and self-sacrificing trustee of an intellectual inheritance. Young people mattered to him because they had the brains into which his reservoir of learning could be poured, along with the wine. He looked at us students skeptically, but always with that under-lying hope that, in this or that undisciplined young face, there was yet the outward sign of a brain large enough and dispassionate enough to capture some of the accumulated knowledge of mankind, and which could carry that knowledge through life without spilling it, until finding another brain into which it might be discharged.[11]

It is clearly a target-rich paradigm. I will not be concerned here, however, with those critiques that address the particulars of any theory, such as the advocacy of a particular curriculum or teaching method. (As I acknowledged in chapter 1, those critiques frequently seem quite justified to me.) Rather, I want to focus on major criticisms that apply broadly to the paradigm itself, and therefore to most or all theories that fall under it. Nearly all of the significant claims of this paradigm have generated debate—the value of enculturation, the authoritative construction of a canon, the focus on the life of the mind, the view that encountering great texts can shape character, and the alleged link of such an education to a flourishing life.

Prominent among objections is that the transmission of culture model presumes a false human homogeneity. Whose culture is to be transmitted in this paradigm? On its face, it seems to presume a shared or unified culture, which defies reality; or it arrogantly projects Western European culture upon other peoples—an intellectual colonialism. In either case, it is woefully unsuitable for our multicultural world.

Adler addressed this concern head-on and gave little ground:

> There may be other great ideas and other great conversations
> about them in three or four of the cultures in the Far East—
> Hindu, Buddhist, Confucian, and Taoist. But these are not only
> quite separate from one another, they are also extraneous to
> the great conversation about the 102 great ideas in Western
> literature and thought. At this stage in the history of the world,
> a world cultural community does not exist, and a global set of
> great ideas cannot be compiled. The future may hold the possi-
> bility of one global great conversation, but that lies far ahead of
> where we are today.[12]

This is, of course, the sort of supercilious response that proves
the critics right. Adler has no compunction about nominating a
few Eastern cultures in which "there may be other great ideas"—
though he doesn't sound confident that they will turn up; nor does
he equivocate about the precise number of "great ideas" in Western
culture. Moreover, he states flatly that there is no global cultural
treasure to transmit, no set of global great ideas, because there is
not (at least not yet) a global culture. Culture seems synonymous
with religious tradition in his account, though Islam appears to
be forgotten, and the notion of a multicultural conversation is
apparently impossible. Adler's rebuttal seems, in the end, to have
conceded the point of the critique.

But let us set aside—no, let us jettison altogether—his parochial
notion of where greatness lies. One might argue (still within this
paradigm) that her own culture should have primary, if not sole,
claim on a student's attention; so Adler is otherwise on target,
assuming he is addressing readers in Eurocentric cultures. The
problem is that this doesn't reflect the world we live in now:
whether you think that the forces of globalization will soon
produce a sufficiently unified global culture, or whether you think
that multiculturalism will always prevail, the chance of flourishing in that world (and in many neighborhoods!) would seem
to benefit from a familiarity with more than one's own culture,
or at least from the insight that other cultures have their own
integrity and value. And does it not seem that the conversational
or dialogical model is especially appropriate for a multicultural
society? Moreover, Adler does not imagine that such an education

could actually further a "global conversation" and help create "a world cultural community." To be fair, Adler never witnessed the power of global communications and social networks. While the transmission of culture paradigm does entail both a preoccupation with cultural legacy and the need for selecting worthy texts, it does not require either a single or a particular culture, nor does it prescribe a specific standard of selection. If a flourishing life is the aim, these choices should be made *with sensitivity to the current and foreshadowed culture(s) in which the students will live.*[13]

A deeper criticism is that the transmission paradigm assumes that there is a universal human nature reflected in the cultural legacy (or legacies) of human experience. Moreover, it employs a discredited essentialism to isolate the requisite elements of humanity. There is some truth in this critique, in that this paradigm does assume the relevance and value of prior human experience to successor generations. It presumes that what we share is sufficient for communication, even across generations, and for the thoughts and experiences of one person (suitably encoded and decoded) to be entertained by another. But it need not assume that all people or all cultures are alike; it can help identify and even revel in variation and difference. Empirical research has shown that, beyond biological elements, humans do indeed universally exhibit elements of culture.[14] This paradigm takes "humanity" to be a meaningful concept, and it adopts—if only as a hypothesis to be tested or a working principle to be proven—that all human life has much of importance in common. Among those commonalities is the potential to learn from our differences.

A third objection is against the idea of a principle of selection: however one presumes to deem artifacts or texts worthy of transmission through education, whether based on some notion of "greatness," or social relevance, or political correctness, the principle and the choices made under it are inevitably subjective and arbitrary. Nothing provokes a dispute among academics like a reading list—and these seemingly pedantic disputes can launch culture wars.

Suppose we grant this point: then what is to be done? I noted earlier the press of human finitude on our capacity for reading. Selectivity is required for anyone. Even professors who bash the idea of a canon, in all likelihood, teach in courses in which they have chosen a core reading list, or set the principle by which their students should select their individual reading. Making such selections is one of the responsibilities of educators, either collectively at various levels, or (especially in higher education) individually, as courses are designed. The genuine issue for any educational program under this paradigm—and for all individual courses—is what principle of selection to use, not whether to have one.

I will defer until the chapters of Part III the issues concerning the plausibility of linking this sort of education with a good life and the shaping of character; the larger discussion of values to be developed in that section will be salient to these concerns. I will also pass by the worry that a focus on the transmission of curricular content leads to a passive role for the learner; there are, as I have said, more active-learning versions of this paradigm. But there is one more critique to discuss at this point: the concern that focusing education on the transmission of a cultural legacy occupies students with the past and with the lives of others, not with their own futures. It has indeed been common for advocates of this paradigm to speak of "permanent studies," "universal truths," and the glories of Greece and Rome—and to be either uninterested in or sharply critical of contemporary society and the imperative for relevance to the context of students' lives. Its advocates are educational and often political conservatives, but in the deep sense of seeking to preserve the good, that is, whatever they have found to be valuable. Moreover, the cultural transmission approach seems intellectualist, focused on the life of the mind only—and even then in a narrow sense, traditionally excluding emotion or caring. The human person being addressed is not a whole person, since the model ignores the body, everyday skills and requirements, and concern for personal relationships and roles, whether familial, social, or professional.

In response, I must note that these neglected aspects of the whole person are nevertheless part of the cultural legacy; there are ample resources to address them, texts and works that have encoded human experience with regard to these features of human life. We need to mine them to restore a balance. They will reflect the intellectual climate of their times, no doubt, but still may be revelatory. Yet, nevertheless, we will be dealing with mediated experience: encoded cultural objects are literate or musical or artistic or architectural, and so on, and the very fact of such encoding transforms the experience and "intellectualizes"; the intellect is used to decode and absorb it. But, while we should be sensitive to its limits, it is mediated experience that allows us to extend our individual reach, to connect with others across time and space, and to learn beyond the direct experience of our lifetimes.

This last set of concerns tempts me to play a trump card: these issues are, I believe, addressed and ultimately resolved by the other paradigms to be described. And, to lay all my cards on the table, I believe the five paradigms of liberal education are complementary, that each provides a different approach that ameliorates the problems of another. It is their blending, their balance, and their tension, which release a synergy.

Notes

1 Pier Paolo Vergerio, "The Character and Studies Befitting a Free-born Youth" (c. 1402 CE), in *Humanist Educational Treatises*, trans. Craig W. Kallendorf (Cambridge, MA: The I Tatti Renaissance Library, Harvard University Press, 2002), 45.

2 According to Bowker, "the world's leading source for bibliographic information." These figures are for 2009. For a complete profile, see: http://bowker.com/index.php/press-releases/616-bowker-reports-traditional-us-book-production-flat-in-2009 (accessed November 2011).

3 Vergerio, "The Character and Studies," 59.

4 Harold Bloom, *The Western Canon*. I am grateful to Christopher Cordner for his article, "Literature, Morality and the Individual in the Shadows of Postmodernism," *Literature and Aesthetics: Journal of the Sydney Society of Literature and Aesthetics*, 1998, whose comments on Bloom have informed my own.

5 William Whewell, *On the Principles of English University Education*, 2nd edn (London: John W. Parker, 1838), 37. Immediately following this passage, Whewell makes it clear that literary study is not intended to be the sole element of the curriculum; indeed, one of his larger purposes is to support the place of mathematics in liberal education.

6 Robert M. Hutchins, *The Higher Learning in America* (New Haven, CT: Yale University Press, 1936), 77–8.

7 The three works (of his many) mentioned here are Mortimer J. Adler, *Aristotle for Everybody: Difficult Thought Made Easy* (New York:

Touchstone Books, 1997); *The Paideia Proposal: An Educational Manifesto* (New York: Macmillan, 1982); and *How to Think About the Great Ideas: From the Great Books of Western Civilization* (Chicago: Open Court Publishing, 2000). Information on the Center for the Study of the Great Ideas, including Adler's explanation for the meaning of "greatness," may be found at http://www.thegreatideas.org/index.html (accessed May 2011). For an excellent critique of Adler's views, see Mulcahy, *The Educated Person.*

8 St. John's College, http://www.sjca.edu/ (accessed August 2011).

9 Bloom, *The Closing of the American Mind*, 64 and 344–5.

10 Michael Oakeshott, "The Voice of Poetry in the Conversation of Mankind," in *Rationalism in Politics and Other Essays* (London: Methuen, 1962), 199.

11 Roger Scruton, *I Drink Therefore I Am* (London: Continuum, 2009), 21.

12 Mortimer J. Adler, "The Great Ideas," http://www.thegreatideas.org/index.html (accessed May 2011).

13 Interestingly, St. John's College, through its Graduate Institute on a second campus in Santa Fe, New Mexico, introduced in 1994 a program devoted to "Eastern Classics," the great books of China, Japan, and India, in which students may earn a Master of Arts in Eastern Classics degree (M.A.E.C.).

14 Brown, *Human Universals.*

4

Self-Actualization

But it was to man alone, at the moment of his creation, that God bequeathed seeds laden with all potentialities— the germ of every form of life. Whichsoever of these a man cultivates will mature and bear fruit within him ... we are born creatures who may be what we choose ourselves to be ...

GIOVANNI PICO DELLA MIRANDOLA, *ORATION ON THE DIGNITY OF MAN*

Who am I? What might I become? Do I have a destiny? How might I flourish? These are the questions that launch the second paradigm, which affirms that *liberal education is for self-actualization, leading to a normative individuality.* The distinctive task of education, in this view, is to awaken and nurture valued capacities, dispositions, and talents abiding in the learner. It overlays the normal experience of growing up and draws upon a yearning for fulfillment or completion, combining the hope for betterment with the desire for that which is one's own—the perfection of oneself that I am calling "a normative individuality." This is a "perfectionist" framework, in that it links particular conceptions of the good life to the cultivation and exercise of certain elements of human nature or of individual character (or both). To have a good life thus requires self-actualization, and liberal education is about *becoming.*

The ideal of a self-actualized person may be delineated at various levels of generality from a generic human being to a specific individual. Where does one obtain the normative aspects to be developed? Theorists have looked to theological, naturalistic, socially constructed, or rational sources for sanction. The chosen source of normativity spotlights aspects of the self that are worthy of actualization and, hence, educationally relevant. Combining a level of generality with a source for normativity yields various types of self-actualization theory. For example, some theories in this paradigm are directed only at the self-actualized human being; such a generic account may look to an account of human nature, to distinctively human capacities, or to indices of human well-being and flourishing to determine what should be developed in the learner. Other theories give an account of actualized types of human beings, drawing upon gender differences or social mores or roles for normative qualities. Still others focus on individual development and look to the unique potential and perceived promise of the individual student. Complex theories may layer or blend these levels and sources.

Plato's educational theory, for example, famously gives great weight to social roles, based on a tripartite grouping of the needs of the community: the production of various goods and services, defense and policing, and governance and leadership. It is an individual's potential or aptitude for these roles that is educationally salient, and their optimal realization is the goal of Plato's plan for public education. By contrast, Aristotle's conception of self-actualization is more balanced, based on human nature and recognizing primarily naturalistic indices of well-being as the indicators of flourishing, and yet giving place to such social roles as parent or head-of-household, to (supposed) gender and cultural differences, and to individual variability of, for example, temperament or constitution. Friedrich Nietzsche—though he does not offer a full-blown theory of education—can be placed within the paradigm of self-actualization. The heroic struggle for self-actualization that molds his *Übermensch* is guided by naturalistic and especially individualistic traits, not by social mores or roles (except by opposition to them).

Although it is impossible for any theorist to spell out specific, individualized accounts of self-actualization for even a large group of people, it is clear that some wish to point educational practice in that direction—and others do not. For theorists of the former stripe, liberal education *individuates*, that is, it draws the student toward his distinctive, personal fulfillment; for those of the latter, liberal education *idealizes*, that is, it draws the student toward a universal ideal of self-actualized humanity. For many theorists, it attempts to harmonize both processes. For all, however, it is individual selves that are to be actualized through education.

In contrast to the transmission of culture paradigm, the focus is not on the curriculum so much as on the capabilities of the learner; what is to be studied is dependent upon and derived from the actualized ideal of the student. It is not the need for enculturation that inspires this view: it is the promise of the individual. Under this paradigm, leading a flourishing life requires self-actualization first and foremost.

The Metaphysics of Self-Actualization

There are interesting variations in the language of this paradigm, and they hint at different metaphysical underpinnings beneath the educational surface. The educational process and its aim may be variously described as: *finding* or *discovering one's self*; as *self-definition, self-realization*, or *self-actualization*; as *self-formation* or *self-creation*. It all begins, of course, with *self-knowledge*. Each of these interpretations intimates ontological commitments that differ in regard to exactly what exists when, and what happens during the proposed normative alteration of the self. Primal yet metaphysically complex concepts, such as the self, individuality, possibility, potential, and actuality, are deeply embedded in the paradigm; some paradigmatic versions also invoke the concepts of talent, destiny, or fate. Superficially subtle differences in expression may be tied to profound differences in the metaphysical account of the process.

We can mark these subtle differences in epigrams and clichés. The famous Delphic motto was "Know thyself!" The poet, Pindar, wrote, "Become what you are." But there are also imperatives that we should become more than we are: "Be all that you can be," urges the United States Army. "Be your best self," encourages Oprah Winfrey. Is the intended educational process to be one of coming to know oneself and celebrating what one already is, perhaps becoming aware of one's prejudices and limits; or of finding one's singular destiny or *daimon*, and learning to "love one's fate"; or of nurturing a contingent development, growth, or actualization; or of choosing and acquiring something valuable but not inherent and making it one's own?

In fact, the paradigm of self-actualization accepts a range of theories that blend processes of discovery, understanding, nurturance, acquisition, and assimilation. The variation in these conceptions turns largely on two factors: (1) whether the relevant aspects of normative individuality are nascent in the individual, and (2) the sort of process required for an individual to render them effectively operational. But all interpretations claim that liberal learning offers students a better version of themselves than would likely be attainable through simply growing up and older, and this self-actualization entails moral development.[1]

The more individualized versions of self-actualization also offer the student a realized *identity*—a sense of one's self that has both individuality and authenticity. The flourishing life to be sought is not just a good life, it is somehow *one's own life*—a life that displays one's uniqueness, the life one was meant to have, one's true vocation, a life that one claims for oneself. The supreme aim of liberal education is given an individualized interpretation: it becomes, for each of us, the search for a compelling vision of *my* good life, and the cultivation of that life. Any educationally adequate interpretation of a flourishing life must, for those who have this outlook, incorporate the actualization of individual potentials.

The Actualizable Self

Three basic assumptions about the self in this paradigm are: (1) that its potentials are knowable; (2) that some of these potentials are worthy of educational efforts; and (3) that at least some of the latter group are actualizable.[2] To say that one's potentials are knowable does not require that the self be transparent; it might take considerable effort or expertise to determine one's potential. Theories of human nature, accounts of what features of human beings as a species should be developed through education—these are debated in the public arena, benefitting from dialogue and billions of actual cases. Determining an individual's potential, however, is a much more constrained process. How do we learn what someone has the capacity to do or to become?

One method in common use today is to rely on the use of diagnostic instruments, ranging from genetic screening to tests of aptitude, intelligence, or personality—each intended to reveal something relevant about the individual. Another method is to rely on the reactions expressed by the individual to various experiences: we expose them to different activities, to various cultures, to a breadth of study, to see which, if any, generate interest, satisfaction, or passion. As we know from history, there is ample room in both approaches for social and personal prejudice: what is tested and its chosen indicators, who is tested and for what purpose, and how results are used, can distort the view of what potential a person presents. In many respects, it matters whether one's potential is known to oneself or to others only or to both. The struggle to understand or forge one's identity is the basic plot of much of literature, from heroic epics to coming-of-age stories. That struggle is, in this paradigm, put at the heart of liberal education.

Second, there is the assumption that some, only a subset of, human potentials are worthy of being developed through education. This claim is a two-edged sword: it states that each person has precious potentials that can be developed into valuable, functioning virtues, skills, qualities, and so on; but it also suggests that we may have other qualities that should remain undeveloped or be suppressed. We all have, in short, the potential for good and for bad. Many philosophies of human nature have bifurcated the self, decreeing that some aspects of human beings are noble and deserve cultivation, while other aspects are base and must be restrained or escaped if possible. It is Plato, of course, who began this splitting of the human psyche, proclaiming that the mind's ability to grasp ideas and reason is noble, but the body's depravations and decay constitute an unfortunate and embarrassing debilitation. Our bivalent self is one clue that this earth is not our home; this life, not our real life. For these thinkers, our true calling, our best life, our destiny, lies elsewhere. Other philosophies—Aristotle's, for example—embrace an integrated view of the self, and are more likely to find this world our home, and this life our only one or the only one that matters now, though this does not remove the responsibility for choosing among all our potentials. On the individual level, however, there are more agonizing choices than those between one's brighter and one's darker possibilities; sometimes we have to choose between goods. Imagine a young woman who has the potential to become a champion golfer, a political leader, or a virtuoso violinist—but, who cannot, for practical reasons easily imagined, develop all three talents optimally. Any would represent a flourishing life and a blossoming of her individuality, but each would require the rejection of the other lives (a reality Aristotle recognized in noting that *privation*, as he termed it, is a cost of *actualization*). Our understanding of our potentials, our live options, also depends on our circumstances—who knows how many such young women there might have lived in ancient Athens, but since golf and the violin had not been invented, and since women generally were not welcomed in politics or thought to be capable of leadership, none were found and none were hunted.

The third assumption, that the valuable traits or capacities are actualizable, affirms the effectiveness of human educational effort in shaping self-improvement. The requisite process may be somewhat mysterious, but may engage the full range of educational techniques: practice, habit, experience, self-reflection, self-expression, articulation, gaining information or knowledge, emulating role models, and so on. Unlike the transmission of culture model, self-actualization privileges active learning; in many versions, the "self" in "self-actualization" is both object and agent of the change. Various individuals, various potentials, may require different modes of education for effective self-actualization. In the more individualistic version, there is likely to be an emphasis in practice on finding the proper fit between the individual and the teacher, the school, and the content and method of instruction.

Advocates and Exemplars

Among advocates of self-actualization, horticultural metaphors and images abound. German educator and author, Friedrich Froebel (1782–1852), recognizing that children have individual needs and potentials, developed a concept of early childhood education for which he coined the term "kindergarten." In this "garden of children," one needed first to understand what sort of plants were seeded, which was largely discovered through play; then it was a matter of providing the appropriate nutrients in the environment to encourage each child to grow and bloom. "The mind grows by self-revelation. In play the child ascertains what he can do, discovers his possibilities of will and thought by exerting his power spontaneously."[3] The tendency to replace verbs like "transmit," "instill," and "inculcate" with verbs like "nurture," "cultivate," and "develop" indicates a shift from content-centered to child-centered pedagogy.

Different plants require different conditions in which to thrive, of course, but once the right encouragement is offered, the educational garden must rely on the child's own nature. This approach is affirmed by the Italian educator, Maria Montessori (1870–1952):

> Scientific observation has established that education is not what the teacher gives; education is a natural process spontaneously carried out by the human individual, and is acquired not by listening to words but by experiences upon the environment. The task of the teacher becomes that of preparing a series of motives of cultural activity, spread over a specially prepared environment, and then refraining from obtrusive interference. Human teachers can only help the great work that is being done, as servants help the master. Doing so, they will be witnesses to the unfolding of the human soul and to the rising of a New Man who will not be a victim of events, but will have the clarity of vision to direct and shape the future of human society.[4]

The notions that self-actualization is the hope and purpose of education and that it requires the kind of freedom found in play and in artistic expression attracted progressive educators both in Europe and the United States. In Britain, the impact was greatest at the primary and secondary levels. A. S. Neill's (1883–1973) Summerhill school, founded on the Continent and moved to England in 1923, and still in operation, gives its students radical personal freedom, and finds in such freedom the basis for happiness and growth. But in the United States, there was an impact in higher education as well. New "experimental" colleges were founded, or new curricula and pedagogies with a "progressive" approach were instituted at long-standing institutions. They were avowedly student-centered and celebrated student self-expression; they expanded student freedoms and introduced self-designed studies; they awarded academic credit for artistic pursuits and internships; and they claimed to awaken the unique potential of each student. The early wave crested in the 1920s but included such institutions as Antioch College (1852), Rollins College (1885), The New School (1919), and Bennington College (1932); a second wave, rising in the spirit of the 1960s, included New College of Florida (1960), Hampshire College (1965), and The Evergreen State College (1967).

This sampler of advocates and schools does not reflect the rich theoretical work on self-actualization produced from Aristotle onward. To exemplify such theories, I want to consider a work of the American philosopher, David L. Norton (1930–1995). It is perhaps an odd choice because, although Norton advances a provocative and fully elaborated theory, he does not present it as a theory of liberal education—and, as we shall see, he rejects certain traditional educational claims. The theory is beautifully laid out in his 1976 book, *Personal Destinies: A Philosophy of Ethical Individualism.* Its opening chapter, titled "The Ethical Priority of Self-Actualization," expresses the affirmation that identifies his theory with this paradigm: the first priority in cultivating a good life is self-actualization. This is a linkage he, too, identifies with Aristotle's conception of *eudaimonia.* Although Norton presents his theory as universal in application, it celebrates the particular: it is not primarily about *human destiny*, but rather about *personal destinies*—which, he believes, are possessed singularly by each and every human being. He invokes the image of Socrates listening to his "inner voice" or *daimon*, and adopts that term—the meaning of which evolved from "guardian spirit" to "character" to "personal destiny" or "fate" to "demon." A good life is not to be defined by externalities: it must grow from a personal search, freely undertaken, for one's own *daimon*; then one must embrace and "live" that choice. While life as a human being offers infinite, genuine possibilities for one's life, among these is one's "ownmost possibility." Self-actualization thus involves self-discovery and the realization of one's ownmost possibility through living out one's destiny.

Norton's metaphysical assumptions seem retro to some. The late Richard Rorty, American philosophical provocateur and neo-pragmatist, stated in a recently released film interview: "I think the Socratic ideal of self-knowledge is replaced, among contemporary intellectuals, by the Nietzschean idea of self-creation. The life of the intellectual is not a matter of finding out what has been inside himself or herself all the time, it's a matter of becoming someone new."[5] But Norton is explicit and forthright about his metaphysical commitments. He writes, in a chapter titled "The Metaphysics of Individualism": "[There are] two ultimate presuppositions that are distinctive to self-actualization ethics. This ethics presupposes the normative authority of individuated possibilities. Accordingly, it presupposes, first, that possibility is an ultimate, underived, and irreducible modality of the real and, second, that possibilities subsist as an incommensurable multiplicity of discrete individuals."[6] Furthermore, shaping a future requires alternative possibilities and the freedom to choose among them. Through a sustained and historically informed discussion of these presuppositions, Norton strives to clarify the ontology of self-actualization, the choice to make explicit or actual that which is implicit or possible—yet real. As Norton puts it, "The individual's choice of what is to be done by himself is the choice of his ultimate possibility, a possibility that *is himself* as a fulfilled person."[7] And again, "What one chooses wholeheartedly is the self one shall strive to become, a becoming that contributes actual worth to the world."[8]

One of the best attributes of Norton's theory is its recognition of life's stages—childhood, adolescence, maturation, and old age—and the distinct tasks each brings. Adolescence is the period in which the individual discovers her autonomy, her sense of uniqueness, and begins the search for identity and destiny; maturation is the period in which one recognizes his mortality, commits to his destiny, and lives according to its lights. What are the marks of self-actualization? Norton believes that it requires "whole-heartedness" and brings with it personal integrity—indeed, "the life of the integral individual [may be seen] to constitute but a single act spread over time."[9] Because the self one has actualized is one's "ownmost" possibility, it also displays authenticity. The subjective marks are a type of happiness, an end to "peevish striving," and a sense of being in place, being where one ought to be and doing what one ought to do: what one—*this* one individual—*must* do.

Like most robust ethical theories, when seen from other angles Norton's account also may be interpreted as a theory of personhood, a theory of human psychology, and a theory of education. Viewed as an exemplar of the self-actualization paradigm I have described, his theory lies among those that emphasize the actualization of the unique, individual self; though we should keep in mind that other theories under this paradigm may emphasize the actualization of universal or generic human qualities, such as moral virtues, self-reliance, social skills, or intellectual capabilities. It is rare for any theory to reject one of the polarities completely. In practice, both concerns are usually in play—how can one actualize one's individuality without actualizing one's more generic human capacities? Even Norton presents a *general* theory of human *individuality*.

Educators who staff schools must, of necessity, plan an education for groups of students; they naturally tend to address common human capacities and identify generic objectives. But practitioners of the self-actualization model also understand that differentiated and individuated learning opportunities are required if individual student potentials are to be developed—and therefore they allow an individual student to explore alternatives. But this is where Norton cries "Halt!" The way a student explores life possibilities, he believes, is through "participatory enactment"—an imaginative entering-in to attractive alternatives. He says:

> Exploration consists in enactment of alternatives, followed by evaluation by each youth himself, aided by teachers skilled in hermeneutics. Because knowledge is to be gained by the method we have termed "participatory enactment," the classroom is an inadequate arena, and education must enter the world by such means as a work-study program and apprenticeship structures. For it is an experimental *doing* that is to be analyzed for the evidence of innate potentiality it affords. Classroom study is no substitute for the required doing because it is its own distinctive sort of doing. Indeed it is a highly constricted sort of doing, physically inert, focused upon books, and natively congenial to very few sorts of persons.[10]

Dismayed that we identify self-actualization with education, education with schooling, and schooling with the academic classroom, Norton asserts that "We urgently need culturally endorsed alternatives to four years of college in the interest of talented youth for whom academia is purgatory."

One response is that Norton's critique seems directed at the cultural transmission paradigm of education alone, and that he construes education to be limited to the classroom experience. He finds this sort of education, "focused upon books," to be neither utilitarian ("Bluntly put, a college degree is an impediment to seventy percent of the vocations for which the degree is presently required ...") nor valuable in itself—"except for the small numbers whose true vocation is scholarship."[11] This was, of course, written decades ago, and experiential education has become an ascendant mode of learning in the liberal arts experience. But the social imperative to earn a college degree has, if anything, intensified, although current economic conditions have triggered a renewed debate. It is important to acknowledge, however, that Norton is not rejecting learning, but only the undifferentiated learning opportunities that are directed toward assumed and hypothetical needs. Surely, self-actualization requires learning as well as choosing and living. Norton is advocating an education that is broader than schooling (or, implausibly, the drastic reform of schooling), but it is in service to the cultivation of a eudaimonistic life. Whatever the response to his metaphysics or his educational advice, we may understand the search for one's *daimon* as the search for a compelling conception of a good life, a good life of one's own.

Critiques of the Self-Actualization Paradigm

The central insight of this paradigm seems intuitive and even obvious: education is about a betterment of the individual that improves prospects for a good life. It shines the educational spotlight on the learner, usually the learner as an individual, toward whose development curricular and pedagogical plans are framed, guided by the learner's natural capacities and interests. These "progressive" features do not, however, shield this paradigm from criticism.

There are critiques that challenge the metaphysics on which the paradigm is constructed. Perhaps the most ominous are those that deny the existence of the key entity: the self. The concept of self-actualization does not require that we take the self to be a thing among others, like tables and chairs, but it does require some conception of a self that has both stability (or continuity) and the capacity for change. Some reject the concept of human nature, which is crucial to any perfectionism that purports to derive its notion of flourishing from the nature of human being or human beings. (Accepting such critiques would have momentous repercussions for the concept of education itself.) The special and hypothetically distinctive characteristics and capacities of human beings used as normative by some theorists are contested by opposing philosophies and by empirical research. Many previously nominated features by theorists—such as tool-making, means-end reasoning, play, communication through speech—have failed, after sustained research, to separate humans from all other animals. Other research questions whether humans indeed exhibit such features: are we rational beings? Or are we routinely influenced by unconscious and irrelevant factors, oblivious to what is mattering to us, "predictably irrational"[12]?

Less sweeping—and more persuasive—is the criticism of theories like Norton's that postulate the pre-existence or subsistence of one's ownmost possibility—the idea that there is a preordained personal destiny for each of us that we may find and live out, reject, or tragically miss altogether. But we need not employ such an individualized version of Platonism to construct a self-actualization theory. We would still need some rationale for the normative evaluation of a person's potential or possibilities, but it would be broader in its openness to more than one possibility as representing flourishing for the same individual. Remember our talented young woman with mutually-cancelling potentials in at least three directions? We need not assume that only one of these lives is the child's "ownmost possibility," representing her authentic self—her personal destiny; we might well believe that any such future self is worthy, authentic, and fully flourishing. Neither theory gives much guidance to the young person who must make such a choice, of course, but a theory like Norton's that elevates a single possibility, weighs more heavily and makes the choice, literally, fateful.

Perhaps the most ready-to-hand criticism of the self-actualization paradigm is that it is, well, self-centered! To base education fixedly on the self seems patently to disregard human relationships, one's cultural inheritance, and the practical and ethical dimensions of social life. Surely, liberal education is not, for each of us, "all about me." There are at least two lines of response to this concern. The first is that, as specific theories are framed within this paradigm, the self may be conceived as contextual, situated, and relational; and self-actualization may well involve a normative quality of relations with others and social action. No one has said that the flourishing self flourishes alone. Norton himself invoked Plato's "principle of the congeniality of excellences," claiming that virtues arise in complementarity, having relations of mutual support.[13] The second response is simply to remember my view that self-actualization is but one of the strands of liberal education and is supported by the others, which together address or at least ameliorate this concern; and—to repeat a claim not yet fully defended—most robust theories of liberal education include elements of all five paradigms.

Finally, one might wonder whether self-actualization is not the aim of education *tout court* rather than a distinctive paradigm within liberal education, and whether, in that case, it is empty of useful content. It does seem correct that all forms of education—whether vocational or religious or liberal—imply a "betterment" or normative change in the learner. But the liberal education paradigm I have described is more commanding than that: it instates the sort of betterment that conduces to a good life; its normativity is drawn from different sources; the betterment of the individual is its aim, not a by-product of achieving another goal; it concentrates educational efforts on the self and its development. While a cascade of increasingly specific theories and plans would certainly add further content, these differences alone show the distinctiveness of self-actualization as a paradigm of liberal learning. Moreover, if we were to make that misidentification, we would lose the question of whether a focus on self-actualization does in fact lead to a flourishing life.

The elevation of self-actualization, in the great majority of accounts, introduces the importance of self-reflection and celebrates a rich, inner life as an aspect of flourishing. It reminds us that our social and objectified selves are not all; our inner lives can be impoverished, desolate, humdrum, or the opposite. Many advocates of the transmission of culture model claim that the enhancement of one's inner life is a great benefit of reading the great works.[14] Self-actualization seems to reverse the priority: enlarging and enriching the dimension of inwardness in one's life may be the whole point.

Notes

1 Nietzsche might seem to be an exception, but even though Nietzsche self-consciously rejects conventional moral standards, there is a normative individuality (for Nietzsche, *der Übermensch*) that is to be achieved through heroic struggle. This anti-morality, "beyond good and evil," nonetheless functions as a moral prescription.

2 Even those versions that speak of creating a new self must acknowledge that the success of any such efforts is actually contingent on the potential of the individual. The old self must have the potential to adopt the new self if it is to "take."

3 W. T. Harris, "Editor's Preface," in Friedrich Froebel, *The Education of Man*, trans. W. N. Hailmann (New York: D. Appleton, 1891), vi.

4 Maria Montessori, *Education for a New World* (Oxford: Clio Press, 1989), Introduction, n.p. First published in 1946, this text is available through the Montessori Teachers Collective at http://www.moteaco.com/abcclio/world.html (accessed July 2011).

5 Richard Rorty, interview in the film *American Philosopher*, prod. and dir. Phillip McReynolds (2011), http://vimeo.com/21268165 (accessed July 2011).

6 David L. Norton, *Personal Destinies: A Philosophy of Ethical Individualism* (Princeton, NJ: Princeton University Press, 1976), 128.

7 Ibid., 189, italics original.

8 Ibid., 195.

9 Ibid., 224.

10 Ibid., 350, italics original. (This citation includes the next quotation as well.) Norton extracted the term "participatory enactment" from Thomas Nagel's famous article, "What Is It Like to Be a Bat?", *Philosophical Review* 82, no. 4 (October 1974), 435–50. He develops the concept well beyond Nagel's brief introduction and quick rejection of the role of imagination. See the long footnote: Norton, *Personal Destinies*, 249–50.

11 Ibid., 350–1.

12 Sigmund Freud's psychoanalytical investigations into the subconscious manipulation of our conscious selves was a forerunner of many such accounts. There is now a huge literature of experimental and neurological work that challenges human rationality. One of the most widely read popularizations of such research, from which I have taken this phrase, is Dan Ariely,

Predictably Irrational: The Hidden Forces That Shape Our Decisions (New York: HarperCollins, 2008).

13 Norton, *Personal Destinies*, 40 and 306–8.

14 I cited Harold Bloom on this point in chapter 3.

5

Understanding the World

*Since men turned to philosophy in order to escape from a
state of ignorance, their aim was evidently understanding,
rather than practical gain.*

ARISTOTLE, *METAPHYSICS*

*Liberal education is for understanding the world and the forces
that shape one's life*—so affirms the third paradigm. In this strand
of theory and practice, the educational focus is not inward on
the possibilities of the self, but outward on the actualities of this
world. As Albert Einstein said, "To understand the world, one
must not be worrying about one's self."[1] "The world" is meant to
encompass not only the physical world of objects and processes,
but also the social, cultural, economic, and psychological realms,
as well as the world of abstract ideas—what Sir Karl Popper
termed "World 3."[2] (The self appears in this world, of course, but
only as an objectified self, as an entity among others in the world,
an object for study.)

Surely it is plausible to claim that in order to pursue a flourishing life, one must understand one's circumstances: *Where am I?
What sort of place is this in which I live and move and have my*

being? With what forces must I contend? These inchoate questions begin in wonder about startling events and mundane cycles, and they fly quickly to grander reflection on the human predicament and prospect. The encounter with the dangers and confusions of the world may lead us to humble supplication before powers greater than ourselves and to the development of rituals; or it may lead us to assertive attempts to manage or control these forces and to the invention of crafts.[3] But there is also a third response: it may lead us to the awful (in the original sense of that term) attempt to comprehend. All three of these responses, in their own ways, attempt to make the world a familiar place. But to understand the world is to try to grasp it *on its own terms, as it is,* not as a projection of our own fears or needs. Liberal education, on this paradigm, seeks both to refine these questions and to advance answers. In so doing, it presents the most judicious conclusions from the accumulated, progressive, and collective inquiries humans have reached in the attempt to understand the world. For the student, this effort involves not only the absorption of information and the acquisition of knowledge, but the development of cognitive frameworks and forms of discourse within which meanings can be created. Not just facts or theories, but structures of knowledge and methods of inquiry are the vehicles for understanding.

Structures of Knowledge

The curriculum is, once again, central in the paradigm, and epistemology now comes to the fore. The knowledge students should acquire is apportioned from the current store of human knowledge of the world. Knowledge is not a morass of information; it is structured. In educational practice, the epistemic structure of human knowledge intersects with the practical need for selectivity (we can't teach everything known) and the pedagogical structure required for sequential learning (some things must be learned before others). The curriculum tends to be conceived as important knowledge of our world packaged as a set of "subjects"—biology, physics, economics, and so on.

The list of available subjects or "disciplines" has evolved during the long development of liberal education. "Philosophy," as the "love of wisdom," once comprised virtually all areas of study and speculation. The medieval *quadrivium* included arithmetic, geometry, music, and astronomy, accompanied by the methods studies of the *trivium* (grammar, dialectic or logic, and rhetoric). Since then, of course, the natural sciences have divided and subdivided, the social sciences have emerged, and the number of recognized academic disciplines has increased exponentially. Today, forms of inquiry are manifold, and the structures of knowledge highly elaborated and incommensurate. The formation of new disciplines, like speciation in evolutionary biology, is a phenomenon difficult to explain (and more difficult to predict), yet one that is crucial to any comprehensive theory of the development of knowledge. The result of centuries of progress in the cooperative and collective attempt at understanding our situation, this evolution reflects the continuous interaction of expanding information or facts, theories and paradigms, and technological developments.[4]

We may try to define a discipline by its epistemic objects, the things it theorizes and seeks to explain, or the aspects of experience it problematizes; or we may refer to the methods and concepts it employs to undertake such study and record its findings; or we may interpret it as a form of discourse, a language game; or we may (as I have done with liberal education) define a discipline as a distinct tradition with a continuous narrative of self-definition and a refined legacy of knowledge. But, however we conceive them, the number of forms of knowledge that now beckon the student and assert their place in comprehending our world is bewildering—and ultimately beyond the range of any one student.

Moreover, the list of salient "forces that shape one's life" alters through time and circumstance. After all, it is not only our knowledge of the world that changes, but our world itself. Electronic media, chemically-assisted agriculture, and the global demand for oil certainly affect our lives today; we need to have some understanding of them, among other factors, if we are to understand our situation. Yet none of them would have been applicable just a century and a half ago—and all farming was organic until 1945. But technology is not the only such force; changes in religion, politics, education itself, the arts, work, and human rights represent powerful forces that situate us in a life-context. These factors contextualize liberal education and their changes help energize its continual reform.

In our time, we contend with "the information explosion"; knowledge advances so rapidly that we now speak in terms of its period of doubling and its rate of obsolescence or depreciation.[5] We face the need for both comprehensiveness and selection; especially in the last century, the pressure to find some principles by which to select, organize, and manage a finite curriculum has grown.

How can educators structure the requisite knowledge of our world? The history of liberal education displays many different ways to structure such a curriculum, with the "subjects" framed as disciplines, forms of thought, practical problems, research problems, area studies, interdisciplinary fields, and so on. Whatever the scale and structure of the universe of knowledge from which the theorist draws, however, two principles are generally adopted: *breadth of study* and *integration*. Any object of study—whether a person, place, thing, abstract idea, or event—has no meaning in isolation, without reference to a context. Perspective engages context; increasing the number and integration of perspectives enriches meaning and enhances our understanding.

Take water, for example. How are we to understand water? We learn much about water by studying it from the perspectives of physics (hydraulics) and chemistry. But we enhance our understanding by studying its role in biology; by examining it from economic, political, sociological, anthropological, historical, aesthetic, philosophical and religious perspectives; we can examine it through the lens of environmental science or comparative literature or mythology. As we gain multiple perspectives, we acquire greater intellectual facility, a depth of understanding, an increase in our repertoire of cognitive methods, and an enlargement of meaning, as we connect various aspects of the world in multiple frameworks of interpretation. Moreover, the inevitable limits and narrowness of one perspective can be revealed and corrected by taking others. These ideas provide the public rationale for the distribution requirements that are a staple of college degree programs, prescribing a minimal number of courses in the arts, humanities, social sciences, mathematics, languages, and natural sciences.

The second principle, *integration*, rejects two temptations: reductionism, the attempt to reduce these various studies to one—the one we believes give the true picture of what is real; and intellectual compartmentalism, the hermetic separation of the perspectives into alternate views of the world, leaving us with the need for a kind of gestalt shift to change from one to another. Although it is true that we enlarge our cognitive resources by drawing on the perspectives of several fields (perhaps seeing a connection between economic models and evolutionary models, or applying molecular tools to issues of whole organism zoology), and while breadth of study also provides an intellectual cross-training (assuring, for example, that chemists can produce research proposals that are written effectively, or that economists skillfully employ mathematical modeling), the second principle draws us into the self-reflective, intellectual challenge of assimilating and integrating what we learn.

One might ask whether this endeavor is not simply a version of the transmission of culture model—but with a focus on current knowledge of the world rather than great texts. That interpretation, however, whether of theory or in pedagogical practice, would miss the mark. Though it is true that we must rely extensively on the testimony of others in trying to comprehend our world, the aim of understanding goes beyond the delivery of informational content; it involves an initiation into methodologies, technologies, and standards of inquiry. Under this paradigm, students do not simply read the great works of science, but learn the scientific method and some of its embedded ideas and most recent conclusions.

It is helpful in this to draw upon the insights of what is now called "virtue epistemology."[6] Its central point is that knowledge is a human good that represents an achievement—not a useful collection of lucky guesses. Achieving knowledge requires effort and attention; it draws upon intellectual and sometimes moral virtues; it takes time and requires skills; and it entails making conceptual connections. Information can be transmitted; knowledge must be earned. Even Aristotle acknowledged that "learning is no amusement, but is accompanied with pain."[7] It is a distortion, in this view, to analyze knowledge simply by looking to the state of *possessing* knowledge or the act of *transmitting* it; the process of *coming to know* can teach us much about knowledge itself. (For obscure reasons, contemporary epistemologists favor "coming to know" and seldom use "learn" or its cognates.[8]) There is debate about whether *how* one comes to know is relevant to the character of the knowledge one gains, but I find the central point cogent and applicable to both individual and collective human knowledge.

My formulation of this paradigm, however, referred to "understanding" not "knowledge." What is the difference? It does seem that to understand something entails that we have knowledge of that thing. But the reverse is doubtful: I can have knowledge of something, beyond merely having information about it, and yet not understand it. Consider this situation: a cancer patient may look up information about his diagnosis; his oncologist has passed beyond such basic information to achieve genuine knowledge of the patient's type of cancer—and yet even she may not really *understand* cancer. What does she lack? She may still lack additional relevant knowledge, perhaps about the causes, optimal treatment, or full extent of this patient's cancer. Does "understanding" mean "possessing all relevant knowledge"? That seems both too strong and too narrow. Depending on context and object, "understanding" seems to require a fuller integration of knowledge of, a grasp of the explanatory elements and implications of, an empathy with, a direct experience of, or a capacity to take the "inside" perspective of the object of knowledge. Perhaps the oncologist is said to lack understanding because she has never had cancer herself. Think of what it would take to understand, and not merely have knowledge of, calculus, the German language, the political consequences of electronic social networks, Buddhism, or liberal education. If knowledge is taken to be an achievement of value, then understanding seems to be even more so.

Educational Realism and Its Alternatives

Deeply embedded in this paradigm are important philosophical assumptions about the world, knowledge, the human mind, and the good life—and their interrelations. It is worth exposing them, because, as a focus of philosophical debate, they become a source of criticism of the paradigm.

Let us state the traditional position, which is a form of philosophical realism. It asserts that: (1) there is an objective world; (2) we (normal) human beings can gain knowledge of that world and ourselves, at least to a significant extent; (3) genuine knowledge reflects reality, mirrors the world with accuracy; (4) propositions of genuine knowledge are true, and their truth can be justified.

There is a natural fit, in this view, between our mind, the structure of knowledge, and the world itself. To come to know something is an activity or process that is normative, and its normativity is calibrated in response to something outside oneself, to reality. Without the notion of an objective reality, the concepts of truth, inquiry, and knowledge all melt in surreal, distorted ways, like the timepieces in Salvador Dali's painting, *The Persistence of Memory*. How would one explain, for example, the activity of a scientist in a research laboratory without these assumptions? Surely, realists would say, we cannot understand his activities as simply a form of self-expression, or a form of artistic creation, or the enactment of a ritual. Skepticism, in this realist view, is an attitude that has value only in extirpating falsity and certifying knowledge, a tool of inquiry; it is anathema as a final philosophical position.

Immanuel Kant's work presented a powerful challenge to this position. He discerned the limits to knowledge: we cannot know things in themselves; we have no direct knowledge of reality. Moreover, he demonstrated that we construct, in great part, the world we experience and of which we have knowledge. The post-Kantian history of philosophy is marked by attempts to retain some sense of the core concepts (truth, knowledge, reality) in light of Kant's compelling conclusions—pragmatism being a notable example that has also influenced education. We cannot afford to wade into that rich philosophical history here, but I can briefly point to one interesting reconstruction.

It is possible to reject or suspend the assumptions of realism and to interpret "understanding the world" as "creating and expanding human meaning." Charles Bailey has observed that, in this interpretation, "to understand" is to "make sense of something in a way meaningful to me." He analyzes this notion as involving "three key ideas: (i) relationships or linkages, (ii) 'non-arbitrariness,' and (iii) coherence."[9] His analysis seems to tilt toward a coherence theory of truth; other analyses might elevate a pragmatic conception. These interpretations highlight another assumption of our paradigm, one that seems pervasive: the mind finds or creates meaning from such knowledge, thereby endowing our experience of the world with meaning, deepening our understanding, and transforming itself in the process.

Advocates and Exemplars

The nineteenth century educator and divine, John Henry Newman (1801–1890), advocated both principles of breadth and integration in disciplinary studies in *The Idea of the University* (1898), a classic text in the history of liberal education. He defended breadth with an apt metaphor:

> There is no science but tells a different tale, when viewed as a portion of the whole, from what it is likely to suggest when taken by itself, without the safeguard, as I may call it, of others.
>
> Let me make use of an illustration. In the combination of colours, very different effects are produced by a difference in their selection and juxtaposition; red, green, and white change their shades, according to the contrast to which they are submitted. And, in like manner, the drift and meaning of a branch of knowledge varies with the company in which it is introduced to the student. If his reading is confined simply to one subject, however such division of labor may favour the advancement of a particular pursuit ... certainly it has a tendency to contract the mind. If it is incorporated with others, it depends on those others as to the kind of influence which it exerts upon him ...
>
> It is a great point then to enlarge the range of studies which a university professes, even for the sake of the students; and, though they cannot pursue every subject which is open to them, they will be the gainers by living among those and under those who represent the whole circle.[10]

Newman finds integration in the ultimate unity of knowledge and reality, which is confirmed through his Catholicism:

> I have said that all branches of knowledge are connected together, because the subject matter of knowledge is intimately united in itself, as being the acts and the work of the Creator. Hence it is that the sciences, into which our knowledge may be said to be cast, have multiplied bearings one on another, and an internal sympathy, and admit, or rather demand, comparison and adjustment. They complete, correct, balance each other.[11]

This notion of the ultimate unity of the diverse branches of knowledge is captured in the term "university" for complex academies (the etymological meaning is "to turn as one").

Over the next century, disciplines proliferated, and the pressures for a defensible selectivity increased. In the 1960s, educator Philip H. Phenix (1915–2002), formed his proposal for general education around six "realms of meaning": *symbolics* (language, mathematics, and such other symbolic forms as gestures or rituals), *empirics* (all natural sciences and empirically-based social sciences), *esthetics* (all fine arts, including poetry and literature), *synnoetics* (personal, interpersonal, or relational knowledge), *ethics* (normative studies of the moral conduct of free and responsible persons), and *synoptic* (comprehensive and integrative studies, such as history, philosophy, and religion).[12] This proposal, like many that attempt to cluster the forms of knowledge ("realms of meaning") into a coherent and manageable few, suggests both a scope and sequence of study for a liberal education.

At about the same time, philosopher Paul H. Hirst (b. 1927), whose educational writings largely fall under this paradigm, confirmed its link to realism: "A liberal education in the pursuit of knowledge is, therefore, seeking the development of the mind according to what is quite external to it, the structure and pattern of reality." Hirst characterized the presumed relationship between the mind, knowledge, and reality as a "harmonious structure." The relationships are clear: the good life requires understanding; the human mind is peculiarly prepared to learn and understand; the forms of knowledge it can comprehend match the structure of the world; and the structure of the curriculum should reflect the structure of reality. Hirst seemed undisturbed by the historical evolution and profusion of the disciplines, a fact which seems on its face to challenge the notion that our knowledge is organized by *a priori* or necessary structures. Rather, he seemed to believe that the speciation of knowledge is fixed. Indeed, he noted ominously that once one tampers with these assumptions, "the whole harmonious structure is likely to disintegrate."[13]

One might, for instance, let loose the grasp of reality, replacing the view that one has knowledge of *reality* with the claim that one can have knowledge of *experience*. It is a subtle but fateful shift. Non-realist theories like that require reconstruction of key concepts such as truth and reality, not just for clarification, but to retain the grounds that guide and justify education (on this paradigm).[14]

In the end, however, this paradigm is a big tent that can accommodate more than Hirstian realists. Proponents may even debate among themselves to what extent we discover or create the "world" we inhabit; what it is to "dwell" in a world; and what limits there are to our knowledge of our situation. Yet among these versions there is unity in the aim of simply making sense of things, in the value of wonder or curiosity; achieving understanding is always tied to making the phenomena meaningful. And all versions share the assumption that understanding our world is indispensible to a good life (for who would claim that living in profound ignorance or wanton falsity comprises a flourishing life?), either in the strong sense that such understanding and the contemplation of the understood world *is* the good life, or in the weaker and more common sense that understanding the world is conducive to or a component of a good life.[15]

What emerges in this paradigm is a vision of the liberally educated person as someone who has a breadth of knowledge of the world, who understands the forces that affect our lives, and who therefore grasps the human predicament and prospects; moreover, it is a person whose intellect is "broad-gauge," not narrow, whose facile mind benefits from the ability to take many perspectives. Such a person will, depending on other commitments, either deploy these advantages in the cultivation of a good life, or will find them to be intrinsically valuable; that is, they are either instrumental to a good life or a component of it. Newman, as the title of his discourse suggests, takes the latter view: such "knowledge is its own end." Aristotle, similarly, depicted a contemplative life of theoretical wisdom to be the highest human calling, the epitome of human happiness.[16]

Critiques of the Understanding the World Paradigm

If the assumptions of realism are taken to be a necessary element of this paradigm, then any critique of those assumptions impugns the paradigm as well. And, indeed, postmodernist attacks on each and all of them are common—and often convincing. But, as I implied in discussing Hirst's account, we may also take realism to characterize only a subset of those theories that fall under the paradigm. The central terms—reality (the world), knowledge, truth—have a certain degree of elasticity, allowing the paradigm to accommodate positions other than realism. In that case, not all anti-realist arguments need present mortal threats. I do not deny, however, the general principle that the further one must reach to explicate these key ideas and their interrelations, the less likely that this paradigm can work. A full-blown skepticism will deny the possibility of this form of education (and others) outright.[17] What this paradigm requires is an effective epistemology of research, of *coming to know*.

The dean of American educational philosophers, John Dewey, wrote many words over a long career rejecting realism in favor of a thorough-going pragmatism, yet he certainly did not abandon the idea that education may increase our understanding of our world. In his voluminous writings, Dewey said precious little about liberal education specifically, but it is abundantly clear that he would not have endorsed an entirely intellectualist conception of education that focused purely on the furnishing of the mind; nor would he support an interpretation of knowledge or truth that depended upon a foundational experience of certainty. His attacks on dualistic thinking (especially relevant here are the dualisms of subject/object, knower/known, and mind/body) and the "quest for certainty" would rule out such conceptions. In his view, the ultimate aim of education is *growth*. This is growth not as instrumental to some other state, but growth as instrumental only to further growth. To some, this claim has seemed empty or, at minimum, puzzling. But given Dewey's related doctrines, I think that *growth* is best understood as *the increasing ability to derive meaning from experience*—which entails an increasing ability to learn. Dewey's concept of experience is philosophically rich; it represents the interaction of the self-conscious organism with its environment, and thus has polarities that replace the separate entities of the knower/known or subject/object dichotomy. "Experience" is not simply a matter of changes in consciousness or subjectively-generated phenomena; it is interaction with the world and with others. The result is understanding.[18]

A common criticism of this paradigm is that, in aiming simply to understand the world, it falls short. "What good does it do," such a critic might ask, "to understand the world—or to contemplate the world—if that's all that follows? Don't we want to understand the world in order to respond to it effectively, to cope with it, or to control or change it? Knowledge becomes valuable only when it is applied."

There is, I acknowledge, no dodging the fact that this paradigm takes the possession of genuine knowledge (or understanding) to be a good, and its acquisition to be a virtuous achievement. And some theories within this paradigm—those that value knowledge for its own sake alone—resist attempts to value knowledge of the world as means to more practical ends. Indeed, Aristotle stands such critical concerns on their heads: instead of viewing theoretical contemplation (*theoria*) as a means to practical reasoning (*praxis*), he claims that we should engage in practical reasoning in order to make a safe space and ample time in our lives for theoretical contemplation. And we have seen that Newman defends the pursuit of "knowledge [as] its own end." Nevertheless, although adopting this paradigm means accepting understanding as an achievement and a good, it doesn't necessitate the rejection or devaluing of practical or applied knowledge. Dewey, even in proposing growth for the sake of growth, believed that increased meaning derived from experience carried the increased ability to solve a wider range of problems. One can claim, with full compatibility, that the judicious application of knowledge is also an achievement drawing upon intellectual and moral virtues, and a human good. This is Aristotle's view as well.

But why not bring practical concerns to the fore and make the solving of problems *through* the acquisition of knowledge the aim of education? To this reasonable question, there are three dominant lines of response. The first is that this would reverse the priority of values. To understand is indeed a good and precious thing in itself, though other goods may follow from it. The second response is that we must remember the ultimate focus of liberal education: the good life and one's life as a whole. Although it seems unquestionable that solving problems would be helpful throughout one's life if one is to flourish, the pursuit of knowledge, the attempt to understand the world, makes demands and responds to values that are different from those found in the search for relevant practical information. Gaining a cognitive perspective is more deeply transformative than acquiring the relevant information to solve a problem. Moreover, recognizing a situation as problematic in the first place, defining the problem, knowing what sort of solutions are possible, imagining solutions, selecting appropriate methods, knowing the limits of one's methods, considering unintended consequences, and recognizing when the problem has been solved—all of these require a broader cognitive perspective. It requires that we focus our efforts, as Charles Bailey has put it, "beyond the present and particular." The third response—the now familiar one that would override the others—is that this paradigm, in the end, represents but one strand of liberal education; it is complemented by the others, one of which includes a paradigmatic focus on engagement with the world. And thus we turn to the fourth paradigm.

Notes

1 The quotation may be apocryphal: it is frequently included among quotations of Einstein, but always without citation; I have not located the source.

2 Karl Popper (after Gottlob Frege) termed "World 3" the realm of abstract ideas, in distinction from "World 1" (physical objects and events) and "World 2" (subjective mental states) in several works, including *Objective Knowledge: An Evolutionary Approach*, rev. edn (Oxford: Oxford University Press, 1979).

3 John Dewey describes these two responses in the opening passages of *The Quest for Certainty*, in *John Dewey: The Later Works, 1925–53*, Vol. 4: 1929 (Carbondale, IL: Southern Illinois University Press, 1984), 3.

4 I have discussed these relationships in "Paradigms and Paraphernalia: On the Relationship of Theory and Technology in Science," in *New Directions in the Philosophy of Technology*, ed. Joseph C. Pitt (Dordrecht: Kluwer Academic Publishers, 1995), 85–94.

5 Calculating such figures precisely is a murky business. Does doubling the amount of information of the Internet equal a doubling of knowledge in that sector? A widely quoted figure is that human knowledge now doubles every five years; another is that a sizeable fraction of what is learned in college is "obsolete" within a decade. But how is one to quantize knowledge? And what is meant by "obsolete knowledge"?

6 This new field of normative epistemology seems to have begun with an article by Ernest Sosa: "The Raft and the Pyramid: Coherence

versus Foundations in the Theory of Knowledge," *Midwest Studies in Philosophy* 5, no. 1 (September 1980): 3–26. This article was reprinted in a collection that expanded his ideas: *Knowledge in Perspective: Selected Essays in Epistemology* (Cambridge: Cambridge University Press, 1991). Other important works in this field include: Linda Trinkaus Zagzebski, *Virtues of the Mind: An Inquiry into the Nature of Virtue and the Ethical Foundations of Knowledge* (Cambridge: Cambridge University Press, 1996); Jonathan L. Kvanig, *The Value of Knowledge and the Pursuit of Understanding* (Cambridge: Cambridge University Press, 2003); and John Greco, *Achieving Knowledge: A Virtue-Theoretic Account of Epistemic Normativity* (Cambridge: Cambridge University Press, 2010).

7 Aristotle, *Politics*, VIII, 1339.

8 One notable exception is Israel Scheffler, *Conditions of Knowledge: An Introduction to Epistemology and Education* (Glenview, IL: Scott, Foresman, 1965).

9 Bailey, *Beyond the Present and Particular*, 64–5.

10 John Henry Newman, Discourse V: "Knowledge Its Own End," in *The Idea of a University* (New York: Doubleday, 1959), 128.

11 Ibid., 127.

12 Phenix, *Realms of Meaning*. See my reference to Phenix in chapter 1 and n. 24.

13 All quotations in this paragraph are from Hirst, "Liberal Education and the Nature of Knowledge," 116.

14 Hirst's strategy in the discussion referenced here is to propose a reinterpretation: the curriculum must therefore be based on the structure of knowledge itself (the disciplines)—but without tethering those epistemic structures to a further reality. A liberal education is thus defined by the scope of knowledge itself, which is acquired to develop the mind (ibid., 122–31). That modification, however, would not only reflect a different metaphysic, but would also redirect the aim of education from understanding the world to developing the mind—which would, in turn, threaten to shift the paradigm to self-actualization, since "developing the mind" would likely be understood as a form or component of self-actualization.

15 These views are exemplified in Aristotle's account of theoretical wisdom (*sophia*) in the *Nicomachean Ethics* and Mill's concept of activities that yield "higher order" pleasures, in *Utilitarianism*.

16 Aristotle, *Nicomachean Ethics*, X.

17 I have in mind the sort of comprehensive skepticism argued by Peter K. Unger in *Ignorance: A Case for Scepticism* (Oxford: Clarendon Press, 1979).

18 Thirty-eight volumes comprise John Dewey's collected works, plus four volumes of published correspondence. Dewey wrote on a wide range of philosophical topics and, of course, especially on education and schooling, but he was also a public intellectual who often addressed significant social and political issues of the day. It is a curiosity that, within this vast corpus, he seldom addressed higher education specifically, and rarely liberal education. One notable exception is his remarks as chair of the Conference on the Undergraduate Liberal Arts Curriculum held at Rollins College in 1931, of which an unpublished verbatim transcript is extant; Dewey's bits have been extracted and published as "Statements to the Conference on Curriculum for the College of Liberal Arts" in *The Later Works of John Dewey, Vol. 6: 1925–1953*, ed. Jo Ann Boydston and Sidney Ratner (Carbondale, IL: Southern Illinois University Press, 1985), 414–23. For Dewey's arguments against certain dualisms and the philosophical obsession with certainty, see John Dewey, *Reconstruction in Philosophy* (1919) and *The Quest for Certainty* (1929); for his views on experience, see *Experience and Nature* (1925), and *Experience and Education* (1938); and for his sharpest statement on the aims of education and growth, see *Democracy and Education: An Introduction to the Philosophy of Education* (1916). All are available in *The Collected Works of John Dewey: 1882–1953*, ed. Jo Ann Boydston, 38 vols (Carbondale, IL: Southern Illinois University Press, 1972–2008).

6

Engagement with the World

I call therefore a complete and generous Education
that which fits a man to perform justly, skilfully and
magnanimously all the offices both private and public of
peace and war.

JOHN MILTON, *TRACTATE ON EDUCATION*

We now turn to the view that states: *liberal education is for engagement with and action in the world.* It is an approach that reminds us that "flourish" is a verb. A good life is *lived.* This paradigm, like the others, accommodates a generous range of conceptions; in this case as well, they may be differentiated by their interpretations of key terms: "world," "engagement," and "action."

The "world" is foregrounded in this model as in the paradigm of understanding the world, and the same variety of interpretations may apply. In this context, however, the world is not simply an objective realm of multiple entities, but is the arena in which we act, the field of our engagement, or (to use a Heideggerian interpretation), *that wherein we dwell and create meaning.*[1] A full sense of "the world" foreshadows our human prospects in it. And those possibilities help delineate the meanings of "engagement" and "action." They may include, for example: civic engagement, public service, moral action, social criticism, cultural resistance, policy analysis (as an aspect of *praxis*)—even, at the extreme, a principled withdrawal from the world. Thus, liberal education may prepare us to cope with the world, to serve it nobly, to critique it trenchantly, or to reform it.

Within these possibilities there are implicit imperatives, normative injunctions. We are led "to engage with and act in the world" in certain ways that are thought to be good, because they are ethical or virtuous, or because they are effective—or both. As my college's motto puts it: "Do great work." These directives are, in fact, responses to the fundamental questions: *What should one do? How should one live?* In most versions, these directives are personalized, and respond to our individual and primal questions: *What should I do? How should I live?*

Personal effectiveness is thought to be necessary for flourishing, for the living of a good life. This might seem to be more than a nod to the self-actualization paradigm, but they are quite distinct: in this paradigm, it is the realities of the world that serve as a guiding context for action not the potentialities of the individual, and the self-development sought is that which is relevant to deciding, persuading, and acting in normative ways. Normative engagement requires practical wisdom, sound judgment, self-reflection, and considered action; it frequently requires moral virtues like courage, generosity, persistence, sensitivity, and openness of mind; it may also require the building of a good community that can be sustained only by the continual commitment of virtuous and competent people. It may, moreover, require us to go beyond competence to act ethically, gracefully, effectively. A liberal education thus may hope to prepare the student to engage in social service, to do good, to be an involved citizen, to achieve goals, to reform practice, to solve problems, to follow, to lead, to keep one's integrity by withdrawal, to cope with change—and to change the world.

Historically, it has been the public sphere for which educational preparation for engagement and action is directed, not the domestic or private sphere. In societally structured sexism, it was males that were prepared for the public (masculine) realm. The warrior prepares for the battlefield through military training; the liberal arts student prepares for the world of civic responsibility, commerce, and public affairs. We all recognize that one significant line of social progress has been to open this realm to women in many parts of the world, and for men to find place and satisfaction in the private sphere. Some argue for a further reform: liberal education should also prepare its students to be effective in the private or domestic sphere as well. Personal relationships and the roles of spouse or partner, parent, neighbor, and friend are of great importance in the living of a flourishing life, and they need concomitant attention and educational effort. Indeed, serving the supreme aim of liberal education seems to require "preparing students to deal with the demands of everyday living."[2] There are convincing arguments for this reform when one adopts this paradigm and elaborates its relationship to flourishing.

Engagement and Flourishing

John Stuart Mill links such engagement with the world to the good life in a lofty passage in *Utilitarianism*. After dispensing with a list of perceived threats to a eudaimonistic life, he concludes heroically with a robust and complex sentence:

> All the grand sources, in short, of human suffering are in a great degree, many of them almost entirely, conquerable by human care and effort; and though their removal is grievously slow— though a long succession of generations will perish in the breach before the conquest is completed, and this world becomes all that, if will and knowledge were not wanting, it might easily be made—yet every mind sufficiently intelligent and generous to bear a part, however small and inconspicuous, in the endeavor, will draw a noble enjoyment from the contest itself, which he would not for any bribe in the form of selfish indulgence consent to be without.[3]

In Mill's liberal, Victorian vision, the flourishing life is not about "selfish indulgence," but about bettering the human condition, a moral project that demands "human care and effort" and a "mind sufficiently intelligent and generous to bear a part." Throughout this classic essay, Mill works ardently and adroitly to link perfectionism to a Utilitarian framework—drawing upon Aristotle's conception of the good life as a life of practical wisdom (*phronesis*, second best only to philosophical contemplation)—requiring the exercise of sound judgment, normative practical reasoning, and a whole ecology of virtues.

It is important to stress that the aim that defines this paradigm is not socialization pure and simple; it is not merely a matter of preparing the student to *fit into* contemporary culture, to find a professional niche, or to serve a social demand. Theories under this paradigm might, in fact, emphasize social criticism, moral reform, political activism, or (ironically) the need to adopt a "hermeneutics of suspicion."[4] To engage with the world might require, in Brazilian educationist Paolo Freire's terms, an "education for critical consciousness."[5] The stance one is to take in engaging the world, the general objectives one will have, the skills required, and the values to be displayed in one's decision and actions—these are spelled out in the cascade of increasingly specific theories that devolve from this paradigm. In all versions, however, it is not simply the *capacity* to engage with the world effectively that it is the aim: it is also the *disposition* to do so.

The prescribed means by which such learning is to occur have varied widely within the tradition. Through the centuries of liberal education, virtually all its modes of learning have been employed for the purpose of preparing students to act well in the world. In classical times, the methods of didacticism, rhetoric, and dialectic (Plato's favorite) were dominant. In Victorian England, a study of "the Greats" in Greek and Latin was thought to prepare young men for service to the Empire throughout the world. By the 1920s, this approach seemed insufficient, and, beginning at Oxford University, it was largely replaced by the studies known as "PPE"—philosophy, politics, and economics. Of course, it was assumed, most often tacitly, that these curricula were accompanied by the experience of living in college.

One way to prepare to engage with the world effectively is to learn *through* such engagement, preferably in a supervised or protected context. This is an ancient pedagogy that has gained favor especially in the United States in recent years, packaged as internships, externships, work-study programs, service learning projects, student organizations, public debates, model legislature and United Nations programs, practicums, and study abroad semesters. These collected efforts may become institutionally self-conscious and purposeful: many liberal arts colleges feature leadership programs that aspire to develop leadership skills in students. All these methods combine active tasks with encouragement, relevant knowledge, skill development, monitoring, self-reflection, and limits to or safeguards against negative consequences. Even within traditional classroom contexts, there is a rising emphasis on collaborative learning and teamwork as relevant to engagement and service.

From the medieval university onward, student culture presented institutional challenges and disrupted "town-gown" relationships. Although schools hoped to prepare students to act normatively in the world, they were regularly embarrassed by harboring a culture that pulled its students in the opposite direction. For the protection of both their institutions and their students, educators began the attempt to structure out-of-classroom student life. These efforts went far beyond the promulgation of rules. Universities became residential, offering student housing, frequently with faculty in residence. Athletic clubs were organized into official sports leagues. Schools began to sanction student organizations, operate formal orientation programs, and provide a variety of "student services." Beginning in the United States, as these endeavors became more complex, a new cadre of "student affairs" professional overseers were trained and hired. In recent years, the long-standing belief that "life in college" is part of one's education has been taken more seriously as a complementary sphere of learning. We have moved from student life to extra-curricular activities to the co-curriculum and its goals for learning. Student affairs professionals are understood to be educators, though in a different modality from the traditional professor. And the co-curriculum is seen as a natural locus for engagement with the world.

These reforms have not always been well received by alumni, students, trustees, townspeople, and even by faculty. Sometimes they have exacted a toll. Years ago, after one New England liberal arts college had made the bold effort to require students to live in college-supervised housing (and thus eliminate fraternity houses), an institutional accreditation self-study chronicled the change. As I recall it, that report included this weary triumph: "Bigotry, anti-intellectualism, and sloth may not have perished from the earth, but they are no longer an organized force at [our college]."

In chapter 1, I referred to the contemporary morphing of "the course" into a 24/7 learning community. One aspect of this change is the collapsing of the boundary between the classroom and "the real world." Even if registrars do still maintain a clear accounting of what activities received academic credit, the difference between some credit-bearing experiences and some co-curricular experiences is otherwise indiscernible. A music course may require performance in a musical or opera—while the same activity is voluntary and co-curricular on other occasions. Some internships carry academic credit; others do not. Given the current emphasis on accountability and assessment, institutions now find themselves needing to clarify the goals for student learning in whatever context it is expected to occur, so the relationships between the curriculum and the co-curriculum must become more explicit. The goals of engagement with the world are, unfortunately, especially difficult to assess, because they entail complex attributes (discretion, integrity, effectiveness, for example) and are intended to be displayed in life's arena well beyond the years of schooling.

Advocates and Exemplars

Although it seems natural to connect worldly engagement and action with the good life, it may seem surprising to claim a connection to liberal education, indeed to call worldly engagement one of the paradigms of liberal education, since the latter is so often portrayed as elevating theory and disdaining practice. But as far back as its origins in classical Athens, Isocrates—whose school rivaled Plato's and may be considered a prototype liberal arts institution—sought to prepare students to be wise and active citizens, to train them in dialectic and rhetoric, a power to articulate the truth and persuade others that was to be grounded in deep and sound moral commitments.[6]

This aim was famously proclaimed by Woodrow Wilson in a commemorative address he delivered in 1896 as a professor of jurisprudence and political economy at Princeton University, "Princeton in the Nation's Service." It was published in the *New York Evening Post* and reprinted many times thereafter. He observed that "It has never been natural, it has seldom been possible, in this country for learning to seek a place apart and hold aloof from affairs." After duly honoring the benefits of ivory-tower scholarship, Wilson notes that the world is not and cannot be comprised only of scholars. He proclaims:

> The object of education is not merely to draw out the powers of the individual mind: it is rather its right object to draw all minds to a proper adjustment to the physical and social world in which they are to have their life and their development: to enlighten, strengthen and make fit. The business of the world is not individual success, but its own betterment, strengthening, and growth in spiritual insight—"So teach us to number our days, that we may apply our hearts unto wisdom" is its right prayer and aspiration.

This aim was, for Wilson, definitive of the character of his university and mandatory for all others; and it was not purely a matter relegated to the co-curriculum, but a pervasive concern of instruction.

> Of course, when all is said, it is not learning but the spirit of service that will give a college place in the public annals of the nation. It is indispensable, it seems to me, if it is to do its right service, that the air of affairs should be admitted to all its class rooms. I do not mean the air of party politics but the air of the world's transactions, the consciousness of the solidarity of the race, the sense of the duty of man towards man, of the presence of men in every problem, of the significance of truth for guidance as well as for knowledge, of the potency of ideas, of the promise and the hope that shine in the face of all knowledge.[7]

Wilson attempted, with some success, to implant this ethos in Princeton when he was named president of the university in 1902, though his plan to reform extracurricular life by abolishing exclusive eating clubs and building "quads" of student residences was defeated by fierce alumni pressure.

The liberal arts colleges of today embody this purpose; they usually declare it in their mission statements, indeed, they often emphasize it—perhaps responding to concerns about the practical impact of an expensive, liberal education—using such terms as "civic engagement," "public service," "leadership," "making a difference," or "changing the world." To reiterate: it is not merely that one gains special knowledge that is *preparatory* for engagement with the world; rather "student engagement" is a feature of the learning environment itself, from "active" rather than "passive" pedagogy to service-learning experiences, leadership-building programs, advocacy internships, sustainability programs, ethical audits, and even the lauding of exemplary alumni and honorary degree recipients.

Wilson had earlier taught at Bryn Mawr College and at Wesleyan University prior to Princeton. Today's Wesleyan proclaims it is "dedicated to providing an education in the liberal arts that is characterized by boldness, rigor, and practical idealism."[8] Bryn Mawr articulates the contributions of both the curriculum and co-curriculum toward this aim in its mission statement:

> Living and working together in a community based on mutual respect, personal integrity and the standards of a social and academic Honor Code, each generation of students experiments with creating and sustaining a self-governing society within the College. The academic and co-curricular experiences fostered by Bryn Mawr, both on campus and in the College's wider setting, encourage students to be responsible citizens who provide service to and leadership for an increasingly interdependent world.[9]

They are not alone. Gettysburg College asserts straightforwardly at the outset of its mission statement: "Gettysburg College, a national, residential, undergraduate college committed to a liberal education, prepares students to be active leaders and participants in a changing world."[10] The same aim is captured in the statement of Bates College's president: "At Bates, we seek to prepare highly promising young minds from all backgrounds to work, to lead, to solve problems and to serve in the richly diverse and ever-changing world."[11] Indeed, nearly all liberal arts institutions explicitly endorse this educational purpose and employ the paradigm that embodies it.

Advocates for this approach also include service organizations that thrive on the idealism and energies of young graduates. In the United States, both NGOs and government-sponsored programs have created bridges to colleges and universities as channels for world engagement and service. A Princeton alumna, Wendy Kopp, building on a concern for educational inequities and an idea sketched in her senior thesis, founded Teach for America in 1989. The Peace Corps has for over 50 years drawn graduates into international service. The attraction and prestige of these opportunities have helped secure and expand the school and college experiences that lead to them.

Critiques of the Engagement with the World Paradigm

The most frequently heard criticism of theories within this paradigm is that they do not work in practice; that is, they do not in fact prepare students for "real-world" engagement. Either they do not work at all or they work perversely, representing either failure or harm. If they fail, it may be because: (1) there is a disconnect between what is taught or learned and what is required for the goal of effective action in the world—either the link in question is obscure or unspecified, or it simply does not yield the outcomes expected; or (2) the effort is weak and the rhetoric is hollow, unsupported by any serious attempt to define key terms like "leadership" and by any educational effort that has a commanding priority. The best efforts are frustrated by the persistently deleterious aspects of secondary and undergraduate culture. These are, fortunately, performance gaps that might be reformed. Those critics who worry that they will produce harmful or perverse results might argue, however, that there are unavoidable aspects of formal, especially institutionalized learning (such as bureaucratization, indoctrination, power relationships, etc.), that inevitably work against desired qualities and capacities—for example, independence of mind, critical thinking, creativity, advocacy, and so on.

Other critics raise concerns that run in a different direction. These programs of learning *through* engagement, they say, are susceptible to cooption by the special interests of corporations, governments, and other agencies. They may degenerate into volunteer labor without an instructional focus or lasting impact. Or they may inculcate political values or reinforce ingrained prejudices while downplaying the importance of understanding and competence.

Please note that these are critiques of particular subsidiary theories and institutionalized practices; they do not, as stated, challenge the paradigm itself—indeed many of these critics endorse the paradigm, but criticize what is done under it; others give up in frustration on the chances for success. The critics effectively challenge the paradigm itself only when the focal point changes from *this* theory or *that* practice, to *any and all* such theories and practices. But upping the ante in this way also seems to alter the nature of the controversy, as the debate turns from largely empirical questions—*Does this practice in fact prepare students for engagement with the world?* Or, *Does that practice actually inhibit creativity* (or *independence of mind*, or *courage to act*, or whatever)—to a set of conceptual questions. Though the questions vary according to the critique, some familiar ones are these: *What is the relationship—if any—between the education of the mind and the shaping of character, between intellectual and moral education? Is "personal effectiveness" a viable educational aim? How is it possible to prepare a student for effectiveness in the world, when that world is changing and will be different in ways unimaginable?*

This paradigm sets an educational aspiration that is beyond the acquisition of knowledge, skills, and attitudes: it seeks the disposition to apply effectively all those aspects of learning in the various spheres of one's life. Whether the focus is on the public sphere (as with the goal of engaged citizenship) or the private sphere (as with the goal of "preparing students to deal with the demands of everyday living"), or both, the intent is to affect the way in which one's learning flows out into judgments and actions. It is true that any such ambition must acknowledge the age-old and profound question of how to bridge the gap between what one knows and how one acts. Any successful and secure bridging involves a transformation of the person, a change that affects values and dispositions, that produces altered perspectives and insistent motivations. I will face these questions in regard to moral dimensions in chapter 10, but at the moment it is important to state some cautions. We should not reduce this issue to a question of pedagogy. The issue is not just whether virtue can be taught; it is whether virtue can be learned. The alternatives would be to assume that one's character is fixed at birth and simply unfolds with normal development, or that one's character is shaped by externalities that cannot be purposefully incorporated within learning. Only after we reject these as the whole story and assume that learning can make a difference can we raise the question of whether such learning may be advanced by a particular educational program.

Becoming someone who can engage with and act effectively in the world certainly seems to be a valuable aspiration for each individual. The value of this paradigm for society, however, depends on the values and skills that are to be manifested in this engagement and action. Cleverness, persuasiveness, problem-solving skills, leadership, and other such capacities may be applied with self-interest alone or with malicious intent. One might become powerful, able to effect one's will in the world, without living a good life. The normative standard should not derive from the skills themselves—the cunning of debate, the adroitness of the decision-making—but from the values they serve.

Notes

1 Heidegger distinguishes a variety of conceptions of "the world," including these two, in *Being and Time*.

2 A reformist goal proposed in Mulcahy, *The Educated Person*, 191. The elaboration and justification of this goal is the point of his chapter titled "Toward a New Paradigm for Liberal Education."

3 John Stuart Mill, *Utilitarianism* (London: Parker, Son, and Bourn, 1863), 22.

4 See chapter 1 and n. 13.

5 His vision of education is developed in such works as Paolo Freire, *Pedagogy of the Oppressed* (New York: Continuum, 1970) and *Education for Critical Consciousness* (New York: Seabury Press, 1973).

6 Excellent accounts of Isocrates in relation to the tradition of liberal education may be found in Takis Poulakos, *Speaking for the Polis: Isocrates' Rhetorical Education* (Columbia, SC: University of South Carolina Press, 1997), and Janet M. Atwill, *Rhetoric Reclaimed: Aristotle and the Liberal Arts Tradition* (Ithaca, NY: Cornell University Press, 1998).

7 Woodrow Wilson, "Princeton in the Nation's Service," in *The Papers of Woodrow Wilson*, Vol. 10, 1896–8, ed. Arthur S. Link (Princeton, NJ: Princeton University Press, 1971); reprinted at http://

www.princeton.edu/~mudd/exhibits/wilsonline/indn8nsvc.html#BM1
(accessed September 2011).

8 Wesleyan University, "Mission Statement," http://www.wesleyan.edu/
about/mission.html (accessed September 2011).

9 Bryn Mawr College Mission Statement, approved by the Board of
Trustees, December 1998, http://www.brynmawr.edu/about/mission.
shtml (accessed September 2011).

10 Gettysburg College Mission Statement, adopted by the Gettysburg
College Board of Trustees on January 25, 2003, http://www.
gettysburg.edu/about/college_history/mission_statement.dot (accessed
July 2011).

11 Elaine Tuttle Hansen, "President's Welcome," Bates College, n.d.,
http://home.bates.edu/about/welcome/ (accessed July 2011).

7

The Skills of Learning

*Life is a tradeoff between spending time and energy
learning new things, and exploiting things already known.
The longer an animal's life span, and the more varied its
niche, the more worthwhile it is to spend time learning.*

J. E. R. STRADDON, *ADAPTIVE BEHAVIOR AND LEARNING*

In this, the last of the five paradigms to be explored, renewed
attention is given to the "arts" of the liberal arts—this time, not as
disciplines or forms of inquiry, but as skills: *Liberal education is
for the acquisition of the skills of learning.* Devotion to the learning
of particular content recedes; there is less worry about whether
instruction includes the coverage of specific material. This seems
a sensible move: after all, knowledge is perishable, either in the
sense that it may be forgotten by the individuals who once learned
it, or in the sense that it is likely to be disproved or reinterpreted
or displaced by new knowledge. What lasts in life is often not the
knowledge we once learned, but the continual need to re-learn the
old and learn the new. Flourishing does not require that we possess
the eternal verities or an unshakeable understanding of certain
truths about the world, but rather that we are adept at learning.
Thus, this paradigm takes seriously the focus on one's life as a
whole and the reality of change. Being "a life-long learner" does
not mean one must continually return to the tutelage of teachers

and trainers; rather, one is equipped to be one's own teacher and to judge insightfully when other educational services are needed. One who is adept at learning truly has acquired the most valuable life skills, those that reign over all others, because she is then able to learn many other skills as needed. An important hope embedded in this aim is that the student will not only *acquire* the skills of learning, but will become *disposed* to use them, and will indeed *love learning*.

There is a vast literature on the distinction between *knowing that* and *knowing how*, introduced by Gilbert Ryle.[1] It includes dilations of each way of knowing, attempts to reduce one to the other, claims on behalf of additional ways of knowing, and elaborations of their relationships. Fortunately, we need not wade too far into these complexities, but some basic points will be useful. (1) Becoming skillful is identified with learning *how*, and that typically cannot be accomplished merely by assimilating information; it requires practice. Active learning is required to acquire a skill. (2) Moreover, it seems that all *knowing how* presumes *knowing that* (which is not to argue the reduction of the former to the latter). Knowing how to play chess, for example, entails knowledge that bishops are pieces that move only on the diagonal; knowing how to speak Italian entails knowing the meanings of words in a basic vocabulary (for instance, I must know that *cucina* refers to the kitchen). We can say that skills are *informed* by relevant *knowledge that*. (3) Most educationally interesting skills are compounded of subsidiary skills. The skill of driving a car involves subsidiary skills, such as estimating distances, observing other drivers, judging the relation between steering and the curvature of the road, smooth acceleration (or proper shifting of gears), and so on. It is possible to be weak in one subsidiary skill and strong in another, and yet all are relevant to skillful driving. Learning complex skills is difficult, in part, because of the need to coordinate the learning of so many different subsidiary skills. (4) It is often difficult to individuate a skill and to describe its boundaries or limits. What exactly is required, for example, to be a skillful lawyer, artist, magician, writer, or orchestra conductor?

When we speak of "skills," we may refer in a neutral way to various applications of *knowing how*, the way one refers to ice skating, or cooking, or poker as skills one might possess—or not (as in, "I'm sorry, I don't *know how* to skate."). But "skill" can also imply excellence in performance, as when we refer to a "skilled poker-player" or a "skillful politician." Skills and crafts have normativity, a sense of quality that is derived within the activity itself, not from the uses made of the skill; so one may be a "skillful driver" but use that skill for an unworthy purpose, say, to drive a get-away car from a crime. The highest reaches of quality in a skill, we term "mastery." A master chess-player or carpenter is one who is very highly skilled and who performs with excellence.

Learning to Learn

In each of the four paradigms examined previously, skills play an important role; each paradigm privileges or elevates certain skills that conduce to the educational aim. So, for example, the transmission of culture model values the skills of scholarship and exegesis; the engagement with the world model values the skills of practical reasoning and persuasion. But learning depends on previous learning: learning the skill of textual critique relies on one's having acquired the skill of reading, which in turn relies on one's having learned the alphabet. Learning skills is, therefore, a central part of liberal education under any conception. One cannot, under any of these paradigms, become liberally educated simply by knowing *that*; one must also know *how*.

This fifth paradigm, however, not only places the acquisition of skills as the guiding aim, but it focuses on a special set of skills: its most fundamental claim is that learning is not merely a process; it is a complex skill. This is an interesting claim, one worth careful attention. I noted in the Introduction that we can learn unconsciously and unintentionally as well as deliberately and with full attention; while it is true that the performances of skillful people have many unconscious and unintentional aspects, it is doubtful that they could have learned the skill itself in that way. The now-skillful driver is not attending consciously to all aspects of driving, but no one learns to drive unconsciously. To think of learning as a skill is, then, to concentrate on purposeful and deliberate ways of learning.

When we watch different people learning the same skill, say learning to play the cello or to solve algebraic equations, we commonly observe that people learn at different rates and in different ways. Often we relate the rate of learning to natural aptitudes. Individuals also vary in patience and persistence. Recently, researchers have discerned patterns in the effective ways we learn and have described different "learning styles." But this paradigm suggests that skillfulness may be relevant as well, and that some people are more skilled at learning than others. Moreover, it claims that there are generic skills of learning transferable from one subject or activity to another and effectively applicable in many areas.

What skills might these be? One popular choice is *critical thinking*. Though definitions of this skill diverge, a common thread is the application of reason (especially the canons of logic) to arguments, beliefs, and claims. It therefore may entail questioning assumptions, applying considered principles, and assessing evidence. The National Council for Excellence in Critical Thinking has published a detailed definition of the term: "the intellectually disciplined process of actively and skillfully conceptualizing, applying, analyzing, synthesizing, and/or evaluating information gathered from, or generated by, observation, experience, reflection, reasoning, or communication, as a guide to belief and action." Moreover, this statement is explicit regarding the transferability of critical thinking: "In its exemplary form, it is based on universal intellectual values that transcend subject matter divisions: clarity, accuracy, precision, consistency, relevance, sound evidence, good reasons, depth, breadth, and fairness."[2] The centrality and significance of critical thinking for intellectual activities and decision-making have led to all the apparatus of a national movement in the United States: advocacy organizations, workshops, numerous texts, training, and a robust theoretical literature. Most U.S. and Canadian colleges and many high schools now offer courses in critical thinking; in Britain, a course titled "Critical Thinking" is offered to sixth-form students (usually sixteen- to eighteen-year-olds) as an A-level subject, and an advanced-level course is available.

Among other skills frequently nominated are: *communication skills, active listening, information literacy, quantitative reasoning skills, ethical reasoning, social skills, creative and imaginative skills*, and a cluster commonly called *study skills. Communication skills* also represents a cluster, and may include skills of writing, speaking, visual presentation of information, and effective presentation of oneself and one's message through television and other media. *Active listening* may also be considered a communication skill, but so little educational attention has been given to the reception end of the communication process, that it is worth its own mention.[3]

Information literacy is a broad term generally understood to include the skills of recognizing when information is needed and what sort of information would be salient, as well as the abilities to locate, evaluate, and effectively present or apply the relevant information. Our era is often labeled "the Information Age," and while our access to information is unparalleled—there has never been a better time to be a scholar—we are, as many have said, drowning in information. The skills of coping effectively with this bounty (or curse, as some would have it) are therefore receiving greater attention; it no longer refers to competency with computers—which has become a basic skill. What is now intended are skills of research and application. Some would even argue today that "information literacy" refers to an emerging field within the liberal arts: the study of "the nature of information itself, its technical infrastructure and its social, cultural, and philosophical context and impact."[4] I would go further: a crucial skill of learning today is deciding wisely what *not* to learn. Life is short, and how is one to handle not only the growing superabundance of valuable information, but the flood of technical instructions, software updates, "apps" for almost everything imaginable, and works in ever-expanding media? It is a highly-refined and valuable skill to determine cannily which tasks of learning to bypass and which to pursue.

Quantitative reasoning skills or *numeracy* begin with basic calculation skills and build to a wide range of competencies in the selection, use, and evaluation of various forms of mathematical information and reasoning. It is yet another special form of communication skills. *Ethical reasoning* is a basket term that includes skills of recognizing values conflicts, engaging in values clarification, thinking through a considered personal position on ethical issues, and employing cognitive tools to resolve moral conflicts. The *social skills* that advance learning are, for example, the skills of understanding and learning from other cultures and those who are different, along with the skills for working collaboratively and learning within groups. *Imaginative skills* refer, for instance, to the abilities to take creative approaches, generate counterexamples, visualize possibilities, and develop alternative solutions. *Study skills*, commonly taught in pre-college years, include organizing complex material, using reference works, creating an outline as a structure of thought, and knowing one's own most effective learning styles.

Emerging from these ideas is a distinctive image of the liberally educated person as a person who knows how to think and how to learn and who employs those skills aptly—someone who listens actively, thinks critically, knows how to access and package salient information, can employ appropriate quantitative techniques, reasons thoughtfully about moral issues, can learn from others who are different, is creative in imaging solutions, and is capable of marshaling best personal practices for learning material (to invoke just the skills I have listed). Being educated is therefore less about knowing certain things, assimilating great texts, actualizing all one's talents, or being an activist in the world, and more about possessing the skills of learning—although those skills may well incorporate the subsidiary techniques of the other paradigms.

Advocates and Exemplars

Advocates often arrive at a skills-based educational paradigm by expanding the model of basic skills, the foundational skills on which more advanced forms of learning depend. The ironic slogan of "the three Rs"—referring to "reading, 'riting, and 'rithmetic"[5]—is used to define the mission of early education, but it suggests not only "ladder" skills that lead to higher learning, but life-long skills—skills that are used to learn and to function in the world as long as one lives. Focusing on the needs of every student for "readiness" for the twenty-first century, one prominent K-12 educational advocacy group has added the "four Cs": critical thinking and problem solving, communication, collaboration, and creativity and innovation.[6]

This approach is echoed in higher education, and it is not new. No less a figure than John Henry Newman seemed to reflect this paradigm when he wrote:

[The kind of education a university should provide] is the education which gives a man a clear conscious view of his own opinions and judgments, a truth in developing them, an eloquence in expressing them, and a force in urging them. It teaches him to see things as they are, to go right to the point, to disentangle a skein of thought, to detect what is sophistical and to discard what is irrelevant. It prepares him to fill any post with credit, and to master any subject with facility. It shows him how to accommodate himself to others ... how to influence them, how to come to an understanding with them, how to bear with them. He is at home in any society, he has common ground with every class; he knows when to speak and when to be silent; he is able to converse, he is able to listen; he can ask a question pertinently and gain a lesson seasonably, when he has nothing to impart himself ...[7]

The Chicago School critic, Ronald Crane, developed this idea in repletion in a private letter to Chauncey Boucher (both were colleagues of Robert Hutchins and Mortimer Adler at the University of Chicago):

Forming or developing what may be called basic intellectual habits [is] basic in the sense of being fundamental to all more advanced and specialized intellectual effort whether within the University or without. The ability to see problems, to define terms accurately and clearly, to analyze a question into its significant elements, to become aware of general assumptions and preconceptions upon which one's own thinking and that of others rests, to make relevant and useful distinctions, to weigh probabilities, to organize the results of one's own reflections and research, to read a book of whatever sort reflectively, analytically, critically, to write one's native language with clarity and distinction—the development of these powers would seem to me to be no less the business of "General Education" than the communication and testing of knowledge, and I am not sure that they are not, in the long run, the most important and valuable fruits of a well-considered "General Education."[8]

Today, we find an emphasis on skills in institutional presentments as well. For example, The Annapolis Group, representing about

130 liberal arts colleges, states that its member institutions "regard the overarching purpose of a liberal arts education as developing students' intellectual and personal capacities," which seems to reflect a self-actualization approach; predominant among the list that follows, however, are to "think clearly, analytically, creatively, and critically"; "make effective use of technology"; "work collaboratively and successfully within diverse social environments"; and "communicate effectively."[9]

The focus on skills, no doubt, responds to three aspects of our contemporary educational environment: utilitarian concerns, rising costs, and the demand for documented outcomes. A liberal arts education might be seen as practical, even worth the considerable financial and opportunity costs, if its graduates can acquire demonstrable, useful skills. Some institutions have chosen to reinforce the practical nature of taught skills by emphasizing their applicability to career success; others focus on the personal empowerment that skills of learning can provide over a lifetime. Most liberal arts colleges elevate skills in their self-presentations, but few organize their curricula around specific skills or focus thoroughly on *learning how* in pedagogy.

An exception is Alverno College, a Catholic liberal arts college for women. Alverno seems to celebrate a self-actualization approach, emphasizing the uniqueness of students: "Your education should be all about you, helping you to become the best version of yourself and to realize your potential by becoming the person you haven't yet imagined." In its program, "self-actualization" is addressed through (if not reduced to) the acquisition of skills. Its program is "ability-based and focused on student outcomes integrated in a liberal arts approach." The curriculum stresses eight abilities: "Communication, Analysis, Problem Solving, Valuing, Social Interaction, Developing a Global Perspective, Effective Citizenship, and Aesthetic Engagement." Alverno claims that these eight "core abilities"—a significant characterization—"represent the very building blocks needed to create an effective and relevant learning experience. These abilities are the building blocks for learning ..." Furthermore, it advises prospective students: "In every area of study, you'll be expected to show evidence of learning. And you'll have numerous opportunities to showcase your command of the eight core abilities; the same abilities needed for effectiveness in your work, family and community." Yet it also says, "We help you reach for something far more valuable than a career."[10]

Reed College states forthrightly: "The goal of the Reed education is that students learn and demonstrate rigor and independence in their habits of thought, inquiry, and expression." But, like most liberal arts colleges, Reed does not structure its curriculum in an instrumentally direct and explicit way toward the acquisition of these skills. Some educationists would conclude that this is problematic, that this reveals a disconnect between methods of teaching, curriculum, and stated educational goals. For those critics, institutions that preach skills but do not pursue a skills-based curriculum, fail in self-awareness, laze in murky thinking, and lack integrity in practice. In fact, the situation may be much more complicated and there is some empirical evidence for a subtler, if not "murkier" approach.

Empirical research on cognition presents important findings for skills-based theories.[11] The research addresses both the individuation of skills and optimal ways of learning skills, and the results should caution theorists about the supposed generic transferability of skills. Reading skills, for example, seem to vary across subject matter; writing and problem-solving skills are also subject-specific. Being skilled at reading literature does not entail being skilled at reading philosophy. One can be adroit at writing history, but unable to write poetry. An adept solver of problems in economics may be stumped by problems in chemistry. Moreover, and in part as a consequence, skills need to be taught in the context of their use, drawing upon both background knowledge and contextual information; they must be practiced promptly and in a relevant context to be retained. These observations challenge the claim that there are isolable, transferable skills of a comprehensive nature that could be used as the goal of education; rather, all such generic skills are actually names for a cluster of related but subject-specific skills that are applicable to different contexts.

Let us say we elevate communication as a central skill. One research-supported approach would be to recognize that—once we are past a very basic level—different fields have different communication conventions. Communicating in chemistry, for example, might involve the skills of keeping lab notebooks, articulating clear research hypotheses, writing abstracts of research findings, presenting work in a poster format for professional conferences, writing grant applications, and so on. These are quite different from the communication conventions of, say, philosophy, which would include formulating arguments using well-defined concepts, identifying fallacies and counter-examples, writing papers that advance a thesis, responding critically to the arguments of another, and so on. Both build on basic writing skills, but their elaboration diverges sharply. As the flamboyant Princeton sociologist, Marvin Bressler, once said, "My students say they don't want to learn content, they want to learn to think. I say, 'Fine, let's think a little about Sociology'."[12]

Objections to the Skills of Learning Paradigm

Some may find it surprising that skills would be given any significant part in liberal education, except perhaps as early preparation. Skills involve training and practice—which are often contrasted with education and theory, respectively—and surely no account of liberal education could make those processes central. But there is ancient authority for such claims within the liberal education tradition. Plato's proposed curriculum for leaders included the capstone study of dialectic, the skill of talking things through until a clear understanding could be achieved. The *trivium* of the medieval university was essentially training in the skills of grammar, rhetoric, and dialectic. The liberal arts programs of today regularly use training and practice to teach academic skills: pronunciation in foreign languages, use of instrumentation in the natural sciences, statistical reasoning in the social sciences, listening techniques in music appreciation, and so on.

But, in the tradition of liberal education, whenever skills have been elevated, they have been embedded in a larger context of knowledge and qualities of character. From Cicero's essays to Newman's *Idea of the University*, the commended skills are to be displayed in ways that reflect a breadth of knowledge and intellectual and moral virtues. These attributes opened up an appreciation for style. Focusing on skills alone is a characteristically modern approach: if education hones the skills of reading, for example, it leaves to individual wills the choice of what is to be read. Though students may be directed to acquire skills of learning, *what* they should learn through their lives may be left open.

One might object that isolating skills from knowledge and virtue gives them a free-floating quality and reduces them to competencies. The larger sense of mastery of a craft and its ethos is lost. Competencies are then prone to be narrowed further, as process and performance are reduced to outcomes. Once again, we have a problem that can be prevented by the application of the other paradigms as complements. The concern for assimilating culture, gaining an understanding of the world, actualizing one's potential, and preparing to engage in the world—with these in place, we have the context to give skills their salience and style. Perhaps one could then argue that the acquisition of the skills of learning does not represent a paradigm at all—at least not on a par with the other four. One could, in much the same way, imagine a paradigm organized around a set of qualities of character: *Education is for the development of intellectual and moral virtues.* Intellectual curiosity, open-mindedness, clarity of thought, appreciation of difference, honesty, the courage of one's convictions—these and others might find a place in such a panoply; and, indeed one can find such virtues celebrated in the mission statements of many liberal arts programs.

Do the skills of learning really comprise a distinct paradigm? I acknowledge that it is a matter of judgment, for I have not claimed *a priori* status for them; though they arise naturally, I say, from working out the implications of the ultimate goal of cultivating a good life.[13] There are considerations against it: to elevate learning skills as the core idea of a paradigm reverses important means-ends distinctions, and achieving the aims of each of the other four paradigms entails the acquisition of relevant skills. These points notwithstanding, it seems to me that the skills of learning are being taken as an influential paradigm in contemporary liberal education, and we lose the opportunity to examine it as fully if we do not call it into focus.

This concludes Part II and the exploration of the five distinctive paradigms. In Part III, we will take them together, describing their complementarity and the themes they share, and using their perspectives to understand the values and moral aspirations of liberal education.

Notes

1   Gilbert Ryle, *The Concept of Mind* (New York: Barnes & Noble, 1949). For an early response to attempts to collapse the distinction, see Jane Roland, "On Knowing How and Knowing That," *Philosophical Review* 67, no. 3 (July 1958), 379–88.

2   Michael Scriven and Richard W. Paul, *Critical Thinking as Defined by the National Council for Excellence in Critical Thinking* (1987); published in "Defining Critical Thinking," *The Critical Thinking Community* (website of The Foundation for Critical Thinking), http://www.criticalthinking.org/aboutCT/define_critical_thinking.cfm (accessed September 2011).

3   For information on effective listening, see the website of the International Listening Association: http://www.listen.org/.

4   Jeremy J. Shapiro and Shelly K. Hughes, "Information Literacy as a Liberal Art: Enlightenment Proposals for a New Curriculum," *Educom Review* 31, no. 2 (March/April 1996), http://net.educause.edu/apps/er/review/reviewarticles/31231.html (accessed September 2011). I will return to this issue in the final chapter.

5   The phrase is apocryphally attributed to Sir John Curtis, in either a speech or a toast given before the Board of Education in London in 1825. It is hypothesized by some that the third "R" may have been "reckoning," which was a common nineteenth-century term for arithmetic calculation—but, of course, that wouldn't rescue Curtis from the second "R."

6   The Partnership for 21st Century Skills, http://www.p21.org (accessed September 2011).

7   Newman, *The Idea of a University*, 192.

8   Ronald Crane to Chauncey Boucher, 1931; quoted in John W. Boyer, *Three Views of Continuity and Change at the University of Chicago* (Chicago: The University of Chicago, 1999), 52.

9   "About the Annapolis Group," http://collegenews.org/about-the-annapolis-group (accessed July 2011). The list also includes other important elements that reflect the influence of other paradigms.

10 All quotations in this paragraph are from the Alverno College website: www.alverno.edu (accessed September 2011). See especially these web pages: "About Alverno," "Our Ability-Based Curriculum," and "Mission and History."

11 An informative summary of the educational implications of such research, though now a decade old, is: Jennifer Cromley, *Learning*

to Learn: What the Science of Thinking and Learning Has to Offer Adult Education (Washington, DC: National Institute for Literacy, 2000), http://literacynet.org/lincs/resources/cromley_report.pdf (accessed September 2011).

12　"Conversation on General Education with Professor Marvin Bressler, April 1, 1979," transcribed in *Report of the College Planning Committee, October 1980* (Winter Park, FL: Rollins College, 1980), 282. In this paragraph, I have drawn on the current, goal-based curriculum of Gettysburg College. One of its goals is "Effective Communication," which has several aspects, including requiring each department or program to teach the "communication conventions of the field," normally to be demonstrated in the capstone experience of the major.

13　The skills of learning paradigm was not included in either article in which I first developed many of the ideas in this book (see the Preface and Acknowledgments).

PART III

The Values and Moral Aims of Liberal Education

8

Core Values of Liberal Education

The function of education in a democracy is... to liberate the mind, strengthen its critical powers, inform it with knowledge and the capacity for independent inquiry, engage its human sympathies, and illuminate its moral and practical choices.

ISRAEL SCHEFFLER, "MORAL EDUCATION AND THE DEMOCRATIC IDEAL"

A good way to begin the excursions of this chapter is by taking stock, giving a succinct summary of the account of liberal education presented thus far. To this point, I have presented liberal education as a vital tradition of educational theory and practice that is defined by the supreme aim of forming a compelling conception of a good life and cultivating a life in which one flourishes. Within this tradition have arisen five competing yet complementary paradigms, which are each defined by a subsidiary aim: transmission of culture, self-realization, understanding the world, engagement with the world, and acquisition of the skills of learning. Each paradigm inspires and accommodates many more specific conceptions of liberal education; indeed these paradigms represent the first step in a cascade of increasingly specific theories,

practices, and institutionalizations of liberal education. Attempting
to deflect or reject common critiques, I have distinguished between
the critiques directed at particular theories and practices and
those that are directed at the concept of liberal education and the
aim that defines the tradition. I have pointed to the evolutionary
dynamism, complexity, range, and openness of this tradition—
largely produced by the interaction of these paradigms that respond
to intellectual, cultural, and technological changes—as both the
context for comparing particular conceptions of liberal education
and as the matrix for contemporary and future developments.

In this chapter, I hope to enhance this account by exploring the
relationships among these paradigms, both their differences and
their complementarity. Then I will turn to the ways in which they
are manifested through certain "core concepts" or themes that
are often associated with liberal education: *freedom*, *autonomy*,
democracy, and *truth*.

Contrasting the Paradigms of Liberal Education

Though it is a simplification, we might think of the first four paradigms
as directional: *transmission of culture* looks to the past; *engagement
with the world* looks to the future; *self-actualization* looks inward to
the self; and *understanding the world* looks outward to the natural
and constructed context in which we dwell. The *skills of learning*
paradigm is omni-directional. These directionalities indicate different
sources of the educational content or curriculum: the transmission of
culture paradigm draws upon the encoded human experience of texts
and works; self-actualization looks to a reading of human nature and/
or the potential of individuals; the engagement paradigm draws from
the phenomena of the world, from a realistic view of nature itself,
from the structure of knowledge, or from the elements of human
experience; the engagement paradigm looks to a problematized view
of the possibilities of human action and creation—to a sense of what
may or must be done; and, finally, the skills of learning paradigm
draws upon an account of human interests and needs.

In addition, each of the paradigms elevates a set of skills and
correlated virtues. For example, the skills of literacy, including

translation and interpretation, are especially salient for the transmission paradigm's aim of receiving and assimilating the worthy
works of writers and artists; whereas the skills of practical
reasoning and persuasiveness are brought forward for the aim
of engaging with the world. And while curiosity is a cardinal
virtue for understanding the world, self-awareness is favored for
self-actualization.

These distinctive aims, skills, and virtues are instantiated in
differing models of the educated person, or rather in sketches or
caricatures of the educated person until given more detail by the
specific theoretical conceptions that arise under each paradigm.
Under the paradigm of transmission of culture to successor generations, the educated person is a scholar, one who knows great works
and the symbol systems in which they are constructed; one whose
mind is furnished and enriched by literature, history, philosophy,
and art, and whose imagination is endowed by a cultivated
memory; one who may enter into "the Immortal Conversation"
with an informed and yet personal perspective. The self-actualization paradigm envisions the educated person as one who knows
herself well, and has employed that understanding to achieve self-
mastery and the development of a range of talents and virtues; the
accomplished individual, the person who continually seeks new
challenges and pursues his highest aspirations, one who successfully climbs the hierarchy of needs; the sage whose wisdom derives
from self-knowledge; and the authentic person who embraces his
life as his own—all are images of the self-actualized person. To
understand the world and the forces that shape one's life is a goal
embodied in the polymath, a person with broad interest in and
knowledge of the ways of the world, the disciplines, and of contemporary findings of research in the natural and social sciences.
The engagement with the world paradigm aspires to produce
an effective person—an executive, civic activist, social critic or
reformer—who will act normatively and persuade others. And
the skills-based paradigm models an astute and life-long learner, a
self-reliant and competent soul who possesses the know-how and
disposition to learn whatever is needed or of interest.

It should be clear that these paradigms represent different polarities of educational thought and practice. Taken separately, they
would construct divergent educational programs. The proponents
of one often disparage another. Their contrasts have fueled intense

debates about curriculum, pedagogy, and institutional purpose. In the history of liberal education, though they rise and fall in fashion, none has been decisively abandoned. And for good reason—or so I have claimed: these comparisons identify features that differentiate these approaches to liberal education, but the paradigms are complementary as well as competitive.

The Complementarity of the Paradigms

What does the assertion that the paradigms are complementary mean? First, it means that, tied to the ultimate concern for living a flourishing life, these five strands are interconnected: often, one aim is subsumed as means to another's ends; sometimes, the elaboration of one leads to another; and at other times, more than one strand, even all five, are declared boldly as pluralistic ends of equal status—leaving to the learner the task of discovering their relationship.

For example, one might interpret self-actualization as ultimately requiring both knowledge of and engagement with the world: Aristotle is identified primarily with the educational aim of self-actualization, of developing and exercising virtuous traits in a flourishing or eudaimonistic life; but Aristotle thought such a life was expressed through understanding one's world (*sophia*, or theoretical wisdom) and engaging in action with virtue (*phronesis*, or practical wisdom). Or, one might see the assimilation of transmitted culture as a path to self-realization: Michael Oakeshott is known for valuing the transmission of culture, interpreting our intellectual heritage in the image of a grand conversation, in which we must "learn the voices"; yet Oakeshott also asserts that entering this conversation, "our common inheritance ... is the only way of becoming a human being, and to inhabit it is to be a human being"—expressing thereby an ultimate, motivating hope for self-actualization.[1] Such interconnections among distinguishable aims are commonplace in both theory and practice.

Note how elements of all five aims appear in the following excerpts sampled from the current mission statements of three liberal arts colleges:

The power of a liberal arts education ... help[s] students develop critical thinking skills, broad vision, effective communications, a sense of the inter-relatedness of all knowledge, sensitivity to the human condition, and a global perspective, all necessary to enable students to realize their full potential for responsible citizenship ...[2]

Amherst College educates men and women of exceptional potential from all backgrounds so that they may seek, value, and advance knowledge, engage the world around them, and lead principled lives of consequence.[3]

A liberal education cultivates the mind and the imagination; encourages seeking after truth, meaning, and beauty; awakens an appreciation of past traditions and present challenges; fosters joy in learning and sharing that learning with others; supports taking the intellectual risks required to explore the unknown, test new ideas and enter into constructive debate; and builds the foundation for making principled judgments. It hones the capacity for critical and open intellectual inquiry—the interest in asking questions, challenging assumptions, seeking answers, and reaching conclusions supported by logic and evidence. A liberal education rests fundamentally on the free exchange of ideas—on conversation and questioning—that thrives in class-rooms, lecture halls, laboratories, studios, dining halls, playing fields, and dormitory rooms. Ultimately, a liberal education promotes independent thinking, individual action, and social responsibility.[4]

These institutions are not, at least in their public presentments, governed by one paradigm, but by a blend of all five.

The second aspect of complementarity is that the narrowness and defects of any one approach are offset or corrected by the involvement of the others. Thus, for example, the concern that preoccupation with self-actualization might lead to self-absorption is answered by the ways in which other paradigms put the attention outside the self: in the attempt to assimilate the cultural legacy left us by others, or in the compelling endeavor to understand the world around us, or in the call to respond to people and events. Similarly, the objection that the transmission of culture paradigm may stress intellectual development only and promote a bookish isolation from domestic and public spheres is countered by the empirical effort to understand the world we dwell in and the forces that affect our lives, by learning how to learn collaboratively, and especially by the moral and pragmatic focus of the aim of effective action and engagement. As we saw in the previous chapter, the objection that the skills, even the skills of learning, should not be taken out of context or separately from values commitments is addressed by the combined impact of the other four paradigms.

Indeed, the paradigms seem necessarily interrelated—which is not surprising, given the natural connections between the primal questions they address (*Who am I? What may I become? What is my situation? What may—or must I do? How may I answer such questions?*). Any one approach seems incomplete or oddly blinkered when walled off from the others. Rarely does a theorist work within one paradigm only without giving way at some point to at least a nod to the others; institutions that aspire to educational purity by adhering to one paradigm only are distinctive, but eccentric, rare, and vulnerable. Robust theories of liberal education may be distinguished by the balance and blend of the five strands they weave. It is a central thesis of this book that the paradigms have relations of mutual support and that liberal education optimally includes the influence of all five.

There is a third aspect to the complementarity: there are significant themes that thread through and bind these strands of liberal education, conceptual continuities of values that are often given moral weight. They tend to function not only in regard to the aims or aspirations of a liberal education, but also within the process of liberal education itself. These ideals are commonly associated with liberal education and are frequently invoked in discourse about the liberal arts. The rest of this chapter is devoted to consideration of four such thematic concepts, their ties to the ultimate aim of flourishing, and their manifestation within each of the paradigms.

Freedom

One such theme (reflected in the often misunderstood term "liberal") is *freedom*. In the long history of the tradition of liberal education, there are many meanings, diverse associations, given to the link between *freedom* and *liberal education*, which, in part, reflect the historic alterations in the concept of freedom. The original terms commonly translated as "liberal arts" (*eleutheriai technai* in Greek, *artes liberales* in Latin), could be rendered equally well as "the skills of freedom." One ancient interpretation is that these terms denote that set of studies suitable for a free man as opposed to a slave or a brute—or a woman. (A slightly shaded version of this interpretation is that the liberal arts are studies that may be applied in a condition of freedom.) This is, of course, the origin of the notion that liberal education is necessarily aristocratic, elitist, or sexist. But that charge presumes that free human beings necessarily comprise only a subset of the population. As freedom is extended, the core of this interpretation may be applied without the taint of aristocratic or colonialist superiority.

It is certainly the case that, for centuries, educational theory was preoccupied with the proper education of those who would rule, but that is understandable given the typical political structure: the education of the prince and his noblemen would clearly represent the most pressing of concerns. (There is a parallel in the theory of emotions, which during ancient times seems preoccupied with the emotions of anger and fear—a reasonable worry, however, in a time of tyranny and absolute rule.)

Another equally ancient interpretation is that the *septem artes liberales* are the studies that liberate: a liberal education is a liberating education. Freedom, in the ancient Western philosophical tradition, is an accomplishment, not an inalienable right. It is achievement, requiring discipline and self-mastery, the guidance of reason, and a sense of one's limits and place. To be ignorant is true enslavement. Epictetus, for example, states in his *Discourses* that although "the many" may assert that only free men should be educated, philosophers believe that only educated mean are free.[5] Liberal education thus proceeds from and for freedom.

The conception of the liberation that education offers is colored distinctively by each of the five paradigms; each strand offers its particular form of freedom. The cultural transmission ideal offers liberation from a timeless, meaningless, unconstructed present. Imbibing a heritage of works that comprehends human experience across the years and miles helps to free the learner from parochial prejudice and to expand the intellectual and moral imagination. The self-actualization idea offers liberation from confused and imposed identities, from the frustration and alienation of stifled, untested, or suppressed potential. It promises the liberation of one's authentic self in the realization of one's ownmost possibilities. Yet a different form of liberation is suggested by the ideal of understanding the world and the forces that shape one's life: this is liberation from superstition, ignorance, and error; and such understanding can have an emotional impact as well, freeing us from reflexive fear and hostility. The ideal of effective engagement with the world aims to commission the student; it provides liberation from powerlessness, false constraints, and social entropy. This is liberation from helpless by-standing, a freedom of agency, the ability to shape one's will to one's judgment, to fulfill one's best judgment, and to act on behalf of one's values. And finally, acquiring the skills of learning empower the student with the freedom to grow, to discover, to know, and to understand. In concert, these ideals would free us (and obligate us) to be morally mature persons together; collectively, these forms of liberation permit us to flourish, to have the greatest prospects for a good life.

The theme of freedom is indeed pervasive in the tradition of liberal education; especially important are its expression in the classical liberalism associated with the Enlightenment and its relationship to truth. To explore these connections expeditiously, we must first open some other related themes, beginning with *autonomy*.

Autonomy

Autonomy, the capacity of willing and making one's own choices, is a theme that appears in the tradition of liberal education both as a goal of the educational process and as a constraint upon it. Foundationally, the will and decisions are one's own because they are *freely* willed and chosen, neither coerced or imposed nor stifled or suppressed. This is, of course, why indoctrination is condemned as an ethical violation, and why appropriate methods of liberal education are at pains to prevent it.[6]

The process of learning should honor the value of autonomy; only then can the means be consistent with the ends.[7] Just as the basic task of parenting is to nurture the child into an adulthood in which she is capable of making her own choices, so a liberal education should yield a person who is autonomous in a more profound sense, something beyond normal ascription of adult responsibility. That profundity is a function of the scope and quality of one's choices, a measure of an individual's live options and empowerment. The person who believes and acts and feels as he does because he knows no other way is, from this perspective, the antithesis of a liberally educated person. His prospects for a flourishing life are sadly constrained. Autonomy in the fullest sense requires a reservoir of imaginative possibilities of thought, action, and emotion—possibilities of content and of style as well—that can be deployed in determining one's will and one's own choices. They may be foundationally one's own because they are freely willed, but they are finally one's own because they are freely *selected* from other possibilities.[8]

Superficially, the theme of autonomy is probably most visible in the paradigm defined by engagement with the world. The focus on becoming someone who is effective in the arenas of human action entails autonomy in the fullest sense. Nonetheless, autonomy is a theme in the self-actualization paradigm as well. It should not be construed, in that context, as simply one capacity among others to be developed in the realization of a normative self; rather, autonomy is seen as fundamental to a self-actualized mode of living. It is given special prominence and enhanced interpretation in those conceptions that elevate authenticity or choosing one's ownmost possibilities as the guide of self-actualization. In addition, to acquire the skills of learning is to become one's own teacher, to obtain and evaluate the information one needs, to be given the tools to extend one's grasp. Autonomy resonates in the other paradigms as well: any assimilation of the cultural legacy adds to the learner's reservoir of imaginative possibilities, as the encoded experience of the thoughts, feelings, and deeds of other lifetimes is absorbed within the learner's personal experience; and, of course, understanding the world and its formative forces allows a better grasp of one's options and the likely consequences of one's actions.

In postmodern times, autonomy is sometimes derided as a relic of the Enlightenment despite its ancient roots and perennial blossoms; it is charged with reflecting atomistic individualism, celebrating self-sufficiency, and ignoring human relatedness and dependency. But autonomy may also grace the "situated self" when understood in other ways—for example, as what enables the exercise of human capabilities in response to one's situation, or as a condition of moral agency that shapes relationships.[9] Having the capacity to influence one's own life in response to critical reflection may even be essential to the concept of a developed self—situated and related, or not.

The autonomy valued in liberal education is not merely a metaphysical or moral construct; it also includes the outlook that psychologists call an "internal locus of control." This arises from the belief that one's life is largely affected by one's own actions and choices, and not determined by others or by chance. I may not control everything that affects my life, but my efforts are relevant to a significant extent. Those with an internal locus of control reject as a life-defining attitude the giving up one's life to "external" control—to superstition, to powerful others, to "the system," or to blind chance—in favor of self-efficacy. Flourishing is not primarily a matter of luck; each of us may shape our lives.

In valuing autonomy as means and end, liberal education thus affirms a fundamental human capacity, an essential determinant of identity, the confidence and desire to shape our lives, and an instrument and component of a flourishing life.

Democracy

Although there is a manifest connection between the first two themes and that of *democracy*—the political vision in which freedom and autonomy are enshrined—it may seem odd to claim either a conceptual or a traditional connection between liberal education and democracy, since one striking historical change in liberal education is its metamorphosis from the classical model of an exclusive education suitable only for leaders—free, aristocratic, leisured men—to the contemporary vision of an education required of all for effective democratic citizenship. But, in fact, the connection was there at the outset: after all, it was the emergence of democracy and the correlative threat to aristocratic values in ancient Greece that provoked consideration of the best education for such citizens and the establishment of competing schools to offer it. To be sure, the Athenian conception of democracy, though radical in its forms of participation, was severely restricted in extending the eligibility to vote: citizenship in the democratic years of ancient Athens was limited to free, native-born males.[10] Its native sons, such as Plato and Isocrates, were able to found and own schools that professed to prepare citizen-leaders; on the other hand, Aristotle, a resident alien from Thrace with Macedonian connections, had to rent property for his school, in which the scholarly mission was more directed to research. The xenophobic Athenians never fully trusted foreigners, whether they were itinerant philosophers, wholesale merchants, or ingratiating diplomats.

Through the fits and starts of a punctuated social evolution, our collective sense of who is capable of and entitled to such citizenship has become increasingly inclusive—and the need for liberal education more widespread. If we are to shape our political destinies together, each one valued as a moral equal, then promoting education becomes more than a private and public good: it becomes a political imperative. The moral climate of democracy, understood in the Deweyan sense, in which each individual's experience is valued as relevant to the construction of the good, a society in which virtually all adults may shape their own lives—and therefore the lives of others—depends on liberal education for its very survival as well as its thriving. In such a climate, the concern for one's life as a whole and for what it is to live a flourishing life becomes a live issue for all.

This hopeful conception is opposed to the view that democracy is simply that political system in which individuals have the greatest scope to satisfy their desires—desires that are given, not considered, informed, mediated, or reconstructed. That is the vision of a consumerist society in which freedom and autonomy merely mean getting whatever one wants. Education, especially liberal education, involves the normative alteration of one's desires and wants. The very motivation for education is lodged in what Harry Frankfurt called "second-order desires": *the desire to desire X*, or, *wanting to want X*.[11] Second-order desires produce "a new volition"; they create a normative realm within or upon the natural realm. Educators want their students to come to want what will be conducive to their flourishing; they hope their students will come to share such second-order wants for themselves—and that this will eventually transform their first-order wants. This does not mean that every citizen in a democracy needs fully to share a conception of the good; on the contrary, it permits and even values a diversity of conceptions. But it does imply that every citizen desires to lead a flourishing life, and that everyone understands that such lives have relations of mutual support.

Truth

Truth is a touchstone within the tradition of liberal education. Despite that fact, I do not intend to wade into a review of philosophical theories of truth, because the tradition has, I believe, given genial accommodation to most conceptions of truth—though they ramify differently and may require parallel reconstruction of other key concepts. The views that truth is correspondence with reality, coherence with other embedded beliefs, whatever works in experience, or an epistemic social construction—all these accounts and others significantly reconstruct the nature of truth, but do not displace or discard it as an educational touchstone. At the deepest level, the generic concept of education, when used normatively not descriptively, seems inescapably related to truth, however obliquely and under whatever interpretation. The supreme aim of liberal education, the ideal of a good life, of flourishing, also seems to be tied to truth. These relationships appear sharpest when we consider the alternative: *How could education or a flourishing life rely upon error, falsehood, the illusory, the fake, and the deceptive?* To be led from ignorance to error is no educational progress. To seek a life based on illusion and falsehood is perverse; the very notion of a good life implies one that is *genuinely* good. The various accounts of truth elevate different benefits that truth may convey—certainty, correctness, a sense of coherence, reliability, usefulness in action and in learning. How could a life be said to flourish if the opposites were its grounding—uncertainty, error, incoherence, unreliability, and dysfunction in action or in learning? Truth matters. It is indeed a touchstone: it is one of the cardinal values that define the normativity of education.

The five paradigms embody a concern for truth in interestingly distinctive ways. Self-actualization values self-knowledge and rejects self-deception as an end; many versions seek a form of authenticity—a form of lived truth. The aim of engagement with the world may seem to downplay truth or to displace other theories in favor of a pragmatic effectiveness in action. Superficially, the engagement paradigm does seem most friendly to a pragmatic account of truth, but the qualifications one stipulates to make "engagement" normative may invoke other senses of truth: for example, if we aim to act *with integrity*, we may imply a sense of coherence; if we aim to make the world *a better place*, we may invoke correspondence to reality as a test for our actions. In any event, engagement with the world is, in this paradigm, incomplete without some normative qualification—and those qualities are linked to some conception of truth and its implications for action. A similar point might be made about the skills of learning paradigm. An important normative qualifier of the learning process is the truth—while we may learn falsehood, why would we seek to learn it? Moreover, many of the skills of learning serve the aim of discovering the truth.

The other two paradigms represent a provocative contrast in regard to truth. The canon that represents the distillate of one's cultural legacy is, in part, compiled for the truth (or truths) its works are thought to embody. Many theories formed under the transmission paradigm would have us draw from the vast reservoir of encoded human experience the greatest works; "great" texts are those that have enduring and compelling value because of the truth they speak—and which each generation must protect and transmit. Such transmission implies a fidelity of meaning, an accurate (that is, truth-preserving) rendering of the content of the works. On the other hand, the aim of understanding the world conveys a search for truth that will be shaped into increasingly elaborated cognitive structures: facts, theories, knowledge, disciplines, cognitive perspectives, and world-views. Because of the contrasting emplacements of truth, these paradigms have often been in opposition and produced conflict. In short, one seeks to preserve and communicate truth; the other to discover it.

The opposition is traceable to the conflict between Socrates and the Sophists over methodology. The Sophists elevated rhetoric as the supreme educational method. In rhetoric, as with the transmission of culture paradigm in general, the truth is already in hand; the task is to articulate it clearly and communicate it persuasively. The truth reposes in the cultural stock one has inherited. Socrates, by contrast, championed dialectic, a method in which one seeks the ever-elusive truth by talking things through. While rhetoric assumes possession of the truth and aims at bringing it to power in the world, dialectic acknowledges ignorance and seeks the truth through dialogue. In actuality, each approach uses the other, though only in a subsidiary way—rhetoricians employ dialectic in scholarly investigations of texts, and dialecticians employ rhetoric in the statement of their hypotheses for consideration.

Bruce Kimball organized his history of liberal education around this conflict between rhetoric and dialectic, titling his book *Orators & Philosophers: A History of the Idea of Liberal Education*.[12] After centuries of domination by rhetorical methods, dialectic spawned the "New Philosophy" that shaped the Enlightenment, a scientific method that rejected the authority of received opinion in favor of a reasoned and empirical search for truth. Experimentation replaced conceptual analysis ("talking things through"). One might claim that this opposition between rhetoric and dialectic generated the divide and still defines the difference in ethos between "the two cultures" of the humanities and the sciences. That idea is, at most, an insightful caricature, but it ignores the fact that each "culture" makes significant use of the dominant method of the other.

Truth and Freedom

There is a particularly interesting relationship between the themes of truth and freedom—especially in light of the "two cultures" contrast between paradigms. In a characteristically trenchant and pungent essay, Richard Rorty distinguished between two political poles in educational theory—the right and the left—in terms of the perceived relation between truth and freedom. "The right usually offers a theory according to which, if you have the truth, freedom will follow automatically." Since these conservatives hold that our cultural legacy embodies truth (or even the Truth), our educational task is to absorb it through "the natural light of reason" and to cherish and transmit it faithfully and diligently, for "only the truth can make us free." Taking the viewpoint of the rhetorician, the right believes that freedom is a reward for our assimilation of the profound truths of our tradition, an achievement threatened chiefly by our own internal flaws, such as disruptive passions and sin.

Those on the left, Rorty says, invert this construction, inter-preting cultural transmission as "a triumph of acculturation" that imposes an identity and stifles human freedom. Thus, for the left, the struggle is for individualization in the face of socialization, and the threats are primarily external: they are obstacles to freedom, such as social convention, prejudice, and economic and political constraints. The left asserts that freedom is the first priority; and "if you take care of freedom ... truth will take care of itself."[13] The claim that freedom of inquiry is foundational derives from dialectic—though any ancient dialectician would caution that we must struggle for the truth—it doesn't just appear when we are freed.

Although Plato arrived at his vision of the ideal state dialec-tically; although his curricular proposal placed dialectic as the capstone study; and notwithstanding his banishment of poets and artists, Plato's totalitarian utopia operates on rhetoric. The philosopher-king has seen and possesses the truth; citizens are told the truth (as abridged by the wisest, and in so far as the citizenry can grasp it—two significant qualifications); they will thrive, Plato believes, so long as all arrangements and actions are grounded in truth and reason. Liberal democracy, by contrast, denies any shared or establishmentarian vision of the truth; rather, it seeks to secure a freedom in which citizens may pursue their own understandings.

Rorty observes that our practice, especially in the United States, has been to adopt the view of the right for education through secondary school, and the view of the left in higher education. We teach the cultural legacy first; then, in college, establish freedom to critique the received views, establish one's own perspective, and pursue one's own truth—an arrangement Rorty largely endorses, because one must be reared in a culture and gain some of its tools in order to equip oneself for the task of individualization.[14] Ultimately, however, Rorty embraces a Deweyan conception that synthesizes elements of both views: the tradition we inherit should be seen as one of gradual human liberation and democratic openness—and that rejects elements of both, especially concepts of absolute truth and an authentic self separable from society.

This move seems to me to be in the right direction. Educational polarities should not be ossified as dualisms. In the matter of rhetoric and dialectic, both are needed throughout our lives; their rhythmic interplay is also necessary in learning. Rhetoric emphasizes understanding in the old sense of *standing under*, submission to received stimuli (whether ideas, images, sounds, and so on) for the purpose of deriving meaning. Dialectic involves the self-assertion of articulation and projective thought as hypothesis or critique.

I like to think these complementary relationships are expressed in one of our most familiar monuments. The traditional symbol for dialectic's search for the truth is the torch; we carry the flame to negotiate the darkness of our ignorance and illuminate the truth. The symbol for rhetoric is the scroll or book or tablet: the precious record of received truth. Think now of democracy's "new Colossus": cradling the text (inscribed "1776") in her left hand and holding aloft the torch in her right, she wields both rhetoric and dialectic to break the chains at her feet and proclaim freedom democratically for all—as she is formally called, "The Statue of Liberty Enlightening the World."

Notes

1 Michael Oakeshott, "Learning and Teaching," in *The Voice of Liberal Learning*, ed. Fuller, 45.

2 Gettysburg College, Mission Statement: http://www.gettysburg.edu/about/college_history/mission_statement.dot (accessed July 2011).

3 "The Mission of Amherst College," https://www.amherst.edu/aboutamherst/mission (accessed September 2011).

4 Bowdoin College, http://www.bowdoin.edu/about/purpose/index.shtml (accessed July 2011).

5 Epictetus, *The Discourses*, 2.1.25, http://classics.mit.edu/Epictetus/discourses.html (accessed November 2011).

6 It is not an easy matter, however, to determine precisely when a student is being indoctrinated. The usage of the term is hobbled both by conceptual confusion (on which the literature is imposing) and disputes over values (over which curricular battles rage).

7 For a sustained account of the relationship between autonomy and liberal education, see Meira Levinson, *The Demands of Liberal Education* (Oxford: Oxford University Press, 1999). Levinson, however, is concerned with education in the liberal state, not specifically liberal arts education.

8 I have examined the relationship between forms of clarity, the imagination of possibilities, and education in "The Philosopher, the Teacher, and the Quest for Clarity" in *Philosophical Reflections on Society and Education*, ed. Creighton Peden and Donald Chipman (Washington, DC: Rowman & Littlefield, 1978).

9 The "capabilities" approach was famously developed by Amartya Sen in *Commodities and Capabilities* (Oxford: Oxford University Press, 1985) and applied by Martha C. Nussbaum in *Women and Moral Development: The Capabilities Approach* (Cambridge: Cambridge University Press, 2001).

10 This is a sound generalization, though special conditions sometimes applied. Minimal property qualifications were vestigial, but eventually "native-born Athenian" came to mean that both parents had been born in Athens. Young men had to complete basic military training before gaining the right to vote. In any event, Athenian democracy did not enfranchise women, children, slaves or former (emancipated) slaves, or resident aliens. For a more precise historical account, see John Thorley, *Athenian Democracy*, 2nd edn (London: Routledge, 2004).

11 Harry G. Frankfurt, "Freedom of the Will and the Concept of a Person," in *The Importance of What We Care About* (Cambridge: Cambridge University Press, 1988), 11–25.

12 Bruce A. Kimball, *Orators & Philosophers: A History of the Idea of Liberal Education* (New York: Teachers College Press, 1986).

13 Richard Rorty, "Education as Socialization and Individualization," in *Philosophy and Social Hope* (London: Penguin Books, 1999), 114–15. See also Richard Rorty and Eduarto Mendieta, *Take Care of Freedom and Truth Will Take Care of Itself: Interviews with Richard Rorty* (Palo Alto, CA: Stanford University Press, 2005).

14 Does the notion of a proper sequence or rhythm apply to the five paradigms of liberal education? Is it best, for psychological or pedagogical reasons, to begin with, say, the skills of learning, then move on to understanding the world, and so on? In short: no; not if the point is to devote different segments of one's education to different paradigms. The paradigms apply to education comprehensively; they are not modes of instruction—though they do inspire specific practices—and they function, I have argued, in complementarity.

9

Intrinsic Value

Whatever is a component of a human being's flourishing is good for him. But should we also accept the converse: that whatever is good for someone is a component of his flourishing?

RICHARD KRAUT, *WHAT IS GOOD AND WHY*

Flourishing, as the supreme aim of liberal education, has intrinsic value. Although it is a continuous and emergent end, it is an end-in-itself.

The concept of *intrinsic value* is recurrent in the tradition of liberal education—one that might be included with the core concepts of the previous chapter. It is an idea of deceptive simplicity because it holds within itself a hierarchical view of values, difficult questions of justification, a portrayal of the experience of human valuing, and implications that undergird the moral claims for liberal education. This chapter is devoted to exploring these and related aspects of intrinsic value in order to understand its role in liberal education.

The Basic Distinction: Extrinsic *versus* Intrinsic Value

The concept of intrinsic value is always introduced comparatively: on the one hand, there are those things which we value instrumentally, as means to end, whose value is *extrinsic* in that it derives from something outside the thing itself—from its instrumentality, usefulness, or conduciveness in relation to something else; on the other hand, there are things that we value for their own sake, as ends in themselves, whose value is *intrinsic* in that it derives from the thing itself, from its essence or nature, or from our experience of it—from its inherent goodness. We are all familiar with the basic ideas: someone takes the commuter train in order to get to work, so riding the train has, in that respect, purely extrinsic value—the purpose and value of riding the train derive from the need to get to work. Of course, the job itself might be seen instrumentally, simply as a means to an income. And so on. Aristotle, who (as I noted in chapter 2) is largely responsible for this teleological view of values, thought that these chains of *doing A in order to do B, which is done in order to do C* must end; they must converge in a terminus. At that endpoint, the question, "Why (for what purpose) are you doing *X*?" has no answer other than "Because *X* is good for its own sake—it has intrinsic value." He believed, of course, that the ultimate end, the *summum bonum*, of a human life is *eudaimonia*, a self-actualizing happiness. I have similarly claimed *flourishing* as the governing aim of liberal education.

There is an asymmetry in this duality in that the ends "govern" the means. The means, which have extrinsic value, are determined and judged by the ends they serve; that which is of intrinsic value is, in some sense, "higher" than that which has value only as a means to it or is prerequisite for it. This is the hierarchical aspect of this scheme. We *employ* means in the context of *purpose, desire, will,* and *action*, and we monitor their extrinsic value in terms of such measures as *efficiency, effectiveness, appropriateness, costliness,* and *permissibility* (and their opposites). We *experience* or *realize* ends-in-themselves, which may involve *fulfillment, normative activity or quality, contemplation, enjoyment, appreciation,* and attributions of *worthwhileness.* All of our strivings, our pursuit of one thing to achieve another, are meaningless unless lit by the attractive glow of the intrinsic value of the end.

Valuing Intrinsically

This basic, binary distinction may seem clean and clear, but within the human realm of purposeful action and delight, things are more complicated. Return to the daily ride on the commuter train: there might be someone on board who simply delights in riding on trains, or who enjoys watching the people and the scenery on this particular train; he might reject the use of more efficient means to get to work, if available, because they would not provide the same experience. For such a person, riding the train has both extrinsic and intrinsic value. Oh, he might not ride the train endlessly or board it if he had no need to get to work, but he values it for its own sake. We need not assume that riding the train is his *summum bonum*; that is, we should not assume that the "ultimate end" or "highest good" (if there is such) is the *only* intrinsic good available to each of us. Those theorists who adopt a monistic theory of the good (the view that all values are ultimately reducible to one) would, of course, claim that our happy train-rider finds that train-riding *instantiates* the highest and ultimate good, or has a strong relationship to it. But we need not take that position: we may conclude that there are several goods, each of intrinsic value, which are irreducible to each other—in which case, life will sometimes offer painful dilemmas of choosing between irreconcilable values.

There are further subtleties. An instrumentality or means may be taken to be (or may become) an end in a different way: for example, a key or a password is a means to an end only, but if I can't find my car key or remember my password, their value becomes conspicuous; recovering them becomes my end; and I may move heaven and earth, disturbing those around me, in feverish attempts to accomplish that end. This is a matter of indexing the end from one's intentional object; locating my key is an "end-of-the-moment." That status does not, however, give it intrinsic value.

There is another complication: something may be valuable instrumentally in an indefinitely large number of ways; it may serve many purposes; its poly-instrumentality may become so significant, we come to see it as being valuable in itself. Literacy and critical thinking are commended, as we have seen, as skills of such transferable utility, such fecundity, that they come to be regarded as having intrinsic value. In the case of literacy, however, it is worth remembering that reading and writing were once the special skills of trained professional scribes, a utilitarian skill of instrumental value. Socrates famously disparaged writing as a medium for philosophy. As with the information literacy skills of today, such a shift from an extrinsic to a bestowed intrinsic value is contingent upon the cultural embedding of the skill. There is a gap, however, between transcendent utility and intrinsic worth, and there are inherent dangers in taking any means (however useful) as the end-in-itself.

Still another subtlety is especially relevant to our educational topic: something which is originally of extrinsic value can be absorbed within the end to which it leads; it can cease to be a means only and become a necessary component or definitive constituent of the end. (Note the difference from the previous case, in which the means are taken to be of intrinsic worth without reference to the many ends they may serve.) Indeed, such a transformation, which is often gradual and psychologically subtle, is an enrichment or expansion of meaning of that which has intrinsic value.

This point was crucial for John Stuart Mill in his classic, *Utilitarianism*, as he tried to fend off the objection that Utilitarians do not value virtue because they have made happiness the highest good and sole end of human conduct. Mill explained, "The ingredients of happiness are very various, and each of them is desirable in itself ... besides being means, they are a part of the end." This process is not always salutary, however: Mill discusses how money or power or fame may be elevated from being desired as a means to being desired as an end in itself, or as a necessary part of the happiness they were to produce. But, says Mill, "Virtue ... is a good of this description. There was no original desire for it, or motive to it, save its conduciveness to pleasure, and especially to protection from pain. But through the association thus formed, it may be felt a good in itself, and desired as such with as great intensity as any other good ..."[1] Thus being virtuous may become, for some, an essential element of being happy. It is as though the end-in-itself is a magnet, drawing in its proximate means, and ultimately embracing them.

This process is important in understanding the relation between each of the paradigms and the supreme aim of liberal education: the assimilation of worthy texts or the understanding of important aspects of our world may be seen as means to the supreme end of cultivating a good life, but each may also become an inalienable element of such a good life. Through such a process, the participation in the Immortal Conversation or the pursuit of scientific research may come to have intrinsic value. A darker possibility, however, is that these aims might be elevated as ends-in-themselves, attributed with intrinsic worth, their connection to the original aim vestigial or abandoned altogether. (This is an educational perversion, a forgetting of the governing aim, to be considered in chapter 12.) Nonetheless, Mill's account helps us understand how the subsidiary aims of the four paradigms are thought by many advocates to have intrinsic worth.

The two types of values, extrinsic and intrinsic, seem to structure our sense of time differently. Chains of means are both dynamic and sequential; ends-in-themselves are stopping points, with a timeless quality. If we take happiness to have intrinsic value, for example, we do not attempt to "get through" happiness efficiently or effectively; rather, we hope it lasts because the quality of time it brings with it cannot be surpassed. The experience of intrinsic value involves what psychologist Mihaly Csikszentmihalyi has called "flow."[2] In such experiences, time "flows" of its own, there is an "immersion" in the activity, a loss of self-consciousness, an alignment of emotions, and an alert focus. Furthermore, there is an attitude of "holism" to such an experience. The person who simply rides the train to get to work only cares about certain instrumental aspects of the experience of the train ride; it is just a means of transportation. The person who finds intrinsic value in the ride takes in many aspects of the experience and finds all the particulars salient—an experience of "flow."

Throughout its history since Aristotle, liberal education has often been identified with *leisure*. For some brusque critics, that association is evidence that this sort of education is elitist, for leisured aristocrats, not for practical, working, "make-a-difference" folks. That is an unfortunate and superficial interpretation— and it is wrong in its implications. It is true, of course, that one cannot pursue an education in conditions of violence, famine, extreme poverty, and illness; education requires a circumstance that permits sustained attention and self-reflection. Adults who return to the classroom realize they must create such circumstances in the midst of work and family obligations. But these needs are tied to circumstance; they need not be tied to status. Aristotle's point is more profound, however. He divided our time into three sorts of activities: work, recreation, and leisure. Both work and recreation were periods dominated by extrinsic value: we work to earn a living, and we recreate in order to restore ourselves so we can work again. Leisure is that precious portion of our time that is focused on intrinsic values, in which we engage in activities for their own sakes. In such periods of freedom, we pursue activities as an *amateur*, a lover of the art, not as a professional who works for pay. Leisure opens a window for whatever we find genuinely worthwhile.[3]

Liberal education not only is aimed at a convergent intrinsic value—flourishing—but it also views the experience of intrinsic value as an essential element of flourishing. One's life is richer the more activities one can engage in for their own sake. Being able to appreciate many things, finding fulfillment and enjoyment in many pursuits—these are a boon to the spirit. This is yet another sense of "breadth" in liberal education. A person is "narrow" who finds few things interesting, who values intrinsically only one or two pursuits, especially if these activities are suitable only for the young, or require specific resources, or diminish the person's capacities in the long run. Intrinsically worthwhile activities one may pursue throughout one's life are the best insurance for flourishing in a long and chancy life.

Karl Marx and Max Weber, in works written from quite different perspectives, honor the value of honest work.[4] The craftsman and the bourgeois merchant are not leisured in the sense of having a life of unstructured time, yet their work has value beyond its instrumentality, its contribution to production and trade. Does this notion conflict with claims about intrinsic value? Not as directly as it might seem. Work is alienating when it is only given instrumental value, and when the employee is used only as a means to the employer's ends, without the dignity that comes with intrinsic value. Many men and women find intrinsic value in their craft; many are fulfilled in their professional work. In some cases, they would choose to do their work without pay (assuming they could still be financially secure); some consider it a vocation; some find it painful to withdraw in retirement. Such people have made their work a component of flourishing. No doubt that is easier with some jobs than with others: education for the traditional professions—the ministry, medicine, law—grew from liberal arts foundations not just because they were specialized skills constructed on a body of knowledge, but because they offered intrinsically valuable work. Liberal education, in aiming toward a flourishing life, not only leads the student toward fulfilling careers (intrinsically valuable work), but also cultivates the attitude of finding intrinsic value in the work one has to do.

The Justification of Intrinsic Value Claims

There is a feature of the concept of intrinsic value that is troublesome: it is a *terminus*; it is an end to reasoning; it silences dialogue. Its ascription denies the need or the possibility for any justification—at least for justification by purposefulness. If all our striving is for our happiness, then it is pointless to ask "Why do we want to be happy?" Do we hope to be given a reason beyond happiness itself? We don't seek happiness *in order to get something else* (which further goal would then justify our pursuit of happiness); rather, in this example, we do everything else *in order to be happy*. Flourishing, experiencing or realizing intrinsic value, is thus self-justifying.

Not only does this put genuine flourishing beyond reproach, but its throne may seem thereby to occupy a cul-de-sac, disconnected from further purposes, an inert and self-contained position. Thus when one asserts the intrinsic value of pure scientific research (understanding the world), or when Newman asserts that "knowledge [is] its own end," it appears to celebrate uselessness and to preempt the possibility of any demurral. Such a self-righteous stance is bothersome to anyone who wants knowledge to be put to use and research to yield applications that improve the human condition. One could, in light of the eliding of means and ends, respond that understanding the world is a good that has *both* intrinsic and extrinsic value; or, in a more sophisticated move, one might claim that we ultimately gain more instrumental value from knowledge when it is pursued for its own sake.

But there is a deeper question lying behind the annoyance of the practically-minded: can any such claim to intrinsic value be validated? Does anyone—Aristotle, Mill, or Newman included—have any basis whatsoever for ascribing intrinsic value to something? Even the brilliant Mill was backed into a corner with this question, and said that the only basis (the only "proof") was that people who know such an activity well will find it so.[5] Though Aristotle developed a normative concept of generic human thriving, he identified happiness as the highest good after a thoughtful review of what people actually desire. Newman points to Cicero's claim that it is in our nature to seek knowledge and proceeds to argue that philosophical knowledge goes beyond the particular, transforms the mind, and is therefore a treasure in itself (note that there is an element of the generically useful being deemed to have intrinsic value in this account); ultimately, however, for Newman, all value flows from God. There is a sense, in these related but various accounts, that the recognition of intrinsic value derives from both a quality of experience, from its natural connection with other experiences and activities, and from the ordering provided by that ascription. Intrinsic value is not only a terminus then, it is a *source*. It is the well-spring of other, instrumental values.

John Dewey was another philosopher troubled by this axiological cul-de-sac and argued that we should not fix upon any particular content as the goal of education, elevate nothing as having permanent, intrinsic value—except growth. He insisted that "growth itself is the moral end," and to "protect, sustain and direct growth is the chief *ideal* of education."[6] As I noted in chapter 5, this concept of growth is not empty, but is open and points to the increased capacity to derive meaning from experience. But although Dewey's conception of growth constitutes a rejoinder to the pursuit of self-affirming, pre-defined, intrinsically valuable ends, he also acknowledged the unifying, qualitative, sublime "experience of the whole" that can overwhelm us in aesthetic or religious experience.[7] As a pragmatist, Dewey believes (my apologies to David Hume) that theory is and ought to be the slave of action; indeed theorizing is a form of indirect action. Meaning is both brought to experience and found in it through action. Contemplation, however, is attention to and enjoyment of such meaning, and when such meaning is unifying and intimates a wholeness to experience, it is indeed a culmination.

Worthwhile Pursuits

It is one thing to claim that flourishing is tied to intrinsic value and that liberal education cultivates multiple sources of such value, but it is another to claim that some sources are better than others. As we have seen, normative claims are unavoidably part of educational theory, and they appear at each level in what I called "the cascade of specificity." Normative judgments are implicit in setting educational aims at every level, and they also appear in the necessary selection of curricula, teaching methods, and planned co-curricula. There are, for example, many pursuits that individuals might find intrinsically valuable—from chess to physics, from cooking to philosophy, from surfing to sociology. How are educators to determine which pursuits to include in their program? Implicitly or explicitly, their choices represent judgments that some pursuits are better, "higher," or more significant in some way.

Typically, the tradition of liberal education has asserted that it cultivates those activities that are the most "worthwhile." This means, of course, that other ways to spend one's time and energy are less worthwhile, and so the fully-elaborated result is often an opposition or hierarchy of "higher" and "lower" pursuits. Philosophy and physics outshine cooking or surfing or chess every time. But why, exactly? To answer this question, theorists have several options. First, they can claim some greater utility for the "higher" pursuits; they might even claim that the most worthwhile pursuits are those that help construct a flourishing life. That approach, of course, reverts to the mean-end hierarchy, and ignores the claim of intrinsic value. Second, they can claim that there is some other standard against which they can compare intrinsically valuable activities, some measure of "worthwhileness" that is not reducible to usefulness. They might claim that their favored pursuits possess both sorts of worthwhileness, though usually one sort is more decisive than the other. Cutting across these options are the issues of subjectivity *versus* objectivity, and relativism *versus* universalism: *Are the judgments validated only by individual perceptions or may they be confirmed publicly?* And, *Is the label "worthwhile" applied relatively—worthwhile for one student, but not necessarily for another—or is it intended universally, that is, worthwhile for all?* Though combining these options generates numerous theoretical possibilities, I shall focus on the one that has dominated the tradition: the view that worthwhile activities may be ranked as good-in-themselves, without regard for their usefulness, and that these rankings are objective and universal. Philosophy and physics are simply "higher" than cooking, not because of their usefulness, but because of their intrinsic worth—and that is true objectively for every student.

Plato is usually credited with (and often derided for) launching this game. Based on his metaphysical commitments, Plato elevated the mind over the body: theory is higher than practice; intellectual activities are more valuable than physical activities; white collar vocations are nobler than blue collar jobs; and the beautiful outshines the utilitarian. And, one is tempted to say, the rest of Western culture is history. These judgments and so many that follow from them are so deeply embedded in the Western psyche that they seem almost necessary truths. (Plato did, nevertheless, demand excellence in all levels of activity, whether in physical training or in dialectic.)

Despite deep metaphysical differences with his mentor, Aristotle echoed many of these ideas when he wrestled with the question of what pursuits are worthwhile. In trying to describe the sort of activity that defined a happy (eudaimonistic) life, he was quite explicit about his criteria: (1) the activity should engage the best aspect of human nature, which is the intellect—and which grasps the best knowable objects; (2) it should permit us to engage in it continuously, not occasionally or episodically; (3) it should offer pleasures that are pure and enduring; (4) it should be self-sufficient rather than dependent upon numerous contingencies and external supports; (5) it should be loved for its own sake, that is, pursued for its intrinsic value; and (6) it should therefore be undertaken in leisure, that is, in a time and manner that allows for doing something for its own sake and not for money or other utilitarian gains. Aristotle, a paragon of perfectionism, also requires that it be pursued with excellence and come to characterize "a complete term of life."[8] Based on these criteria, he concludes that contemplation (*theoria*), the active understanding of the world through theory, is the highest, most worthwhile activity of all. Although practical studies and activities can be valuable and even necessary (Aristotle cites political and military leadership as examples), the ultimate point in doing them well is to make one's world safe for contemplation.

These antique arguments and prejudices, bolstered by the concept of intrinsic value, redound through the history of liberal education. The basic notion seems intuitive: some activities are more worthwhile than others. Superficially, one might wonder how anyone could object to this idea—after all, who would want to initiate students into worthless activities? But of course, that begs the question of just what we mean by "worthwhile," and the subsequent question of what activities fit our description. Contemporary philosophers have been at pains to validate the notion that some studies are, independent of any practical value, intrinsically worthwhile, and that some shortlisted pursuits are more worthwhile than others.

R. S. Peters proposed that education is the initiation of students into worthwhile activities and modes of conduct. He used the term "initiation" because he intended that students would not simply learn about such pursuits, but would come to understand them "from the inside," experientially.[9] He devotes an entire chapter in *Ethics and Education*, a landmark text of twentieth-century analytic philosophy of education, to the explication of the concept of worthwhile activities. Peters interprets activities to involve rules and standards and to have "some kind of point." In general, he finds that activities that give more occasions for "exercising skill in dealing with the unexpected" are more absorbing; there is a joy in mastery of such activities. But there is a deeper normative aspect, and one can reach it only in a second-order, reflexive sort of way: Peters claims that anyone who questions what activities are worthwhile is taking a "noninstrumental and disinterested" stance, and that the choice of activities will "derive from the nature of the activities themselves and the possible relations between them within a coherent pattern of life." Ultimately, the activities that are most worthwhile are those that are most salient to answering the question, "What activities are most worthwhile?" This is why philosophy and physics and history are more important, more worthwhile, than checkers, belly-dancing, and carpentry, according to Peters, and why they deservedly claim curricular space.[10]

Does this sort of transcendental argument seem contorted, a verbal analog to one of Escher's impossible staircases? It has seemed so to many critics, and a number of its proponents, including Peters himself, ultimately offered revised arguments. Does it recall Mill's predicament of trying to prove why one pleasure is "higher"

than another? Some theorists have indeed embraced a version
of the Millian argument: we know some activity has a certain
intrinsic value because "many people, in every age, have claimed
it to be so—in other words, our appeal is to what would now be
called intuition."[11] This is by now a familiar cul-de-sac, no more
persuasive than the transcendental argument.

A radical critique of this whole enterprise of determining
worthwhile pursuits was promulgated by the former Cambridge
don and current MP and Minister of State, Oliver Letwin. In his
academic years, Letwin wrote one book of serious philosophy: a
provocative, compact work, titled *Ethics, Emotion and the Unity
of Self*.[12] In that book, he argues that the attempt to identify and
justify certain pursuits as "higher" or more worthwhile than others
is a fatuous and hollow exercise that betrays philosophical prejudices. He traces this game to "philosophical romantics"—those
philosophers who bifurcate the self into "higher" and "lower"
components, dividing mind from body, reason from passion, moral
from non-moral value. This world, to them, is not our true home,
and they leave us with the predicament of two desiccated, warring
half-selves locked in perpetual tension unless the "higher," better
self can transcend this life. The hierarchy they produce, Letwin
says, is "a myth." He then adduces many proposed justifications,
some historical and influential (like Mill's), and others speculative
and designed-for-the-occasion—and he rejects them all. He does
acknowledge, however, that *within* an activity, there may be better
and worse examples. He does still have standards. But for Letwin,
no one has any basis for claiming that poetry is more worthwhile
than football—though some poems are more deserving of our
attention than others, and some games are excellent football, but
not all.

Letwin's arguments are too extensive and detailed to be treated
fully here, but some features can be summarized handily. Among
the criteria others have proposed for distinguishing "high" activities from "low," he rejects: a higher or purer quality of pleasure
offered; inherent moral quality or moral effects; the display of
greater beauty; the permanence of its effects; the drawing upon
capacities that are more generically and permanently applicable;
the durability of the objects to which it attends; difficulty or
complexity; influence and impact in the world; edifying effects on
the devotee or on humankind as a whole; the extent to which it

draws upon distinctively human capacities. He does not, unfortunately, consider Peters' argument directly, but presumably, since he rejects the question itself, he would avoid the transcendental presumptions, and Peters' proposal would be superfluous. Some of Letwin's rejoinders seem less well thought out than others, but there is little question that he raises considerable doubt about trying to validate the normative ranking of pursuits by referring to the intrinsic qualities, aims, or effects of the activities; or to the capacities, motives, and experiences of the participants; or to the quality of the objects with which the activity is concerned. What, one might ask, is left?

There are several things to say in response to Letwin's provocations. In the first place, the arguments he marshals to reject *any comparison of pursuits* in terms of their "worthwhileness" would, if valid, remove the justification for finding *any pursuit at all* to be worthwhile. (His acknowledgment that there are better and worse performances within a pursuit does not provide a reason for engaging in any particular pursuit.) In this case, to destroy the comparative use of the term is also to destroy its substantive affirmation. And that result—that no activity can be judged worthwhile—is unacceptable, especially if we seek a flourishing life.

Second, one might in fact affirm some pursuits as worthwhile for a *unified* or *integrated* self; the normative criterion for activities need not be based on a good-self/bad-self dichotomy (although, as I said, Greek prejudices lurk indelibly in our collective psyche). Third, if calling something "worthwhile" is a recognition of its intrinsic value, we should not expect a proof for that appellation; in my experience, no one is *argued into* finding an activity intrinsically worthwhile anyway. A devotee can always point to features of the activity he finds salient as justification, but he cannot—as Mill recognized—prove its intrinsic worth.

Finally, particular conceptions of a good life bestow value on various activities, recognizing some as more worthwhile than others. But the one is not a *proof* of the other; it is a *reflection* of the other. Several of Letwin's arguments that football is as good as poetry seem to point to different individual constitutions, different preferences, even different conceptions of a good life—rather than to undermine the concept of worthwhileness. He never allows for the possibility that divergent and subjective judgments of what is worthwhile may employ the same concept of worthwhileness.

Differences about normative claims need not indicate differences in conception at the meta-level. To say this in another way: just because two people differ in their judgments about which activities are more worthwhile does not imply that they differ in their conceptions of "worthwhileness." They might, but they might not—they may simply judge differently. To determine which it is, one would need to hear them articulate and then compare the salient features that led to their judgments.

Letwin does not address education directly, and his conclusions leave adrift the educator who must select among pursuits to define a curriculum. His larger point is clear: intellectuals have undervalued the physical as part of human life. Point taken. Theorists are misguided when they claim that a liberal education contains *within itself* all life's truly worthwhile activities. That claim elevates the activities required for the various paradigms—knowledge, skills, and so on—and ignores or denigrates family life, the cultivation of the physical, the world of work, and so on. Rather, liberal education is intended to help students cultivate what is worthwhile; though, as Peters suggests, the student may also, in the course of learning, experience some of these "from the inside."

Liberal education is not, and should not aspire or pretend to be, completely removed from the world. While it may require a place and time for self-reflection, it is oriented toward the world because it is directed toward a flourishing life. And it is of the world, because it is fed by and helps to feed social, intellectual, and technological change. To seek intrinsic value and worthwhile activities is not to sever whole dimensions of life, but to reach out to the whole of human experience.

One's Life as a Whole

One significant way in which liberal education reaches into human experience is its concern with one's life as a whole. As we have seen, liberal education presents learning as continuous with living, as a *life-long* endeavor. Schooling may end, but the learning is never finished. Life keeps surprising us, we age and change, and we may grow in ways the paradigms envision; the tasks of learning under each of the paradigms are infinite tasks.

There is, however, a deeper significance than the endlessness of learning: it is that the concept of one's life as a whole is to be used as a normative guide. Throughout his attempts to characterize a flourishing life, Aristotle keeps qualifying his description by such phrases as "if it is allowed a full life," reminding us of the importance of both contingency and continuity.

The focus on experiencing intrinsic value and engaging in worthwhile activities might convey a sense that a flourishing life is one that is full of moments of goodness—episodes of "flow," self-contained beatitudes, or periods of personal welfare and fulfillment. What is missing from this description—which causes it to fail as a complete characterization of flourishing—is the active guidance of the notion of one's life as a whole. When an individual thinks of her life as a whole, she places its episodes—good, bad, and indifferent—in a larger context of meaning; they become related to other episodes in the past and possible ones in the future. Indeed, "episodes" may be replaced by larger units of meaning. For brevity, let me sketch just two ways this might be done.

John Rawls proposed that we may interpret a good life as the realization of an individual's *rational life plan*, an integrated set of aims that derive from the individual's self-reflection and considered desires.[13] Such a plan is continually revised throughout the individual's life in response to resources and life circumstances. Even when implicit, a rational life plan gives purpose to our actions, directs and sequences both first- and second-order desires, and particularizes the notion of flourishing. I might note, however, that, at least in the language in which it is thusly framed, the notion of a rational life plan may seem to regiment one's life, to turn the unplanned into the meaningless. Perhaps that can be corrected. A second way, favored by psychotherapists and many humanities scholars, is to think of one's life as a *narrative*, a personal story: a good life is one with a good story. Episodes are then part of a larger plot; themes develop; uncertainty, contingency, and failure contribute to the story, along with one's intentions and will. The devices of a rational life plan and a life narrative are two ways of grasping one's life as a whole, of personalizing the concept of a good life, thereby creating and finding normative guidance. One may still live in, enjoy, and celebrate the moment; but one lives that moment for and in the context of the sort of life one desires and affirms.

I beg patience for one more recollection of Plato. Actually, "recollection" is the appropriate term, because I want to refer to the great fantasy in which Plato explains his doctrine that all learning is remembering or recollection (*anamnesis*): the conclusion to the *Republic*, known as the Myth of Er. Gravely wounded in battle, Er has what we would call a near-death experience in which his soul leaves his body, moves toward a great light, and is drawn into a procession of the recently deceased. After being cleansed of sins or rewarded for virtue, the souls are drawn majestically past a series of magnificent and mysterious splendors toward the very wheelhouse of the cosmos, the Spindle of Necessity. Eventually, the crowd of souls assembles before the Fates. In front of them are spread tokens representing possible lives, lives they may live in their next incarnation. They are given to understand that they will choose their next life by selecting its token. Some make seemingly foolish or bizarre choices, some choose well; but each soul happily gets the token it desires, and each soul and chosen life are sealed by the Fates and by the assignment of an individual *daimon* (in this context, a guardian spirit or destiny). The throng, now weary from these intense events, is led to a vast plain, where they drink from the river of forgetfulness and sleep, submerging all memory of their disembodied time between lives. At dawn, they are born into their new lives, "like shooting stars." Except, of course, Er, who does not drink the water and awakens on the battlefield to report the wonders he has seen.

As a culmination to the *Republic*, this powerful but obscure myth seems to serve many functions for Plato. The value of justice—the focus of the text—seems mocked and thwarted by the "natural lottery," the disparate situations into which we are unfairly thrown at birth; but Plato seems to find justice even there: in some sense, we are responsible for the lives we have. It also offers another argument for the living of a just life: reward and punishment in the afterlife. Furthermore, it weaves together chance and choice as determinants of human life—ultimately, they seem to elide into fate. Of course the myth also offers a theory of learning as recollection: we learned everything we'll ever know between lives, when our soul was free, but forgot it at birth; teaching is prodding memory to consciousness. All these and more are at work, but I want to highlight yet another lesson. The *Republic*, which Jean-Jacques Rousseau pronounced "the

most beautiful educational treatise ever written,"[14] argues that
the human prospect, both individual and communal, depends on
education. In the transmigration Er witnesses, the individual souls
confront the adoption of their next life with whatever wisdom,
whatever experience, whatever character they have. What the myth
tells us is that, ultimately, education is for the choosing of a life,
our own life; it is our best human hope to craft our fate.

Notes

1 Mill draws on an associationist psychology to explain this
   transformation of means into ends, and, though he affirms that "there
   is in reality nothing desired except happiness," he views the desire for
   virtue alone, without its link to happiness, as a pious perversion. This
   discussion and the quoted passages are from Mill, *Utilitarianism*, IV,
   "Of what sort of Proof the Principle of Utility is Susceptible."
2 Mihaly Csikszentmihalyi, Flow: The Psychology of Optimal
   Experience (New York: Harper, 1991).
3 Aristotle discusses leisure in *Nicomachean Ethics*, VII, 4–6
   (1146b1ff.) and *Politics*, VII, 14, (1333a30–b5) and 15 (1334a11–
   40). For an extended discussion of these ideas, see Josef Pieper,
   Leisure: The Basis of Culture, trans. Gerald Malsbary (1948; South
   Bend, IN: St. Augustine's Press, 1998).
4 Their views of this issue may be found in, among other writings,
   Karl Marx, *Economic and Philosophic Manuscripts of 1844*, trans.
   Martin Milligan (Amherst, NY: Prometheus Books, 1988); and Max
   Weber, *The Protestant Ethic and the Spirit of Capitalism*, trans.
   Talcott Parsons (New York: Scribners' Sons, 1958).
5 Mill, *Utilitarianism*, IV, "Of what sort of Proof the Principle of
   Utility is Susceptible." In context, Mill actually made this point
   comparatively: to learn which of two activities is more worthwhile
   (is "higher" in value or has greater utility), one ultimately must
   survey responses from individuals who know both activities well.
6 John Dewey, "Aims and Ideals of Education," in *The Encyclopaedia
   and Dictionary of Education*, ed. Foster Watson (London: Sir Isaac
   Pitman & Sons, 1921), Vol. 1, 33; quoted in Rorty, "Education as
   Socialization and Individualization," 120. The *locus classicus* for this
   claim is John Dewey, *Democracy and Education*, especially chapter
   IV, "Education as Growth" (1916), in *The Collected Works*.

7 John Dewey, *Art as Experience* (New York: Capricorn Books, 1958).

8 Aristotle, *Nicomachean Ethics*, X.7, 1177a.11–1177b.26.

9 R. S. Peters, "Education as Initiation," in Archambault, *Philosophical Analysis and Education*, 87–111.

10 R. S. Peters, *Ethics and Education* (Chicago: Scott, Foresman, 1967), 77–90.

11 R. S. Downie, Eileen M. Loudfoot, and Elizabeth Telfer, *Education and Personal Relationships: A Philosophical Study* (London: Methuen, 1974), 50; quoted in White, *The Aims of Education Restated*, 11.

12 Oliver Letwin, *Ethics, Emotion and the Unity of the Self* (London: Croom Helm, 1987), especially chapter 2, "Higher and Lower Activities."

13 Rawls, *A Theory of Justice*, §§63–4.

14 Jean-Jacques Rousseau, *Emile: Or, On Education*, trans. Allan Bloom (New York: Basic Books, 1979), 40.

10

Educating a Good Person

The work of moral imagination is to increase the control individuals have by enlarging their understanding of the possible ways in which their lives might be made good or better... It is a movement toward a broader and deeper appreciation of the truths that bear on their efforts to live a good life.

JOHN KEKES, *THE ENLARGEMENT OF LIFE*

The previous two chapters have examined the moral concepts and values embedded within liberal education; we now turn to consider the claims that a liberal education will produce morally relevant changes in the student. I noted earlier that I affirm not only the flat and descriptive claim that students are in fact morally affected by the experience, but also the normative claim that the experience is intended to have morally good outcomes: it aspires to equip the student to define and cultivate a "good" life—a qualifier that includes moral or ethical dimensions. Its purpose entails transforming the learner *as learner*, the agent *as agent*. These claims are both complicated and controversial. In some ways, the assertion that education can lead us to a better life is less fraught with difficulties than the assertion that education can lead us to become better persons.

My position is that liberal education necessarily is a form of moral education. Moral education is *the array of practices aimed at moralizing individuals and rectifying social arrangements through structured learning.* I use the verb "moralize" here to mean "to improve the morals of, to make morally better," under any number of interpretations.[1] By "rectify," I mean "to align with moral values, such as justice, fairness, or compassion." Liberal education, as I characterize it, integrally involves such efforts, though of course it also includes more than that: liberal education and moral education are not identical.

Affirmation

The notion that there is a moral component to liberal education is not eccentric: since the classical conception of education as "soul-crafting," the profession (and expectation) that liberal education shapes character, instills moral values, and encourages ethical behavior has been commonplace. The exiled poet, Ovid, writing elegiacally from the Black Sea, tells us, "A faithful study of the liberal arts humanizes character and permits it not to be cruel."[2] Centuries later, this view was embodied in the standard, nineteenth-century capstone of the undergraduate curriculum: a senior course in moral philosophy typically taught by the president of the college.

If we look to contemporary statements of institutional mission or explanations of the liberal arts, we find these venerable expectations are still being affirmed. One liberal arts college, for example, proclaims that it "provides a liberal arts education that develops students' capacity to think freely, critically, and *humanely and to conduct themselves with honor, integrity, and civility.*" Another states that it "educates men and women of exceptional potential from all backgrounds so that they may seek, value, and advance knowledge, engage the world around them, and *lead principled lives of consequence.*" A third claims a legacy in which "the excellence of its academic program is deepened by its *spiritual, moral, and ethical dimensions,*" and notes its "emphasis on *integrity*" and "the College's concern for the uses to which its students put their expanding knowledge."[3] Many of these schools have honor codes, and all endorse and attempt to insure academic integrity. Colleges and universities are clearly embarrassed and disheartened when students, alumni, faculty or other employees are conspicuously unethical, and institutional soul-searching may result if the violations are broad in scale. Most educational institutions lionize accomplished individuals who are also of exemplary character; offers of honorary degrees are—at least frequently—retracted should an honoree's serious unethical behavior come to light. There is little doubt that liberal arts institutions affirm some version of moralization, but these bold institutional affirmations and public practices belie a deeper ambiguity.

Reluctance

Despite these confident proclamations, academic routine, even at liberal arts colleges, celebrates intellectual and even athletic accomplishment far more prominently than ethical behavior, moral stature or character development. In truth, professors are often reluctant to embrace the mission of moralizing students. It is an attitude that grows from many sources. Faculty may see their proper role as a scholar to be neutral, perhaps clinging to a sense that reputable scholarship is "value-free." Or they may deny possessing the relevant expertise, feel inadequate to the task, and, at most, helpfully direct students to somebody else's course on ethics. (After all, are faculty hired for their acuity as moral mentors?) Perhaps they equate all teaching of moral values with the indoctrination of personal prejudice. Maybe the reluctance stems from an inability to assess the effectiveness of any efforts at moralization. (It is true that moral education can often seem less like teaching than dropping a coin in a wishing well.) For whatever reason(s), learning outcomes that are explicitly ethical seldom show up as goals on course syllabi. And the span of one course is, for a project of moral education, rather short anyway; few faculty, especially in larger universities, have sufficient longitudinal interaction with individual students to undertake moralization projects.

Some faculty may be willing to endorse a pastel version of moral education that aims no further than values clarification, deconstruction of ethical systems, or the perfection of an ironic stance in regard to one's own ethical commitments. Many faculty, and certainly most student life personnel, are willing to go further when it comes to the co-curriculum: they are more likely to embrace character education and other forms of moral education as central to the structured co-curriculum. Of course, the same self-doubts about content, expertise, and effectiveness haunt these efforts, but there is an implicit article of faith that goes something like this: whether virtue can be taught or not, it can be learned; and it is best learned through self-reflective experiences of interacting with others.

I do not mean to suggest that faculty always handily outsource any ethical concerns for students. There are many schools whose faculties have instituted general education curricular programs based around values or ethical concerns. (In chapter 1, I named ECLA, which has organized its entire curriculum around contemporary ethical issues.) Many professors see it as a responsibility to examine with their students the ethical issues that surround the subject being taught. Virtually all teachers warm to a concern for academic integrity and ethics in scholarship and research. These endeavors notwithstanding, the reluctance to attempt any intentional moralization of students is widespread among faculty. In short, there is a gap between profession and practice on the matter of moral education; the ethical message of liberal education is ambiguous because the attitude of its educators is ambivalent.

This is not a recent degradation or "demoralization": it springs from the ancient distinction between intellectual and moral capacities and virtues, and the elevation of the former. Various influential conceptions of liberal education have been strongly intellectualist; some exclusively so. Newman's vision of a liberal education for gentlemen, one of the most frequently cited, has long been placed in that camp. In his discourses, he argued for "the enlargement of the mind," for "knowledge as its own end," and rejected the notion that it produced moral virtue in its students—or faculty. At one point, he voices an imaginary critic's vivid mockery of the moralization claim:

> [P]rofessors of this liberal or philosophical knowledge have themselves ... ever been attempting to make men virtuous; or, if not, at least have assumed that the refinement of mind was

virtue, and that they themselves were the virtuous portion of mankind. This they have professed on the one hand; and on the other, they have utterly failed in their professions, so as ever to make themselves a proverb among men, and a laughingstock both to the grave and the dissipated portion of mankind in consequence of them.[4]

Although Newman elsewhere made it clear that a balanced university education includes the moralizing influence of "college" life (that is, residence among a community of learners with vital discourse, personal interactions with faculty, and co-curricular experiences), his focus on the cultivation of the mind has apparently been more memorable.[5]

There is no difficulty in finding contemporary proponents of Newman's narrower intellectualist view. Among the polemical works of Stanley Fish, literary theorist and "opinionator," is a book titled *Save the World on Your Own Time*, in which he exhorts educators to "do your job." In his view, education is directed toward knowledge and cognitive skills; moral education in any form is out of place—"someone else's job."[6]

Though there are age-old issues in play, there are also large-scale developments within education that have exacerbated doubts about ethical goals for students. Within the last century, many colleges and universities founded by religious sects distanced themselves from their sectarian heritage.[7] Public universities and community colleges with avowedly secular and pluralistic purposes grew to become the largest sector of higher education. For much of the public, "ethical" became equated with compliance with professional codes of conduct and legal strictures. Postmodernist critiques of grand, comprehensive narratives challenged moral coherence. Especially recently, an additional factor has come into play: a strident skepticism about institutions and hostility to authority and expertise in general pollutes many interactions.

Are faculty members wise to feel such reluctance? Is there an inherent connection between liberal education and morality? If its supreme aim is directed toward a good life, must there not be such a connection? How could educators have such an aim and leave moralization to other, unspecified, agencies and their purposes?

Denial

Let us take an initial look at the negative position. Put starkly, there are those who believe that liberal education (a) doesn't offer an effective moral education, (b) shouldn't attempt to do so, and/ or (c) can't do so in any event.

Those who affirm (a) only are speaking descriptively. They mean that, as a matter of fact, liberal education is not educating its students morally; they may believe that is the result of a performance gap, a failure of practice, or the need for a shift in paradigms. Like the "worried friends" of liberal education I described in the first chapter, these folks think that flawed practice is the cause of a lack of moral education, not a moral vacuum in the ideal of liberal education itself. We hear expressions of this view whenever a broad ethical lapse makes news: there is soul-searching over whether higher education is failing to instill ethical behavior or moral values, when its students, alumni, faculty, or administrators are caught up in ethical scandals of cheating, fraud, financial corruption, and so on. These doubts question empirical claims about particular contexts, of course, but they point to a large and difficult issue that will demand later consideration: the assessment of moral education.

The view that liberal education should not attempt to moralize its students—position (b)—may be based on various considerations, all of which are hinted at in my speculations about faculty reluctance. (1) There are those who equate intentional moral education with moralizing, in the pejorative sense of preaching platitudes without awareness of prejudicial and otherwise questionable presuppositions. "Moralizing" in that sense violates the values of liberal education, or at least is discordant with its themes of freedom and autonomy. This point might, of course, be useful if it were merely a cautionary claim, but as a sweeping judgment on all efforts at moral education, it seems unreasonably preemptive and usually involves a simplistic reduction of moral education to the inculcation of the content of particular moral judgments. Moreover, it leaves open the question of how one's values *should* be acquired.

(2) Similar doubts about the validity of any moral education come from those who believe that any genuine science (or body of

knowledge) should remain untainted by moral concerns. This view often reflects the positivistic dichotomy between facts and values: knowledge (and truth in general) rests on facts which are subject to verification (or at least to refutation); ethics rests on values that are something else—subjective approvals, desires, emotive responses, or some such. But the news from many sources—which seems not to have reached those for whom this view still reigns (especially, oddly, some in the social sciences)—is that the fact/value dichotomy has collapsed. Philosophers of science, marshaling several lines of argument, have shown that a clean division between facts and values, though useful on some occasions, cannot be maintained. Studying the history of science, the process of scientific research, the personal investment in knowing, the structure of theories and explanations—the dichotomy has been attacked from these and other directions.[8] Even the most hardened defender must at minimum admit that the distinction is contested.

(3) Suspicion of institutional authorities, especially when they engage in moral initiatives, characterizes the reservations of others. Both the political right and left may voice objection to programs of moral education designed by educators and implemented through institutional structures, preferring to place primary responsibility for moral education elsewhere—with parents, extended families, or religious communities, for example. Those with particular religious commitments may be concerned that school-based moral education inevitably projects a secular humanism or liberal individualism. But such advocates must recognize that our values are shaped unavoidably by other sources as well—friends and peers, advertising, entertainment and news media, the culture of work or military service—and these influences, though powerful in impact, may be unintentional, inconsistent, or deleterious. Among such influences, liberal education at least provides resources and tools for reflecting on values, embraces an open and pluralistic perspective, and enables a critical perspective toward externally imposed values. Nonetheless, these objectors would probably deny the wisdom of linking schooling, if not education, to any vision of the good life that included moral content.

The most challenging opposition, however, is from those who hold position (c): whatever its intentions, liberal education simply *cannot* moralize its students. In some formulations, this position denies that liberal education as I have defined it is possible. In certain cases, this alleged impossibility can be tracked to the very notion of morality itself: some postmodernists, for example, regard all morality as a force for control and "normalization"; therefore any effort toward moral education is necessarily inauthentic and misguided. In other versions, this position is traceable to a particularly narrow version of a liberal education paradigm. For instance, some might claim that reading classic texts or gaining scientific knowledge cannot produce moral effects in students—and that it would certainly pervert the process to attempt it. For still other objectors, the issue is time and attention: educators have enough on their plates with meeting cognitive goals of knowledge and skills; there is no available time left over to attend to the building of character. (The assumption that it would require "left over" time is revelatory.)

Underlying several of these objections is worry about the encouragement of moral elitism, a danger that some foresee in tying moral education to liberal education. This is the posture that those who are educated are morally superior to those who are not, and that liberal education imparts a privileged role in determining what is right and good. It is a philosophically interesting issue, leading to questions about moral authority and the relationship between knowledge and values. In principle, one might respond by claiming that this worry is misplaced, or one might defend some form of moral elitism that doesn't identify the uneducated with the immoral.

This completes a brief catalogue of objections to the claim that liberal education entails moral education. Before we can take on some of these issues, we need to think further about the idea of moral education. As I have with "liberal education," so with "moral education," I will strive to delineate a general framework that illumines comparisons among rival conceptions.

Becoming a Moral Person

Let me begin with a naïve question: *Where do we get our moral values?* In a purely descriptive sense, everyone has values—though we might judge some as better than others. *How do people come to have the values they do? And how can they be changed—if they can be?* The query is ludicrously simple, but any adequate answer is dauntingly complex.

A plausible place to begin is with our biology. Humans have evolved neural capacities that enable a moral life and perhaps even preferences or dispositions that tilt or direct our values in a specific direction—toward care for kin, compassion for those visibly suffering, condemnation for those who are caught deceiving us. Any such predilections are quickly elaborated and refined in human interaction—interpersonal, social, cultural. We soak up the patterns of judgment, behavior, and preferences or commitments we call "values" from families, peers, acquaintances, media, spiritual authorities and religious rituals, and many other influences. Simply through normal socialization, as we develop and mature, we acquire some sense of morality. None of what I have described so far is the result of a self-conscious decision: no infant decides to "get values." What are in play are processes of heteronomous learning: unreflective mimicry, compliance with authority, the seeking of conformity, and so on. As a child begins to develop the capacities of self-reflection and autonomy, the possibility of *second-order desires* and *resolution* emerges. Only then might one want to become a better person, try to acquire a virtue through practice, adopt a regimen for ethical reasons, make resolutions for moral betterment, or identify an unjust law that should be reformed.

That is an encapsulated version of the development of a moral agent, a person who has values and may be held responsible for his conduct. There is a very wide application of the term in which the total effect of such influences and development may constitute his "moral education." This is the sense in which Dickens' Oliver Twist and Artful Dodger got their "moral education" in the workhouses and darker streets of London. That is not my usage. I have emphasized both intention and structure in defining moral education as the range of practices aimed at moralizing individuals and rectifying social arrangements through structured learning. In addition to these two aspects, however, there is a third: a moral education presumes to offer "value-added" outcomes; in other words, moral education "goes beyond" whatever morality is hard-wired in our biology and unfurled by simply growing up human; it involves something more than normal socialization. In fact, it may be part of moral education to resist, redirect, or attempt to undo these presentments. If it did not do so, what would be the point? We could simply rest content that the needs of moral personhood did not require any deliberate educational effort—and would not be enhanced by it. But of course we cannot.

Parents, teachers, religious leaders, coaches, youth organizations, schools, social service agencies, and many others work hopefully to moralize the young. Their aims may be expressed spontaneously in "teachable moments," formally in codes of virtuous conduct or structured lessons, personally in responses of reward and punishment. They each may work to enhance or combat other influences on character and conduct. These and other more-or-less formal approaches are self-conscious and intended, if not elaborately planned; they are guided by their own moral norms. Such moral education, like educational programs in general, anticipates both an individual and a social good: it is good to become a moral person; and a society is better if it is just and composed of moral individuals. It affirms that morally-motivated nurturance by others is needed for one to become a moral person—that is, a morally *good* person—or at least will increase the efficiency of the process or the likelihood of its success.

The Content of Moral Education

Moral education has *content*. That content—the intended "value-added outcomes"—may derive from theory or from practice (or both). Every moral theory constructs an image of the moral person from which devolves its conception of a moral education. Cultural relativists, for example, seek to develop people who understand and embrace the values of their society—and perhaps display tolerance to the differing judgments of other societies; Kantians strive to produce persons of good will, self-determined individuals who have strong reasoning skills, a keen sense of duty, and a profound respect for every human being; and virtues theorists focus on the shaping of persons who have moral character, interpreted as a configuration of specific normative traits. I am stating these examples roughly, and each might be dilated into ideals of burnished detail, but my point here is simply that different ethical theories embody different models of the moral person—different senses of what is required for moral agency; of what motives, actions, traits, principles, and practices are morally worthy (and unworthy); of what outcomes or relationships or experiences are good—and that these ideals serve to guide the practices of moral education.[9] Similarly, implicit theoretical models of the ethical community or moral society may yield content for moral education projects aimed at social reform.

Frequently, however, the practices of moral education, instead of being drawn from rarified moral theory, are developed from *practice*, from shared experience or cultural custom. Parents (except perhaps for a few resolute ethicists) are more likely to derive their parenting from the ethos of their own families or religious traditions, or from the mores of their societies—and not from high-flown ethical theory. In these common cases, the programmatic content may be derived from considering such pre-theoretic questions as: *How must we act in order to get along together? What sort of person do I want my child to become? What traits and actions are inevitably self-destructive or harmful to others? What is expected of a decent citizen in our society?*

Whatever their normative guidance, these projects in moral education may also have different levels of aspiration: moral education may take a minimalist approach, aiming modestly at preventing egregious immorality and producing people who are generally decent; or, at the other end, it may be more ambitious, trying to moralize students as far as possible toward *eudaimonia*, supererogation, or some other perfectionist ideal. Today, moral minimalism is likely to be the approach taken by public institutions at every level, perhaps distinguishing the minimum as what is required for democratic citizens, while anything beyond is seen as more subjective or futile. The primary "value-added outcome" from a moral education is one that governs all others: it is the provision of a considered and compelling ideal of moral personhood and a moral community. True, this ideal may be more or less implicit and inchoate or explicit and polished, open and pluralistic or closed and singular, minimal or maximal—but it serves to define the intentionality and structure that make the experience of moral learning a moral *education*.

We can begin to unpack this concept of moral education, by observing that such a project will aim to produce certain outcomes, each made more specific by the particular model of the moral person it enshrines (or by its answers to those pre-theoretic questions). A generalized view is that these outcomes typically include the following objectives:

(1) *The development of morally relevant capacities.* A moral education will seek to awaken and expand the range, sensitivity, and effectiveness of such capacities as, for example, practical reason or judgment, empathy, moral imagination, or the capacity to form caring relationships.

(2) *The acquisition of morally relevant skills.* Moral persons are necessarily competent in certain morally salient skills, proficiency in which is an aim of moral education—for example, the application of principles to cases, consequentialist reasoning, participation in ethically-structured discourse and deliberation, techniques of values clarification, or skills of nurturance.

(3) *The deepening of moral understanding.* Moral education strives to provide the relevant knowledge, perspectives, or understanding that a moral person requires, such as an understanding of oneself and other people, of the implications of social practices, of cultural values, of the moral point of view or of aspects of moral theory itself.

(4) *The development of moral character.*[10] Moral education nurtures virtuous traits and eliminates vicious or morally dysfunctional traits: for example, to develop honesty, courage, persistence, compassion, or tolerance, as settled dispositions, while reducing patterns of deceptiveness, cowardice, giving up easily, carelessness or stinginess.

(5) *The development of moral agency.* Moral education will try to develop various second-order traits relevant to moral agency, metacognitive dispositions that allow a person to monitor conduct and improve as a moral agent, such as: self-reflectiveness, open-mindedness, sensitivity to particulars, emotional integrity, and acceptance of responsibility.

(6) *The making of moral commitments and the alteration of conduct.* Success in achieving the previous outcomes should produce a desired result: students will come to embrace certain values (and reject others) and to act morally (in acts characterized by decency, compassion, utility, care, goodwill, or supererogation, etc.). In short, they will more closely resemble the model of a moral person.

Any robust theory of moral education includes these six objectives; the examples given under each one are meant to reflect diverse theoretical approaches. The "cascade of specificity" applies to moral education as well, whether Kantianism or Utilitarianism or another approach actually produces specific curricula. The six objectives are inseparably intertwined; they are complementary perspectives on morality, and the elements that are plugged in should comprise a complementary and coherent whole.

If this is what moral education in general involves, how is it related to liberal education? In what ways does liberal education further these objectives?

Moral Education and Liberal Education

In the first place, the concept of a moral person is ineluctably tied to the concept of a good life; giving color to one, tints the other. Asking *How should I act?* or *What should I value?* really projects the questions *How should I live?* or *How may I flourish?* with a shorter focal length. Second, as I said earlier, the concept of a good life—the supreme aim of liberal education—includes the notion of a moral life (though I retain the cautionary reminder that "flourishing" involves more than living morally). The five paradigms of liberal education, as we have seen, each promote and embody a particular vision of the good life. It would be possible to assess systematically each of the six objectives for each of the five paradigms—but the execution would be plodding and tedious. It is more helpful here, I think, simply to reflect on some of the more significant points that such an assessment would reveal. We will look at each paradigm, but, for convenience of exposition, take them in a different order from that of their original presentation.

Self-Actualization as Moralization

The self-actualization model seems especially hospitable to moral education: after all, it concentrates directly on the development of capacities, skills, agency, character, and other dimensions of a normative self. As a paradigm of education theory and practice, it seems pervaded by moral values; its well-spring is the moral worth of one's potential and the duty of self-realization; its aim for one's best self or one's "ownmost possibilities" is infused with ethical values, as is the ideal of authenticity. As we've seen, the actualized self is a moralized self—even for those theorists who idolize the heroic flouting or transcendence of conventional morality. Although moral education is clearly intended in this case, by what means does this self-actualization proceed?

The answers are as diverse as the theories that are generated under this paradigm, though many have a common lineage. Aristotle identified three methods, thereby inspiring a flood of derivative programs.[11] His first method of developing character requires practice. If one wants to develop honesty in a child, for example, one must teach the child to behave *as though* he were honest until such a practice becomes habitual and is eventually internalized. This requires supervision, of course, because the child must learn how an honest person behaves. As a moral concept, honesty is difficult to learn: the child may naturally think it involves saying what one truly thinks (without regard for the occasion or the persons within earshot); or may think it is overridden by loyalty to friends or the desire to please the listener; or may think that honesty eliminates fantasy and fiction. One can't avoid the errors in the trials, but correcting them gradually clarifies the concept. Even when the concept is clear, there may be issues of style: being "brutally" honest is not necessarily acting *as an honest person would act.* Through this benign form of pretense or self-deception, one becomes better.

There are two other methods that aid this process. One is the use of a general principle. Aristotle famously recommends being guided by the mean, the proper choice between overdoing and underdoing something (both of which are vices, not virtues). But the mean, the "just right" action is contingent on the situation (culture, time, place, and circumstance) and varies for individual personalities. One should be alert to and try to correct for one's own tendencies to err on one side or another, Aristotle cautions; but in the end, responding to all these variables is an art. That is why we need the third method: role models. Having identified a virtuous—in this case, honest—person, we may look to that person as a guide, trying to act as such a person would. Aristotle believed that the various virtues form an ecology of traits, however, and we can't develop them one at a time, like adding crayons to a box.

Aristotle's legacy includes programs of character education, the virtues approach to moral education, the use of hagiography, and the focus on skills of practical reasoning in determining what is the right act. These approaches function not only at the elementary levels—though Aristotle's point that these are the most valuable and vulnerable years for character formation has largely been upheld—but they appear in more advanced education as well. Inducing students to act as though they were other than they may be at the moment, engaging them in the practical reasoning out of ethical issues that involve conflicting values, and presenting compelling role models as guides—these are techniques of even advanced study.

Engagement with the World as Moralizing

One dimension of normativity for engagement with the world is the moral; there is a natural inclusion of moral education within this paradigm. While self-actualization centers on the development of the moral agent, the engagement model centers on the encouragement of moral action. The world is the arena of moral conduct.

The morally burnished ideal of a person who is effective in the world has been epitomized historically in a succession of paragons (sadly, but unsurprisingly, given centuries of sexism, they are usually male): the heroic and cunning warrior, the statesman, the noble prince or courtier, the proper gentleman, the democratic citizen-leader, the servant leader and reformer. These figures, in whom such qualities as honor, courage, grace, morality, and practical wisdom are conspicuous, have been the focus of many tracts and proposed regimens that draw upon liberal education. Many of their genes are manifest in most contemporary ideals of the liberally educated person—as are the genes of contrasting paragons, like the scholar, the sage, the scientist, the prophet, or the social critic. They are virtuous persons whose actions have impact in the world. They do not simply read great works, they *do* great work.

Historically, various forms of training are often part of the regimen for preparing such a figure: military training—or training in non-violent resistance; training in the contemporary arts of communication, whether oratory, argumentation, or television appearances; training in the social graces and the culturally cool, whether hospitality, fencing, dancing or dress. There is no doubt that this sort of instruction was part of the total experience of liberal education in many eras, but what might we find today that is comparable? In colleges and universities, even in some secondary schools, there is now an elevation of experiential learning as preparation for engagement with the world. These programs (both curricular and co-curricular) include service learning, internships, externships, cultural immersion, collaborative learning and leadership experiences (whether in school organizations or teams, or in correlated community leadership roles). Such experiences position the student as an agent, and the learning occurs through that agency in special settings that combine openness with educational constraints.

The Skills of Learning and the Skills of Moral Agency

There is, I would argue, a significant overlap between the skills of learning and the skills of moral agency. The person who knows how to think critically, engage in deliberation, listen carefully, research information relevant to a matter at hand, discern consequences, enforce self-discipline, and so on, has acquired skills that are important to any moral agent.

A quick objection to this claim is that the list is incomplete, more relevant to certain ethical viewpoints than others. The skills of learning do not include, for example, knowing how to nurture friendships and other caring relationships. That is true—but one might reply that those omissions do not dismiss or diminish the value of all the salient skills that *are* included. A better response is that we need to test this concern against a more robust view of liberal education once we have examined the combined impact of all five interrelated paradigms.

A second, more penetrating objection is that knowing how to do such things does not ensure that one will, in fact, use those skills, or that one will employ them morally. That point is valid as well; there are clever fools and skillful villains. Nevertheless, I must say here and repeat later: no plan for moral education is foolproof; there is no way to guarantee success. Educators can only carry on with epistemic humility, faith that there are better angels of the student's nature, and confidence in the importance of the task. Moreover, when we combine the acquisition of skills with the other two aims examined so far—self-actualization and engagement with the world—we have a more comprehensive approach to teaching character and affecting conduct.

Transmission of Culture as Moral Education

One motivation for the transmission of culture to successor generations is to preserve the mores of the culture; the values, observances, and behavioral expectations that serve to unify and secure the culture. An individual's morality arises within and from such mores. But, as we have seen, becoming a faithful practitioner of the culture one happened to grow up in, conforming fully to its mores, is something less than being morally educated—or less than being liberally educated. Successful enculturation meets only two of the six objectives listed above: the embracing of certain values in conduct and the shaping of character traits; it does not enable an individual to develop her own voice, to take a critical perspective on her culture, to find moral reasons for cultural change.

The transmission of culture paradigm has, nonetheless, traditionally used the study of worthy texts and art works as a force for moral education. The encoded legacy of human experience contains moral content, so exposure to these works conveys cultural norms and provides compelling portrayals of moral exemplars—or so it is hoped.[12] Plato is only the first of many who are so convinced of the moral impact of this approach, both for good and for bad, that curricular selectivity becomes strict public censorship. The need to encounter the "greatest" texts morphs into the need to encounter only the "right" texts.

So far, I have assumed only the more passive versions of this paradigm, those that concentrate on absorption of content rather than engaging in dialogue or finding one's own voice. But, for even the more passive-learning versions, just how moralization occurs is variously understood and often murky. Sometimes mere didacticism, simply being told (through reading or listening) is thought to be sufficient, as though merely absorbing the text will effect a moral alteration. Sometimes, the texts are thought to be imbued with moral authority; great stories and art and music that are compelling for those who merely listen and read, flooding into their porous souls with lasting impact. Often, the process of moralization is thought to rely on a natural tendency for imitation (*mimesis*) or emulation. In any case, what we see and hear alters us; we become what we listen to, read, and view.

Many critics claim, however, that this is all a pipe dream. Given the prominence and plausibility of this skepticism, I want to explore it at greater length, and to that end I will work from a passage by an admirable contemporary theorist.

In an interesting article titled "Conversation as Moral Education," Nel Noddings examines three types of conversation, including "the Immortal Conversation" offered through liberal education.[13] I will quote her at length, both to give her voice and to provide the textual basis for commentary:

> When some people today deplore the loss of traditional liberal education, many of us react with some confusion. We do not think that studying the Great Books or any other canon will necessarily make our students better people, and we reject the haughtiness of those who think their knowledge is Knowledge. However, confusion arises because the questions raised in traditional liberal studies still seem central to human life. We feel that education—real education—cannot neglect the questions, Where do I stand in the world? What has my life amounted to? What might I become? ... What is the meaning of life? Is there a God? What is my place in the universe? ...
>
> It is true that these questions arise and are explored in impressive ways in the great works associated with liberal education, but they may also be asked and explored in other settings. Zane Grey's cowboys ask them while riding the range under starry skies. Old ladies in their rocking chairs, shelling peas or knitting, ask them as the evening cuts off the light of a summer day. Lone fishermen standing on rocky jetties in the Atlantic twilight ask them. Moreover, studying what great thinkers have said about immortal questions is no guarantee that one will be more honest, decent, loving or even open-minded ... Again we have a performance gap.[14]

This is a fascinating passage. Although she rejects the Great Books approach—identifying liberal education with only that curriculum—Noddings does acknowledge that liberal education asks (or once asked) truly important questions—the questions "real education ... cannot neglect." But immediately she focuses on the *setting* in which these questions arise, contrasting the implicitly invoked traditional classroom and its students with idyllic images of adults in nature who pose these same questions. This move involves the second constraint: having narrowed liberal education to the Great Books, she now restricts it to what happens in the didactic classroom, ignoring contextual and institutional factors that shape the experience.

Removing these constraints does not deter the thrust of her argument, however: although the profound questions of life "arise and are explored in impressive ways in the great works associated with liberal education," Noddings does not believe "that studying the Great Books or any other canon will necessarily make our students better people." She corroborates her skepticism with the evidence of good people who are not highly literate and literate people who lack certain moral qualities—a move reminiscent of Newman's scoffer who pointed to the failures that make such claims a "laughingstock."[15] Noddings judges this failure to be "a performance gap," claiming that the moral education attempted (if indeed it is) is ineffective. But in fact she seems to doubt that any program of moral education based on the explication of texts—whatever texts—would succeed. And her skepticism seems to apply not only to the more passive models that emphasize conveying cultural norms, providing vivid moral exemplars, and offering object lessons; she also seems to doubt traditional claims that serious engagement with such texts both requires and develops essential moral capacities and skills.

The assertions that engaging with great texts moralize us by enlarging the scope of moral imagination, by deepening empathy through vicarious subjectivity, and by increasing sensitivity to morally relevant particulars, are empirical claims—but difficult to prove and much contested. Interestingly, many educators, in recent years, borrowed the truth of these claims to critique the traditional curriculum: they argued that in order truly to enlarge a student's moral imagination in a global society, we must expand the range of voices and cultures whose legacy is transmitted. Those reformers (with whom I identify) have largely succeeded, and the heritage of works students typically encounter now is noticeably more inclusive. Martha Nussbaum has recently argued vigorously for the critical importance of the humanities, based in part on such claims.[16] Noddings, however, seems unconvinced that any canon, however constructed, will moralize its students.

(A more cautious, but initially skeptical, approach is taken by Suzanne Keene, a scholar of literature, who questions, "Does reading novels evoke empathy with fictional characters; and, if so, does this really cultivate our sympathetic imagination and lead to altruistic actions on behalf of real others?"[17] Integrating current research on empathy from several sciences, and surveying the history of debates on the issue within the humanities, Keene concludes that the very fictiveness of such works frees readers' responsiveness, compared to the restraint that encounters with "real others" requires. The range of possible affective responses is thereby expanded, and expanded further as we range beyond conventional characters, common plots, and canonical texts. In the end, Keene's study, though sharply focused on novels, is relevant to the larger claims for the development of moral capacities and skills from the engagement with the heritage of cultures.)

In the Noddings passage quoted, she seems to question whether formal learning (or what is sometimes called "book learning") is sufficient, necessary, or even relevant to becoming a moral person.[18] She observes that the "profound questions ... central to human life ... may also be asked and explored in other settings." She paints three lyrical, decidedly non-academic, images: "Zane Grey's cowboys ask them while riding the range under starry skies. Old ladies in their rocking chairs, shelling peas or knitting, ask them as the evening cuts off the light of a summer day. Lone fishermen standing on rocky jetties in the Atlantic twilight ask them." From these vignettes she soon draws a forceful conclusion: "I believe a grave mistake is made when we argue for the traditional liberal studies as the arena in which immortal conversations must take place."[19] Her concern seems to shift from the problem of ineffectiveness (performance gaps) in moral education to the arrogance of exclusivity, that is, to the haughty presumption that *only* in the setting of liberal education and the radiance of great texts can transformative "immortal conversations" take place.

These concerns have deeply challenging elements, though there are casually superficial aspects as well. First, it is not surprising that questions "central to human life" would arise outside the class-rooms of liberal education, even without stimulating encounters with great texts; indeed, that is likely given the vital, universal questions they are. I would therefore restate Noddings' conclusion: it would be a grave mistake to presume that the ultimate concerns of liberal education are confined to academic situations or to scholarly explications of canonical texts.[20]

Second, we should be clear, however, that *asking the question* is only the first, albeit critical, step toward fully *understanding* the question—and it is a very long way from *answering* it. Certainly it matters that Zane Grey's cowboys and old ladies in their rockers and lone fishermen pose such questions; but it also matters what resources—intellectual, emotional, and spiritual—they possess to reflect upon, refine, understand, and answer such questions. Liberal learning is precisely aimed at enhancing one's resources for that purpose.[21]

Having posed such profound questions, do Nodding's exemplars earnestly pursue them? It seems unlikely that Noddings would believe that the mere posing of such immortal questions is suffi-cient, because the context implies a connection between the reflective moment and becoming a good person. She might indeed be simply offering a jibe at academic snobbery and moral elitism, claiming that one doesn't need to hold a liberal arts degree to undertake moral or liberal learning. But, no, she does not imply that her reflective exemplars follow through on the profound questions they pose with plans for informal liberal learning. At this juncture, we encounter the darker point, the deeper challenge: Noddings may be saying that liberal learning, whether formal or informal, *simply does not matter* for engaging immortal questions; being a good person doesn't require liberal learning at all.

Clearly, much depends on what we pack into the notion of a "good person," the ways in which we specify the six objectives of moral education. One might then believe—as Noddings apparently does—that it is possible for an individual to acquire them *sans* the liberal arts, even without informal liberal learning, but from other features of lived experience, such as special relationships or transformative experiences or unusually penetrating self-reflection. That it is *possible* to do so, of course, does not mean it is *probable* or *desirable*. The events of lived experience may change people for the worse as well as for the better, producing qualities that are dysfunctional for or inhibitive of desired moral elements; without purposefulness or structure, normative learning occurs only by happenstance. Purposeful learning both filters and selects, thereby increasing the possibility of efficient, effective, and desired learning.

There is, I believe, a more incisive reply to Noddings' challenge, however: *it greatly underplays the importance of moral understanding.* To make this point, I must turn to the final paradigm: understanding the world.

Understanding the World as Moral Education

Understanding is, of course, pertinent to all the paradigms. One seeks understanding of the cultural legacy, of oneself, of the conditions of good *praxis*, as well as the techniques of learning, but in this paradigm the object to be understood is "the world"— including the natural, cultural, and ideational (and we might add virtual) world—and its implications for us. What relevance has this to moral education?

The succinct answer is that aspects of this understanding are persistently moral under various accounts of morality, and other aspects may become morally relevant on occasion. Depending upon one's moral views, understanding other people and their needs for nurturance, understanding the values of one's own culture or those of another, grasping the implications of social policies and practices, having knowledge of hard-wired human tendencies, accurately foreseeing the probable consequences of one's actions, knowing the code of ethics of one's profession—any or all of these may be essential to inform ethical conduct. The facts of the effect of nicotine on the body are not *per se* moral, but they may become morally relevant in the context of the decision whether to smoke cigarettes.

How important to becoming a good person is the goal of deepening moral understanding? Most of us have doubts about the radical Socratic position that understanding is everything: virtue is knowledge. Aristotle spearheaded that response by showing (convincingly, for most readers) that intellectual and moral virtues differ, that morality requires practical wisdom (*phronesis*) or the art of good judgment, and is threatened by weakness of will and other factors.[22] Knowledge is insufficient. But Aristotle never claimed that knowledge is irrelevant to virtue; that right action is altogether divorced from understanding. Yet, as Australian philosopher Jean Curthoys has written, "[A]stonishingly few philosophers have reconsidered the extent to which moral questions may be questions of understanding. But without some such notion, morality will not have depth and nor, therefore, will the moral philosophy that purports to elucidate it."[23] Curthoys' observation occurs in a review of Christopher Cordner's evocative work, *Ethical Encounter*. She states that Cordner traces our deepest moral intuitions to a "sensitive understanding, which is the core of our moral life." In Cordner's vision, this requires a deep, empathic knowledge of other people, and transformative emotional experiences, as of love, awe, disgust, and reverence. (We will soon turn to the idea of transformation.) As Curthoys notes, "The understanding involved, however, is not of the purely cognitive kind, and is accessible to all, whatever their educational level."

These comments might lead us to conclude that even if we grant understanding a significant place in moral education, it is a form of understanding that won't be achieved through liberal learning. But let us not be hasty. There may be an old, dubious assumption at work in this interchange that takes emotions to be non-cognitive.[24] Moreover, in a sustained analysis of one case of moral understanding, Cordner focuses on the agent's "seeing [another person and her situation] in the light of a "web of meaning." One person can understand another's situation "only so far as he or she can imaginatively participate in that web of human meaning."[25] So, once again, we are led to the need to develop moral imagination and a web of meaning, and it is precisely for these tasks and that sense of moral depth that we turn to liberal education.

I do not mean to deny the moral worth of "simple goodness." Images of simple goodness range from the principled to the sentimental: the dutiful person of goodwill, the kind and compassionate, or the pure of heart. Uneducated virtue is virtue nonetheless. I do claim, however, that such "simple goodness" is always especially vulnerable. It is vulnerable to one's own mistakes and follies, and to the vices and values of others. Without understanding, it is easy for the virtuous to make misguided choices, to produce unforeseen and negative consequences, to ruin a moral action with problems of style and timing, to fail to grasp how one's actions will be received. Without understanding, one's best intentions are more easily manipulated by others. This is not a new insight; it is a very old theme: the vulnerability of the innocent.

Immanuel Kant famously claimed that the only thing that is good without qualification is a good will. A good will, we might say, shines of its own light. But without moral understanding, a person of goodwill is merely someone who "means well."

Gathering the Threads

From the threads of the foregoing discussion, I want to weave a summary position and draw four conclusions. They presuppose my capacious accounts of liberal education and moral education. The first is, by now, familiar: (1) *The supreme aim of liberal education—a good life—is inherently moral, involving considerations of values and ethics and examining one's life as a whole.* Thinking about what makes a good and flourishing life pulls us toward other profound questions of life. This aim gives gentle guidance to educational efforts, creating the "value-added" benefits of formal education. The opportunity to engage in reflection on moral issues at leisure—that is without the immediacy and consequence of "real" situations—is precious and educationally valuable.

The second conclusion is: (2) *All six objectives of a moral education are addressed through the five paradigms of liberal education and the co-curricular context in which it is pursued.* In their complementarity, these paradigms can yield invaluable moral outcomes that would be difficult to achieve by other means: for example, the ability to form, evaluate, and pursue one's second-order desires; the imagination to see one's actions within a larger context of ethical meaning; the imperative to pursue moral understanding. Liberal education provides the resources for informed and adroit moral agency, along with the encouragement of character development and moral commitments.

That claim has an obverse: (3) *Liberal education reduces the vulnerability of the virtuous.* Through the development of moral capacities, skills, and understanding, liberal education informs and guides moral impulses. It helps to secure and protect simple goodness from harm and mistake. It cannot, of course, protect us from all the vicissitudes of life.

Finally, (4) *Taking moral issues seriously will inevitably lead to liberal learning*. Whatever one's situation—whether cowboy on the range, old woman in a rocker, or an undergraduate in the halls of ivy—if one goes beyond merely posing a profound moral question and seeks to understand and answer it, some form and extent of liberal learning will be required. The pursuit of moral learning may not be formal, but it will lead ineluctably to the five paradigms.

Nonetheless, in Noddings' spirit, we might ask: "Can we not acquire such understanding from direct experience—during starry nights on the range, or while shelling peas or twilight fishing?" Surely, we realize that first-hand experience is more effective for changing minds than the mediated experience of instruction? But beyond the inefficiency and unpredictability of effects, the problem is that experience is never pure and unmediated. As Dewey was forever reminding us, the meaning one can derive from an experience is fundamentally dependent on what one brings to that experience, and what we bring includes our memory, skills, character, attitudes, capacities, and our understanding. Learning matters, and previous learning funds future learning. All starry nights on the range are not created equal.

If one—anyone: cowboy, old lady, or scholar—engages any of the "central questions" of human life seriously, one goes beyond merely posing them to seek understanding. Suppose, in a philosophical moment, I am moved to ask, "What is the meaning of life?" or "What is my place in the universe?" To purposefully think through the question requires that I explore alternative responses, weigh implications, discern ambiguities, refine formulations, and develop a deeper sense of myself and "life" or "the universe." I must, that is, undertake the tasks of liberal learning. Learning what other thoughtful humans discovered and concluded (the cultural transmission approach) may enrich my thinking; so may comprehending aspects of the universe (the understanding the world approach); I may need a clearer mind, sharper skills, or refined sensibilities, or find that all this reflection is changing me (the self-actualization approach); or that I need to act on my conclusions (the engagement with the world approach). To pursue my immortal question is to reach out for moral understanding through liberal learning.

It isn't that lived experience is irrelevant or even unnecessary; the point is rather that our lived experience and liberal learning— learning that focuses on our life and living it well; learning that dwells in the full range of human experience; that helps us become who we are, understand ourselves and our situation, grasp the forces that shape our lives, and act effectively in the world— enhance and sustain each other.

Notes

1 It is a sign of social change and evolving usage that the verb "moralize" now commonly connotes "to make moral pronouncements, to preach." Some of the hypothetical objections discussed in the following sections use the term in this pejorative way.

2 "Inguenas didicisse fideliter artes,/Emollit mores, nec sinit esse feros." Ovid, *Epistolae ex Ponto* (*Letters from Pontus*), 2.9.47–8, trans. A. L. Wheeler (Cambridge, MA: Loeb Library, 1924). The letters were made public in c. 13 CE.

3 These three statements are, in order, excerpted from: Washington & Lee University, "Mission Statement," http://www.wlu.edu/x52661. xml; Amherst College, "Mission Statement," https://www.amherst. edu/aboutamherst/mission; and Haverford College, "Statement of Purpose," http://www.haverford.edu/catalog/statement_of_purpose. php (all accessed September 2011), italics added to indicate the moral dimensions.

4 Newman, *The Idea of the University*, 140.

5 The purely intellectualist interpretation of Newman has been helpfully corrected by D. G. Mulcahy in *The Educated Person*.

6 Stanley E. Fish, *Save the World On Your Own Time* (Oxford: Oxford University Press, 2008).

7 For a wistful chronicle of this process of secularization, see James Tunstead Burtchaell, *The Dying of the Light: The Disengagement of Colleges and Universities from Their Christian Churches* (Grand Rapids, MI: Eerdmans Publishing, 1998).

8 These different approaches may be found in, for example: Kuhn, *The Structure of Scientific Revolutions*; Michael Polanyi, *Personal Knowledge: Towards a Post-Critical Philosophy* (Chicago: University of Chicago Press, 1958); and Hilary Putnam, *The Collapse of the*

Fact/Value Dichotomy and Other Essays (Cambridge, MA: Harvard University Press, 2004).

9 I do not mean to suggest that every moral theory presents its conception of a moral person in a singular profile. The theory-derived concept of a moral person may be quite open, comprehending many different qualities and characters with minimal constraints; it may even focus on achieving a society in which different moral perspectives are balanced in a moral ecology; or it may be quite restrictive and homogeneous in its prescription.

10 This is an implication of nearly all programs of moral education, whether they are drawn from "virtue ethics" and "character education" theories or not. Even a hard-edged Utilitarian should encourage such character traits as honesty with oneself (in calculating consequences) and strength of will (to act on one's conclusions).

11 See the *Nicomachean Ethics* and *Eudemian Ethics*.

12 This is the moral analogue to what Rorty described as "know the truth, and it will make you free." See chapter 8, n. 13.

13 See chapter 3.

14 Nel Noddings, "Conversation as Moral Education," in *Educating Moral People*, 123–4. Note that Noddings characterizes "traditional liberal education" as "studying the Great Books," which fits only this one paradigm at best, and not even all theories within it. Note my comments about this fallacy in chapter 1.

15 Noddings writes: "Without mentioning names, I can easily think of four or five superbly educated persons (all of whom deplore the condition of the American mind) who are themselves incapable of hearing or responding generously to views that differ from their own." Ibid. For the Newman reference, see n. 4, *supra*.

16 Martha C. Nussbaum, *Not for Profit: Why Democracy Needs the Humanities* (Princeton, NJ: Princeton University Press, 2010); and Nussbaum, *Cultivating Humanity*.

17 Suzanne Keene, *Empathy and the Novel* (Oxford: Oxford University Press, 2010).

18 The extreme view would be that a liberal education is actually *detrimental* to being a moral person. That is clearly not Noddings' view. It is the position taken by the Renaissance figure, Henricus Cornelius Agrippa von Nettesheim, who in his rant against the arts and sciences, *De incertitudine et vanitate scientiarum et artium, atque excellentia Verbi Dei, declamatio invectiva* (1530), championed

the *idiota* (the humble and ignorant ass) as the model of a moral person. Relevant selections are found in: Agrippa von Nettesheim, "On the Uncertainty of Our Knowledge," in *Renaissance Philosophy*, Vol. 2, *The Transalpine Thinkers*, ed. and trans. Herman Shapiro and Arturo B. Fallico (New York: The Modern Library, 1969), 65–96.

19 Noddings, *Educating Moral People*, 124.

20 This point was made in discussing the concern for a good life in chapter 2.

21 In another article, Noddings writes: "I agree wholeheartedly with [Alasdair] MacIntyre, however, that it would be wonderful if 'fishing crews and farmers and auto mechanics and construction workers were able to think about their lives critically' ... It would be equally wonderful if the same could be said of the graduates of our finest institutions of liberal education. But historical evidence does not support the contention that liberal studies, traditionally defined, produce this result. Some liberally educated people think deeply, critically, morally; many do not." Nel Noddings, "Is Teaching a Practice?" *Journal of Philosophy of Education* 36, no. 2 (2003), 246. This would seem to return us to framing the problem as a performance gap.

22 Aristotle, *Nicomachean Ethics*.

23 Jean Curthoys, "Understanding Others," *Australian Book Review* (2003), 47. I have adopted Curthoys' way of framing this issue.

24 Curthoys does note, however, that the understanding required is "not of the *purely* cognitive kind." Ibid., italics added for emphasis.

25 Christopher Cordner, *Ethical Encounter: The Depth of Moral Meaning* (London: Palgrave, 2002), 170.

PART IV

Obstacles, Threats, and Prospects

11

Persistent Concerns

These arts and sciences, far from deserving such lofty plaudits and panegyrics, are rather for the most part to be scorned and vilified.

CORNELIUS AGRIPPA VON NETTESHEIM, "ON THE UNCERTAINTY OF OUR KNOWLEDGE"

The perdurability of liberal education is remarkable, all the more so because the tradition has continued in spite of natural obstacles and recurrent threats—some of which are perennial while others arise from unique historical circumstances. I am not referring to gaps in performance, such as uninspired teaching, low student achievement, or loss of institutional focus (which are always with us). Nor am I referring to issues of educational practice and policy, such as the threat that declining funding and the rise in cost of a liberal arts degree will be its demise, or the threat that changing demographics will dry up the pool of students aspiring to a liberal education. Both sorts of issues rightly worry educators, administrators, and trustees; they represent mortal dangers, and it may seem irresponsible to pass them by. But in this avowedly philosophical exploration of liberal education, I am concerned primarily with obstacles and threats to the very idea of liberal education and its normative claims. They threaten the vitality of the tradition at its core; it is the prospect of the enemy within that is of concern here. This chapter is devoted to concerns that have dogged liberal education since ancient times but have contemporary nuances; the next chapter will address newfound reasons for alarm. It will deepen our understanding of liberal education to come to grips with these matters, although I am keenly aware that to grasp a problem is not yet to solve it.

Transformation as Alienation

It is an enduring claim that liberal education transforms the student. The term "transformation," carrying connotations of magic and alchemy, suggests that what happens is more profound than the processes of acquisition, expansion, change, or reformation, or even actualization; it implies a profound, metaphysical alteration of the self. I have described it as a transformation of the learner *as learner*, of the agent *as an agent*—a description that is intended to highlight the cognitive, emotive, and moral impact of education on second-order desires. Jane Roland Martin has called it a *metamorphosis*.[1]

In her book, *Educational Metamorphoses*, Martin characterizes this educational transformation as a cultural initiation or migration into a new land, involving the establishment of a new identity. She examines many compelling historical and fictional examples of dramatic educational transformations, case studies in the impact of learning. The inherent educational assumption, of course, is that such alteration is positive, that one's educated self is to be preferred to one's uneducated self—and, indeed, that seems to be the consensus of successive generations who strive to educate their children. But Martin reminds us that in such a metamorphosis, there may be losses as well as gains. Among Martin's case studies is Richard Rodriguez, whose intellectual autobiography[2] describes his transformation through liberal education from a poor, Mexican-American boy knowing only a few words of English to a literary scholar researching in the British Museum. But he also describes with poignancy, the alienation that is the dark side of this transformation: it is primarily an ethnic and cultural alienation, in which even his command of English expresses his loss of Latino consciousness and the intimacy of family. Another case study, this one fictional, is the protagonist of the play (and film), *Educating Rita*.[3] Rita flowers in the world of scholarship, as she also (consciously and unconsciously) takes on new gender roles, identifies with a different socio-economic class, becomes self-confident, and joins the academic culture—a transformation that alienates her from her unambitious husband who no longer understands her. In both these cases, there is no way to undo the change—even if it were desired.

This is a pervasive and troubling, often repressed, idea: that education may result in alienation from family, home, and the life one has lived. Martin emphasizes examples with gender, class, and ethnic or cultural factors. It is not, however, only the first-generation college student who learns much but has little to share anymore with her family; it is also the specialist whose realm of interesting discourse is shrinking, the educated person who, instead of broadly engaging in his culture, comes to inhabit an insular subculture or counter-culture, able to communicate with fewer and fewer people about the ideas that matter to him. And perhaps we should also use "alienation" to characterize the condition of the student who learns to adopt an analytical and critical perspective toward a beloved experience, say music, and as a result gradually loses her enjoyment of it.

Another philosopher, Nicholas Burbules, sensitive to "the ambivalent character of our successes and failures" terms this the "tragic sense of education."[4] And, as in the magic of fairy tales, there is no going back. The autonomy provided by an education, ironically, does not include the choice to become uneducated. Moreover, as I noted earlier, there is no way to inform the student beforehand about the precise nature of this intended transformation. Furthermore, the risk and character of such alienation is highly individual.

The loss that can come with education is a melancholy theme, but before we let gloom or self-doubt overwhelm us, we need to collect our thoughts. It is certainly true that in undertaking an education, whether as teacher or student, we will inevitably be subject to the vicissitudes of life; our best intentions and purposeful efforts can always be stymied by the vagaries of fortune. But that uncertainty, which expands with the complexity and duration of our tasks, bedevils all human endeavors, not just education. It is also the case that some of the unreliability of even our best efforts is not due to external agencies and accidents alone, but is endemic to the educational process. We cannot expect students to be inert, predictable respondents to educational efforts: *the student is not a dependent variable*. There are, alas, students who seem impervious to education, perhaps acquiring skills or information, but without changing in any deeper way—perpetually immature, rigid in values and beliefs, or willfully ignorant. There are also students who hide their weaknesses and avoid being challenged, artfully dodging any experience that might threaten their own self-image ("I am not good at mathematics!") or subjects of which they know nothing ("I have no background in art."). There are also many who are receptive and ultimately become transformed by learning, who are not only more knowledgeable and skilled, but are more confident, compassionate, astute, skeptical, or reflective. Nonetheless, one must acknowledge that the clear potential for failure is a cautionary point and should keep us humble and prayerful in our educational efforts.

There is, however, a deeper anxiety unveiled by Martin and Burbules: the concern is not that education might fail, but that it might *succeed*. Not only is there the possibility of "collateral damage," the potential for incidental harm as a by-product of educational success, but there is also the uneasiness that education's gain carries an inherent loss for the student.

One responds to this sobering concern with praise for the alert sensitivity of such thinkers who attend to the broad and full impact of education, not simply to achievement of preconceived objectives. My second thought, however, is to be wary of the possible romanticization of that which is lost through education. It is a perverse nostalgia that sees all ignorance as innocence. Education is a double-edge sword in this way, but so are all life-altering changes—emigrating to new environments, having debilitating accidents or diseases, winning a high-stakes lottery, or going to war. The liberation from parochialism that comes with education also changes our consciousness, our identity. This is not a threat to liberal education: it is an index of the effectiveness of that education.

In the end, my attitude is one of "nevertheless": despite the possibility of negative effects, we must, nevertheless, educate. Education is not a bond with the angels, nor is it a pact with the devil. We should certainly not deny someone an education out of professional anxiety or timidity; failure to do good for fear of doing harm is not an adequate response.

We must, rather, find appropriate ways of holding on and letting go. When students first arrive on a college campus, it is a threshold day, a day of leave-taking and beginning—full of the ambivalence about the transformation of learning. It is a day of mixed emotions for both the students and the parents and other family members who usually accompany them—full of excitement, wistfulness, joy, anxiety, and relief. On occasions when I addressed this group, I would speak about their mutual need to work out ways of holding on and of letting go. Though a student may come to speak or dress in new ways, to acquire new interests and friends, to change views on religion or politics, to aspire to new goals, the work of "holding on" is ever present.

Martin, who is concerned about such needs, discusses how difficult they can be, these attempts to stay connected, honor, and even serve the "home" culture. The responsibility for "holding on" falls primarily on the learner because the individual situations are so different and the impact of transformation so idiosyncratic, yet there are ways that educational institutions can assist. I once heard of a most imaginative and generous example. It was developed at a college that encourages its students to study abroad for a semester. (Though I never learned which college, it is the idea itself that counts in this context.) Reportedly, many of its students are the first in their families to attend college; the experience of spending a semester in China or South Africa or France is transformative for the students, but it may be an experience difficult to share with their families. With the support of a donor, the college established a fund to permit such parents to join their students abroad and briefly share the experience directly, encouraging bonding rather than estrangement.

Demands for Usefulness

It is a hackneyed complaint that a liberal arts education is not useful. That charge has, indeed, hounded liberal education since the beginning. There is, for example, an early harbinger of that sentiment in Aristophanes' *The Clouds*, in which he mocks Socrates as residing in his "Thinkworks" in the clouds, full of lofty and useless ideas. The perennial complaint has in recent years become a genuine threat because of changes in the political and economic climate of education and because of the multiple ways in which "usefulness" is now understood and promoted. As we shall see, the response to certain of these charges is that a liberal education is indeed useful, though perhaps in ways that transcend the critic's purview; but, in other cases, the proper response is that demands for a certain sort of usefulness would erode or corrode the value of liberal education.

To defend the usefulness of a liberal arts education by observing that it provides a valuable social credential is to miss the point: that is a value gained not from the inherent elements of the experience, but by a snooty social convention. Some advocates of liberal education would prefer to welcome the charge of "uselessness," to reply archly that the indictment is correct but reveals confused values: liberal education is indeed staunchly non-practical (that is, focused on theory) on principle; it is about knowledge for its own sake, celebrating purely the intrinsic values of the life of the mind. That is, as we have seen, a particularly narrow and truncated vision of the rich paradigms and overarching aims of liberal education. A stronger, clearer response can only come after sharpening the ways in which these practical-minded critics think an education should be "useful"—and which they believe liberal education lacks.

In many cases, what the critic means is that a useful education should lead to a well-compensated and secure job; liberal arts graduates do not find natural and immediate places within the job market, they say, and are underemployed and undercompensated. The various (and valid) responses to such a criticism are familiar: liberal arts graduates acquire skills and dispositions that are invaluable in their careers, especially in jobs that give scope to higher human capacities, such as positions of responsible leadership and professionalism. Liberal arts graduates are, in fact, sought after by savvy organizations; they tend to rise faster and go further in the corporate and institutional hierarchies than those who are narrowly trained. Liberal arts graduates are more prepared for the changes in careers that are commonplace among workers in today's world; one doesn't succeed over the long haul by focused and specific occupational preparation.[5] A liberal arts background is required as a foundation for professional education, where qualities beyond mere competence are valued in professional practice. A liberal arts education not only helps one get a job; it helps one know when to leave a job and move on. Liberal education enables a person to view his work, her career, as part of a flourishing life—and not simply as a useful tool for someone else's life.

Despite the readiness of these responses, vocationalism becomes an acute threat when two developments collide: a declining economy and a lack of public understanding of liberal education. Those who do advocate for the liberal arts, such as those who market liberal arts programs, do not help the situation when they buy into the approach of the critics. For example, some colleges are now so eager to show that their liberal arts programs have vocational relevance—especially as "sticker-price" tuition rates have climbed to daunting levels—that they offer career advice with promotional statements like: "an English major can lead to a career as a writer, an editor, a reporter, a librarian, a teacher, or a professor." *Of course* choosing an English major can lead to such a career, but it can (and regularly does) lead to dozens of other careers—minister, politician, lawyer, travel agent, police detective, chef, and on and endlessly on. Such rationales represent a failure of nerve, a "giving in" to the literalist assumptions of the critics that the path from education to job should be direct, as in vocational training. These promotional claims do not educate the public about the practical value of the liberal arts; in fact, they endorse the approach of the critics. Marketing responds to the perceived desires of the market, but liberal education will always be in tension with the market because it seeks to transform the desires of students, not simply to serve them. What is needed is a more forceful, articulate, and public presentation of the arguments listed in the previous paragraph.

There is a different but related sort of charge: an education in the liberal arts is useless in the sense that it does not serve the public good, the needs of the nation—or, at least, other forms of education are more requisite. Noteworthy is the assumption that education should reflect governmental policy and/or social need—a position at least as old as Plato's *Republic*. In the United States today, this sentiment is heard from many quarters; as public concern rises about this country's international stature, domestic prospects, and promise for its citizens, the focus on education (especially on schooling) and demands for its performance and focus become intense. In some quarters, this also involves the elevation of specific types of education, or particular fields of study, and the denigration of others.

A striking example was provided by the current governor of Florida, who just days before I wrote this section, proclaimed: "We don't need a lot more anthropologists in the state. It's a great degree if people want to get it, but we don't need them here. I want to spend our dollars giving people science, technology, engineering, and math degrees." When a backlash developed, he stood firm: "If I'm going to take money from a citizen to put into education then I'm going to take money to create jobs. So I want that money to go to degrees where people can get jobs in this state. Is it a vital interest of the state to have more anthropologists? I don't think so."[6] The out-of-the-blue targeting of anthropology is baffling—philosophers are familiar with such references, anthropologists are not—but let us set that aside as a peculiar choice of political rhetoric; anthropology is the governor's placeholder for the liberal arts (other than applied sciences and mathematics). The governor's argument is that the vital interests of the state should determine funding policy for higher education—a position with initial plausibility—and creating jobs and remaining economically competitive are currently governmental priorities. So what is the problem?

Consider this sweeping generalization: totalitarian regimes have usually supported technical education, never widespread liberal education. Autonomous, critically astute thought and action are not welcomed. When education is centrally structured to serve the needs of the state (as determined by those in power), the lives and careers of students are being used as a means to support a policy goal. A strong nation must of course have well-trained people, and today that includes those in the STEM subjects.[7] Liberal arts education insists that the primary purpose of education is to enhance the lives of individuals—and thereby to create the fabric of a more vibrant society. Of course, that includes a career (not just a "job," incidentally), but there is a great and important distance between feeding the immediate needs of business and preparing students to go beyond competence toward fulfilling and worthy work. Both governmental and business policy-makers tend to focus on the short term; liberal education is focused on the long term. I believe that education, indeed liberal arts education, is a public good; it also is a good that is instrumental for commerce and economic strength. But this good is not achieved—in fact, it is threatened—by the hegemony of other goals and needs over the liberal education of individuals.[8]

Certainly, it is important to articulate and proclaim the impact of a liberal education on "real life" issues; to provide savvy career counseling; to encourage engagement in additional forms of training and learning outside the liberal arts; to incorporate internships that provide opportunities to apply and test knowledge and to reflect on the experience; to teach how to learn; to encourage life-long learners; and to demonstrate the ways in which the liberal arts inform and sustain the professions. It is also important, however, to retain the claim for intrinsic value; to reject a narrow interpretation of "practical"; to educate the public regarding liberal education; to maintain a studied indirectness in the ties to jobs or careers. An enlightened concept of the practical can be embraced by liberal education and yet stand in contrast to technical training.

Illusion and the Frailty of Memory

Plato identified the two hindrances to learning that bedevil education in all its forms: *forgetting* and *false knowledge*. It is worth taking a moment on each of these, not only because they are perennial concerns, but also because they have interesting relationships to contemporary threats as well.

Forgetting is an eternal peril to learning of all kinds. It seems to render futile the effort of education. Forgetting is an especially horrendous prospect for liberal education, because loss of what has been learned suggests one might actually regress, lose whatever "liberation" one has gained. Can we, as T. S. Eliot once imagined, lose our wisdom in knowledge, and our knowledge in information?[9]

Under any common definition of "memory"—for example, "the ability of an organism to store, retain, and subsequently retrieve information"—human beings have, in fact, phenomenal memories. But human beings also forget experiences, including notably what we have learned or are expected to learn. We seem to retain on average only about ten percent of what we are told in lectures; fortunately, visual aids, drama, mnemonic devices, and other techniques, along with active engagement, can increase that percentage. Linking emotional experiences with occasions of learning can also increase retention. Nonetheless, much content is never really acquired, and if we test after some period of time, the percentage of information remembered accurately declines hopelessly. Our memories function selectively and tend to distill or distort what we have learned. But we also seem to need to forget, to dispose of the past; an abnormally retentive memory for all one's days is a disabling phenomenon.

The fact that we forget so much of what we have learned causes us to wonder: *When we forget something, is it somehow still there, latent but available, functioning in a way we may not know? If we forget something and it is irretrievably lost to us, are we still cognitively different somehow from what we would have been if we had never learned it? What does "being educated" require us to remember? Is there a difference between knowing and remembering?*

Some of these questions require, and, in part, have received, answers from empirical research. Cognitive neuroscience has greatly altered and enhanced our understanding of memory and has refined and focused philosophical questions about its operations. Cognitive science, has, for example, revealed the physiological basis for distinguishing our sensory memory, short-term memory, and long-term memory, and each of these has become elaborated into multiple components. It is clear that there is a neurological difference between actively drawing upon those things we know well, and the retrieval process of "calling to mind" things we remember. Memories have been classified by their content (autobiographical or visual memory, for example) and by their "temporal direction" (memories of past events versus memories of one's intentions for the future). The research shows that, although such factors as the strength of a recollection, repetitions, sleep, stress, and other conditions can affect memory, we forget at a predictable and distressingly exponential rate.[10]

What is especially important for our consideration is that we tend to forget unassociated data, disconnected or "orphaned" files of information, most rapidly. Connections across a network of information help both retention and retrieval, and there is indeed a difference between forgetting a datum (a date, a name, the spelling of a word) and losing a "cognitive perspective" one has gained. Say I once learned a great deal about the history of philosophy, but soon began to lose some of the facts—where Schopenhauer was professor or the name of the editor of Aristotle's standard reference—then all too quickly, I may—especially if I am not

teaching or researching philosophy—begin to forget more significant matters (Zeno's paradoxes or Kant's antinomies or Mill's
proposal for evaluating pleasures). But as such erosion occurs, I
may retain the general picture—important issues and schools of
thought, profiles of leading figures, a sense of the flow of ideas, and
so on. Learning is about building long-term memory; education
is about building a vast network of long-term memory. A liberal
education, in developing cognitive perspectives, attitudes and
outlooks, values and world-views, makes lasting alterations in the
psyche. The provision of such networks encourages retention and
retrieval, making relearning an easier task when forgetting occurs.
Active student engagement increases memory, and insofar as liberal
education encourages life-long learning, there is a continuing
battling back of forgetting.

Retaining in memory every aspect of everything we experience
in life would create a huge burden on our psyches. And sometimes
forgetting is a blessing. Yet, because of the sense of loss, forgetting
will always have a tragic quality that mere ignorance lacks—think
of the sense of loss for advanced Alzheimer's patients. In *Philebus*,
Plato asks, "If a man who is full of knowledge loses his knowledge,
are there not pains of forgetting?"[11] Yet, like ignorance, the
forgotten is a continually moving horizon, altering with our
learning and our remembering.

Possessing false knowledge is a continual obstacle to learning.
Plato described this as being in the thrall of illusion: we think
we know the truth, but we do not. It is a form of ignorance,
producing error. But false knowledge is not open to learning; it
is, like willful ignorance, resistant to learning. Why should one
try to learn something one already knows? And how is one to
accept new knowledge that subverts one's own understanding? If
I believe I possess the truth, I lack motivation to learn; moreover,
I may summarily dismiss any other received view as false. I may
reinterpret whatever I hear to fit the explanations to which I hold
fast—false though they be. And if I do grasp a new answer, the
persistence of the old (false) knowledge may be so strong that I
gradually lose my cognitive grasp on the new and resort to the old.

Probably the most famous and vivid demonstration of these
points is the documentary film, *A Private Universe*.[12] Interviewers
asked Harvard seniors, decked in their commencement robes and
eager for graduation, "What causes the seasons—why is it warmer

in the summer than in the winter?" One after another, they confidently explained that the earth is closer to the sun in the summer, which produces greater warmth. "What causes the phases of the moon?" They replied that it was the Earth's shadow. These are misconceptions, false knowledge, that were repeated by otherwise well-educated college graduates, as well as by some faculty and by ninth graders in a nearby middle school. When the students were given the chance to demonstrate their ideas, to inquire about the explanations, and to be proven wrong, they would seem to discard the old explanation and accept the new. Frequently, however, they would try to blend their original (false) idea with the new explanation somehow, and often they would unconsciously resort to the old idea. The old ideas—the eccentricity of earth's orbit and the long shadow of the earth on the moon—seemed logical and could be visualized (if incorrectly). What has struck science educators about this film is how assured the students were in their false knowledge and how difficult it is to learn if you believe you already know. For learning to "take," the old, false belief must be eradicated. We often must unlearn before we can learn.

Plato understood all this and dramatized it in his Allegory of the Cave. The attempt of the freed prisoner, dazzled by the light of the outer world, to return to his comfort level, "towards the things he's able to see, believing that they're really clearer than the ones he's being shown," shows the reluctance to let go of what we think we know. The resistance can be vigorous, even potentially violent: should someone try to free the other prisoners, "if they could somehow get their hands on him, wouldn't they kill him?"[13] False knowledge persists, especially if we rise to defend it as our very own truth, but even if it is just maintained as part of the old, comfortable furniture of our minds.

Outsourcing Cognitive Functions

After considering the erosion of forgetting and the corruption of illusion, we might be tempted to ask whether all that learning is necessary in the first place. If forgetting is inevitable and what we do recall is faulty, why even try to remember? Memorizing is, after all, a notoriously dull and "rote" process of learning. Why not just put the knowledge into external storage—in digital memories, DVDs, computer hard drives, or the Cloud—and retrieve it as needed? Is not access-on-demand the solution to forgetting? And do we not also reduce the subjective factors that contribute to false knowledge when we outsource our knowledge? If asked why it is warmer in the summer, I can simply look up an authoritative explanation. Has not technology solved these two perennial problems with a literal *deus ex machina*? Forgetting is so yesterday. Already there are books devoted to the negative consequences of our becoming a society in which nothing is forgotten.[14] (It is a tragic irony that at the same time, our most feared disease is now Alzheimer's, which devastates an individual's memory.)

Jean-François Lyotard prophesied in *The Post-Modern Condition: a Report on Knowledge*: "We may thus expect a thorough exteriorization of knowledge with respect to the "knower," at whatever point he or she may occupy in the knowledge process. The old principle that the acquisition of knowledge is indissociable from the training (*Bildung*) of minds, or even of individuals, is becoming obsolete and will ever more be so."[15] Is this correct? Is it inevitable? Would it be a good thing?

It is a complex issue, one that—like many of the other questions we have encountered—is worth a book on its own. Outsourcing digitized information in vast, searchable networks clearly has enormous advantages for scholarship, commerce, and for social and political life. When we considered information literacy as a skill of learning, I observed that there has never been a better time to be a scholar; the digitized resources now available for mining are breathtaking. These advantages notwithstanding, I believe that Lyotard's vision, the exteriorization of knowledge and the outsourcing of cognitive functions, also may constitute a peculiar, contemporary threat to liberal education.

The effect is cumulative. First, knowledge is biodegradable for the individual, given our continual forgetting. Second, human knowledge in general seems perishable, given the exponential rate at which it is expanded and revised or discarded by research. Third, we now introduce the capacity to shelve and search vast amounts of information, and to give easy access to all this information. The ironic result is a devaluing of information, perhaps a devaluing of knowledge, even an uneasy sense—as Lyotard asserts—that the training of minds is no longer required to create and use knowledge. In recent decades, we have, with technological advances, separated reproduction from sex—a distinction once imagined only in science fiction, if at all. *Can we likewise separate knowledge from education?*

A first step is to distinguish information from knowledge. Rapid technological progress is permitting us to offload information, to encode digitally images, sounds, and texts, at an astonishing rate and with great detail (that is, with high resolution or fine grain). What we may store personally in our computer hard drives or in online storage is miniscule compared to what the giant information corporations like Google store in their vast "farms" of servers. But vast information is still information. Are we storing knowledge? Well, we are doing more than parking bits of data; we are connecting the data in patterns of access, retrieval, affinity, and usage, and then recording this information as metadata. Is that what constitutes knowledge: data organized by metadata?

Certainly, knowledge implies system and order, the connection of data by logic or by causal implications or by some other relationship in a network. Knowledge inevitably implies a knower with a grasp of the principles and structure of what is known, a cognitive perspective, an active ordering of the information that gives it shape, and an openness toward new learning. Stored information, exteriorized "knowledge," has no impact until it is accessed, retrieved, and recalled. Gaining access *requires memory*: we have to remember how to use the technology, how to frame our query, how and where the information was stored, metadata terms, passwords, and so on. "Recall" requires that a searcher recognize information and "take it in"—which means that the successful researcher becomes a knower who has knowledge. When we refer to the "knowledge" stored in libraries, we are using a trope; it is like saying I have music stacked in my bookcase, when I am referring to music scores. A performance is required to experience it as music.

What then of wisdom? Lyotard does not mention it. But wisdom involves, among other things, a quality of understanding, a sense of salience, a disposition to use knowledge well, and an engagement in continuous learning. Wisdom engages the skills of evaluating information and knowledge. The exteriorization of knowledge can suggest that wisdom may be unnecessary, supplanted by the skills of access. If the response is that, of course, we need to evaluate skillfully the information we access, then the respondent is admitting that knowledge, if not wisdom, is required *in order for access to have value.*

Merely possessing access to the information on the Web—even if one knows how to search for information—does not equal or replace an education. There are devices that equalize and extend human performance: a garage door opener or an elevator—which respond the same to the strong and the weak, to the educated and uneducated. But there are devices like the piano or the computer that widen the range of human performance depending upon talent, skill, and education. No doubt, having a personal computer or an iPad releases creative responses; but the value of these devices increases with one's education.

One of the earliest and most important ways humans found to outsource memory is writing. Making a note, keeping a record, writing a narrative or argument—or pictorially, drawing a map or a diagram—are effective ways of preserving information and sharing it with others. Socrates was concerned that writing was dangerous to philosophy because it outsourced thinking; for him, ideas lost their dialogical vitality when dissociated from the person who generated them, and when written down they were left at the mercy of whoever read them and used them wisely or foolishly. Though Socrates had a point, he didn't understand that writing also opened the possibility of different sorts of philosophizing, allowing for complex, precise, and grand presentations that could not fit a conversational format. We see him as struggling in resistance to the possibilities of a new medium. That is not my stance—or so I believe.

I certainly do not reject the value of information access; nor do I deny that search engines and other advanced programs permit operations that structure this vast information in trans-human ways. I welcome and rejoice at these developments. What I do affirm as well is that liberal education involves the transformation of the individual, which occurs not merely because of what is learned, but because of what happens during the learning process. Liberal education values knowledge, but also understanding, the skills of learning, engagement, and a development of one's talents and capacities; it requires the student to think, evaluate, express, synthesize, appreciate—and remember. Access to all that is known is a wonderful resource, but it is not an equalizer; rather, it seems to be a powerful tool that demands a liberally-educated user.

Notes

1 Martin, *Educational Metamorphoses*.

2 Richard Rodriguez, *Hunger of Memory: The Education of Richard Rodriguez* (Boston: David R. Godine, 1982).

3 Willy Russell, *Educating Rita* (Essex: Longman Group, 1985).

4 Nicholas C. Burbules, "The Tragic Sense of Education," *Teachers College Record* 91, no. 4 (1990).

5 Documented in Michael Useem, *Liberal Education and the Corporation: The Hiring and Advancement of College Graduates* (New York: de Gruyter, 1989).

6 Widely reported in the media, these and similar remarks by Governor Rick Scott were made in various venues. The quotations here were drawn from "Don't Know Much About Anthropology: Rick Scott Censures the Liberal Arts," by Kristina Chew, posted on http://www.care2.com/causes/dont-know-much-about-anthropology-rick-scott-criticizes-the-liberal-arts.html (accessed November 2011). These remarks led to an outcry from academics, students, and a variety of public commentators, generating arguments in defense of the social benefits of liberal arts education.

7 "STEM" is the acronym for "science, technology, engineering, and mathematics"—fields in which the United States is lagging in developing indigenous student talent.

8 In the spirit of full disclosure: my own graduate study in the philosophy of education at Harvard University was supported by a National Defense Education Act (NDEA) Research Fellowship. Imagine a time when becoming a philosopher was thought to contribute to the security of the nation!

9 The familiar lines are:

"Where is the Life we have lost in living?
Where is the wisdom we have lost in knowledge?
Where is the knowledge we have lost in information?"

T. S. Eliot, "Choruses from *The Rock*" (1934) in *T. S. Eliot: The Complete Poems and Plays, 1909–1950* (New York: Houghton Mifflin Harcourt, 1971).

10 For a survey of current science supporting these points, see Alan Baddeley, Michael W. Eysenck, and Michael C. Anderson, *Memory* (New York: Taylor & Francis, 2009), or David Lieberman, *Human Learning and Memory* (Cambridge: Cambridge University Press, 2012).

11 Plato, *Philebus*, 52, trans. Jowett, Internet Classics Archive, http://classics.mit.edu/Plato/philebus.html (accessed November 2011).

12 *A Private Universe*, prod. and dir. M. H. Schneps, P. M. Sadler (Pyramid Films, 1988).

13 Plato, *Republic*, trans. G. M. A. Grube, rev. C. D. C. Reeve (Indianaplois, IN: Hackett Publishing, 1992), 515e and 517a.

14 See, for example, Viktor Mayer-Shönberger, *Delete: The Virtue of Forgetting in the Digital Age* (Princeton, NJ: Princeton University Press, 2011).

15 Jean-François Lyotard, *The Postmodern Condition*, 4.

12

Newfound Threats

Many shall run to and fro, and knowledge shall be increased.
DANIEL 12:4

The outsourcing of cognitive functions—the last issue of the previous chapter—is but one example of issues that, despite ancient resonance, take on new urgency and import as a result of contemporary developments. Changes in knowledge, technology, and culture produce changes in education; seldom are they unproblematic. Evolution implies irreversible processes. When we value a tradition but believe it must remain vital and open to its own evolution, it is difficult but all-important to distinguish the novel and unexpected from the genuinely threatening. Which changes should be welcomed or accommodated, and which resisted or rejected? Misjudgments can make one either a hidebound, antiquated, traditionalist who stultifies the education he values, or a collaborationist dupe who betrays that education and facilitates its demise. Good judgment can't be guaranteed, of course, but it is helped by thoughtful analysis and regular reflection on the defining elements of what truly matters in the tradition. Keeping this in mind, let us consider first the case of specialization.

Specialization

The claim that specialization is a threat to liberal education seems intuitively correct: the nub of the problem seems to involve a conflict between narrowness and breadth. Because I think specialization is sometimes misunderstood, I want first to consider what it entails, what advantages and disadvantages it has, and then explore the ways it might be threatening.

In general, "specialization" refers to the articulation and separation of tasks or roles within a system. From an evolutionary perspective, creatures "specialize" when they adapt to a specific function or environment; their specialization often is reflected in the formation of a particular feature or behavior. The rapid development of prefrontal lobes in *homo sapiens* reflects a specialization, as do the very large eyes of nocturnal creatures, and the koala diet of eucalyptus leaves. These specializations responded to evolutionary "pressure," which is to say they gave a survival advantage to the species that developed them. In the latter two examples, and in most such cases, the specialized developments better suit the organisms to a particular niche, but may also make them more vulnerable to environmental changes or habitats outside their normal range. The increased brain capacity and expanded functionality (such as the ability to use complex symbol systems and to think metaphorically), on the other hand, gave *homo sapiens* increased flexibility in adapting to environments, indeed in controlling environments.

A second conception of specialization arises within a society: we commonly call it "division of labor." Not only as a collective, but as individuals, we stand to gain more if we divide the tasks that need to be accomplished, allowing for individual assignments that reflect skills, resource locations, and coordinated sequencing of tasks. The specialization is not only by general category—production of food, construction of shelter and other structures, defense against enemies, and so on—but it is within each such category. Food production alone is now an enormously complex global web of specialized tasks, from growers and producers of specific food items at the start of the task to home cooks, chefs, and wait staff at the end.

In both the evolutionary and social forms, specialization differentiates advantageously. Cells become specialized for light reception or oxygen delivery or combat against invading disease; organisms become specialized for deep water locomotion or desert survival. In society, people specialize to play specific occupational and social roles; this is cooperative diversification. In both cases, specialization allows for a form of flourishing, for the achievement of goals that are otherwise unattainable. But it also diminishes the ability of the individual to survive outside a system that has all the required component specializations; it creates an ecology in which mutual dependence reigns. Our eyes can only function if the blood and muscle and brain and other tissue do their work, and few of us could survive, let alone thrive, if we were required to meet all our own needs for ourselves—from food and shelter to entertainment.

This elementary analysis applies equally well to specialization in the pursuit and dissemination of knowledge. In fact, I think both forms of specialization apply. Specialized studies and research methods evolve to pursue a particular niche of knowledge; new forms of inquiry give us advantageous perspectives on old issues as well. It is also true that an intellectual division of labor arises to understand complex issues. Specialization in the pursuit of knowledge should allow us to advance our understanding in ways that are otherwise unattainable—and that it has done so is, I think, beyond doubt. It also creates a more elaborate, intricate, reticulated arrangement of scholarship, increasing the dependence of each specialty on all the others. It is rare these days that even highly specialized research does not at least employ tools or techniques or paradigms drawn from another specialty—for example, whole-organism biologists focused on a single species may regularly need to employ tools from molecular biology; or they may adopt economic models as heuristic devices for explaining social interactions.

Specialization also increases the vulnerability of those who specialize: just as makers of buggy whips were done in by the coming of the automobile, so scholars of "Soviet Policy Studies" had to scramble when the Soviet Union collapsed, revealing a panoply of suppressed cultural richness and diversity. Academic specialization is an expensive investment for the individual, yet society benefits from having specialists.[1]

When we talk of the specialization of knowledge, we usually employ spatial metaphors: it implies *deep* understanding of particulars in a *narrow* field. Specialized knowledge is authoritative; to acquire it is to become an expert. This is as opposed to having a *superficial* understanding of generalities across a *broad* area. This is the dilettante, who may be provocative and even creative, but who has no authority or special role in the division of epistemic labor. Or so goes the familiar story. But it is also possible to specialize at any locus or level of study. What I mean is that one can, in principle, become an expert in making connections between two specialties, an expert in collating and interpreting information from a range of research, or in researching problems or topics that connect fields.

How then is such intellectual specialization a threat to liberal education? It is true that the aims of liberal education are larger than securing competence in a narrow specialty, but that does not mean that specialization is hostile to those aims. Only when specialization becomes hermetically-sealed compartmentalization is the possibility of liberal education diminished. If the elaborate network of intellectual relationships, the intricate cluster of mutually-supporting intellectual pursuits, becomes fragmented or forgotten, then the chances for intellectual cross-fertilization and synthesis are reduced. An expert who simply doesn't care about other forms of expertise is practicing tunnel vision of a self-destructive sort; he not only risks the form of alienation described in the previous section, but he also does damage to the epistemic ecology. We encountered this general principle of epistemic ecology once before: the *principle of the congeniality of excellences*.[2] Advocates for and educators in the liberal arts need to make vivid the fact of epistemic ecology, to make explicit the principle that excellences in specialization are complementary, and to apply this understanding in both research and other modes of learning.

The contemporary scene displays hyper-specialization, and it has generated a multifaceted phenomenon that does constitute a serious threat to liberal education: educational compartmentalization, academic tribalism, and the cult of the major.

It is difficult to remember that the concept of a major was introduced to provide freedom and flexibility in an otherwise lock-step curriculum, through the opportunity to pursue elective subjects of special, individual interest;[3] but it quickly (and ironically) became a requirement at most institutions. Today, it is widely taken to be the defining aspect of a degree (one gets "a bachelor's degree *in* psychology," for example); other components of the degree, especially "general education," may be seen at best as simply supportive of the major, or at worst as extraneous requirements to be gotten out of the way so the "serious" work can begin. Students at the threshold of higher education endure a year or more of hearing parents, friends, and counselors ask, "What will you major in?" "What's your major?" becomes a question of identity, reflecting academic purposefulness. The decision to declare a major becomes unnecessarily freighted and stressful, because it is erroneously assumed that choosing a major is choosing one's career—perhaps one's life.[4] No wonder fraught students feel relief when they can finally announce their major.

This is not to say that the choice of a major is unimportant. In practice, declaring a major will signal academic focus, structure the selection of courses, establish an intellectual home, and identify one's closest dialogical peers. But these are incidental to the fundamental purpose: the educational idea of the major is to have students study something *in depth*, to come to know what it is to know something, to gain a modicum of expertise. This is an idea that is compatible with each of the five paradigms, and it now seems to be a permanent fixture of liberal education. Indeed, even many liberal arts faculty think of the bachelor's degree as the major (the important part) plus all the other stuff you have or want to take to gain "breadth." When an academic unit structures a major, the program is frequently composed only of courses offered within that unit, thus assuring that the program is insulated from extramural influences. The stronger students, flush with Advanced Placement or dual-enrollment credits, are often exempted from much of the general education program. The result is lack of intellectual breadth at the collegiate level. Such specialization is too early, too insular, and too preemptive.

This situation has resulted from several mutually-reinforcing factors: the explosion of knowledge giving rise to a profusion of new disciplines, resulting in a dramatic increase in the specialization required to achieve genuine understanding; the increasingly technical vocabulary that is required for intellectual precision; an increase in the scale of institutions of higher learning, with the elevation of the department as a unit of academic administration; and an increasingly elaborated academic tribalism that discourages dialogue about matters outside one's own specialization. What is threatening to liberal education, of course, is that the concern for one's life as a whole and the discernment of a good life become pale, absent, irrelevant, or dismissed as beyond the reach of serious scholarship. Rampant at research universities, these phenomena are incursive at liberal arts colleges as well.

It is, however, too early for despair. The boundaries of disciplines are eroding daily: disciplinary scholarship and research increasingly borrow intellectual tools, models, and techniques from other disciplines, and new interdisciplinary fields of study mushroom around us. The very terms "discipline" and "interdisciplinary" seem somehow outmoded, but we have as yet no good language to replace them. (Academic departments do, however, patrol their borders effectively: I suspect they may outlive the disciplines that once defined them, rather like the historic but arbitrary borders of nation states that no longer bound a culture or a people.) Moreover, concern for addressing social problems and for ethical issues—at least for issues internal to the field and for that larger set of public issues which the field addresses—still resonates in these institutions of learning. And finally, trends toward experiential learning—study abroad, service learning, internships, and so on—may work to reduce disciplinary insularity.

There are also practical steps that can be taken in schooling to reduce the threat. (1) Educators should reform the presentation of the curriculum and common practice so that the specialization of the major—the need to study something in depth—is conceived *as one of the general education requirements* for a liberal arts degree. (2) Educators and counselors should be clear with students and parents that choosing a major is not choosing a career—music majors may become doctors (if they also have the relevant science courses), history majors may become lawyers, and philosophers may become pilots. Yes, there are career paths that require an immediate commitment to a major, but these are far fewer than educators normally convey, and that requirement is largely one constructed by educators themselves. (3) All majors should recognize their relationships to other fields, by programmatically including courses from other departments, by relating language study across the curriculum, by encouraging the importation of ideas from other fields. (4) We need to teach the interdependence of each of our specializations. The tunnel vision we must adopt for focused research in our specialty should be understood as heuristic only; it needs to be balanced by efforts to infuse, to connect, to generalize, to apply to other contexts—to learn from others and to relate to the supreme aim of a flourishing life.

Former law school dean, Anthony T. Kronman—one of the "worried friends of liberal education" I mentioned in chapter 1— has charged that contemporary education has abandoned the key question of liberal education: "What is the Meaning of Life?"[5] Kronman, however, traces that dereliction to the rise within the academy of the German scientific model of education, and especially to the current pervasiveness of "the research ideal." That diagnosis, I believe, just misses the mark. I reject the view that empirical research necessarily undermines humanistic learning, and in fact I have taken the position that it can inform humanistic learning. The threat is not research; it is the divisive effects of specialization—though I acknowledge that the sciences are especially prone to such compartmentalization, and that the scientific ethos has become dominant in much of higher education. Where I agree with Kronman is his concern that a sense of educational holism, a tie to the profound questions that shape liberal education, must be maintained—a concern as we face the next threat: the commodification of education.

The Commodification of Education

A notable trend in the history of education is the increasing complexity of its apparatuses. Curricula expand and subdivide by subject matter and level and lesson; simple spaces for tutoring, practice, and exercise have evolved to become a vast, tiered, bureaucratized network of institutions; instruction under the tutelage of a master has become the project of a large staff of educators with specialized credentials. The Greeks would not recognize the distinction we make in role, for example, between teacher and academic advisor; nor could they have imagined the partitioning of "wisdom" into a plethora of disciplines. This process of the elaboration of educational practice has a feature that can be threatening to liberal education: treating liberal learning as a commodity.[6]

In recent centuries, we have organized schooling into programs of learning that we call "degrees." The degree is the largest, most comprehensive, unit within which we attempt to structure the learning experience, and of course it is also a convenient landmark, enabling us to certify publicly and in writing (a diploma) the level of learning accomplished—at least, in theory. Ancient schools offered no degrees. What we are to learn, however, has long been partitioned into subjects: even the Greeks recognized distinct subjects—geometry and gymnastics, for example—although these were seen as branches of the single tree of wisdom (*sophia*). As late as the nineteenth century, Newman could speak convincingly of the ultimate seamlessness of knowledge. But, as we saw in discussing specialization, we now contend with a burgeoning roster of subject areas, each with distinctive theoretical concepts, methods, technical vocabulary, and long-term projects or problems.

Moreover, we now divide the learning experience further into pre-packaged units we call courses: self-contained, highly structured, and focused learning experiences that have their own landmarks and certifications ("credits"). In most schools, the division goes further into individual class sessions with "lessons" or "learning objects," planned episodes or modules of instruction that increasingly have pre-set and quite specific learning goals. We divide academic time into semesters or quarters. Tuition is priced on the basis of one or more of these units.

Although this process may have been one of systematic division, today's students—and most faculty members—experience it in the reverse, as a process of accumulation. Students complete courses, check off requirements, accrue credits, which are redeemable for a degree, a diploma, and a handshake: "Welcome to the company of educated men and women!" Part of what I find problematic is the reductionism: learning is identified with getting an education, which is reduced to schooling, which means completing a degree, which is "cashed out" as taking courses and accumulating credits, which increasingly is presented as meeting explicit and measurable performance objectives. But it is also the disconnectedness of these units and bundles that threatens liberal education. Serial, self-contained courses—piles of academic credits—are not likely to address questions that are holistic; some connection of the parts, some making meaning of the entire process of education is required if this is all for the purpose of addressing one's life as a whole. Most often educators leave it to the individual student to connect or weave their various courses into a meaningful education, and they assume it will happen without prompting or attention.

All this partitioning of the learning process into topics and time periods, this commodification of education, makes it more difficult to monitor the development of an individual student, except in terms of the growing tally on a transcript; the longitudinal span of learning any one instructor sees is, often, only the length of a term. Yet understanding the individual learner's competencies and potentials is essential for all student-centered pedagogy, for a liberal education focused on self-actualization, and for assuring that the student experience is likely to match the aims of the program design. The role of academic advisor was created in part to address this problem, and an alert advisor can, at best, serve as interpreter for the student of the comprehensive educational experience.

It is natural for faculty to see their courses as the primary units of educational meaning; but what lies beyond that horizon is *terra incognita* for too many. Many professors can envision the major as a unit, a coherent whole to which their individual course makes a contribution. But it is a precious few of today's faculty who take in a degree as a unit of educational meaning, let alone the key unit, and who calibrate their teaching accordingly. They may be the master of their own courses, only a competent contributor to the major, and simply flummoxed in debates about general education and graduation requirements. After all, what does a first-rate molecular biologist really have to say about whether the degree should require one or two years of foreign language study? The faculty may have collective responsibility for the curriculum as a whole and for the structure of the degrees they offer, but many individual faculty members see themselves as qualified and responsible only for their own much smaller curricular estates.

I should note, however, that the conception of a course is changing. I am not referring to the development of online courses, which actually heighten the focus on individual courses as prepared units of content. What I have in mind is a change in the experience of the course, a change that is especially dramatic at residential colleges. The older concept of a course is that of a *class* that meets at designated times each week, for which homework assignments are given. Today, we need to distinguish the *class* and the *course*.[7] When a student registers for a course now, it is less like simply signing up for a class and more like joining a learning community. These ephemeral learning communities (typically, they last a semester or quarter) certainly still meet at scheduled times in classrooms, but they function on a 24-hour clock. They may involve field trips or field work, service learning, film screenings, laboratory or studio work, collaborative projects, study groups, website construction, virtual class meetings, blogging, or wikis—all outside the scheduled class periods. Much of this is enabled by new technologies of course, but it also represents a revised sense of the "space" one is creating as a teacher. Planning for an excellent *class* is only part of the planning; one must now plan the *course*—the full "24/7" community experience. Although this phenomenon can wreak havoc with scheduling and add to the students' imperative for good time management (students are, after all, likely to be enrolled in more than one such "learning community" simultaneously), I think it is a healthy development, because it is one hopeful move toward the reunification of the learning experience: it unites the otherwise disconnected experiences of in-class and out-of-class time—at least within the universe of one course.

Despite my optimism, I believe it is important not merely to celebrate, but also to reclaim effectively, the supreme purpose of liberal education. That involves honoring liberal education as an organic process, not as a collection of discrete learning experiences. A profound educational paradox underlies this situation: one cannot put the supreme purpose of discerning and preparing for a good life as the direct and immediate objective of teaching without thereby distorting the process and likely missing the mark. "Flourishing" is not likely to appear as a learning objective on any course syllabus. One works directly on subsidiary purposes, at most—the study of the cultural legacy or the understanding of the world—or on contributory skills like critical thinking and effective communication. But it is also a mistake to forget about the supreme purpose altogether. When that happens, subsidiary aims rule: education becomes simply about completing courses and gaining credits; there is no value beyond knowing great works, engaging in political action, absorbing a particular body of knowledge, honing a career, or acquiring a skill; moral education may become vestigial; and liberal education fades. The ultimate aim of liberal education—the normative concern for one's life as a whole and for living a human life well—needs to be a felt presence in our educational efforts. At the proper distance and height, yes, but tethered securely, and a felt presence nonetheless. It is the recognition of such a presence that guides the learner and makes a teacher truly an educator.

Losing the Personal and the Communal

For decades now, sociologists and philosophers have worried that our increasingly globalized society induces a loss of the personal, the communal, and diminishes a sense of place. During these same decades, higher education has mounted larger classes, many with hundreds of students; accommodated an increase in commuter (non-residential) schooling; and facilitated an explosion of distance education, with both non-profit and for-profit online programs. These changes have clear-cut rationales: wider access to higher education, efficiency of operation, reduced cost, convenience for students, focused use of faculty time, and so on. They enable new pedagogical possibilities. They also carry *prima facie* an impersonal quality, the absence of a genuine learning community, and an eroded sense of place. These concomitant effects, if real and unmitigated, represent a threat to liberal education.

Both person and place matter to learning. It is a cheap and condescending response to sentimentalize that claim: one pictures nostalgic alumni recalling fondly their callow days with favorite professors in the hallowed halls of ivy. (Nonetheless, it is an interesting truth that persons and places do loom large in graduates' memories of college—often they are remembered more vividly than what was learned.) There is in fact an incisive point to be made about the mattering of persons and places.

The tradition of liberal arts education has long been identified with what I will call *the pedagogy of the personal*. By this phrase I mean the notion that having an interactive relationship between student and teacher matters, and the character of that relationship infuses what is learned. It has the corollary that the personal qualities of teachers are educationally relevant. This is a notion difficult to pin down. It is not merely the obvious truth that how the teacher teaches and grades has a bearing on a student's learning. It involves subtler claims that all knowledge, all learning, is personalized, revealing commitments and individuality; that liberal education involves coming to know *persons*, as well as knowing how and knowing that.

One can display one's personality through the performance and content of a lecture, whether that lecture is to a few, to hundreds, or posted online. Some teachers are masters at the art of the lecture, conveying a rich sense of personality, even intimacy. (I think, for example, of Leonard Bernstein's six Norton Lectures, "The Unanswered Question," taped for broadcast in a standing-room-only Sanders Theater at Harvard University.) Teaching is self-expression and self-revelation, as is learning from and with a teacher. But display of personality is only one part of the process; the whole resides in the view of education as an *interaction* of personalities, in relationships between students and teachers—and among students themselves. When students and faculty form a learning community, new and important learning phenomena emerge and affect all present: diverse viewpoints, contrarian sentiments, spontaneous responses, serendipitous insights, confirmation of one's ideas, support for the effort to understand amid confusion, prompt correction of misunderstandings, surprising questions, and many more.

Students can be challenged in an impersonal way, but an education can also be challenging *because it is personal*. In such an educational climate, there are no bystanders. Students cannot hide in anonymity. Assignments are less likely to be seen as merely "academic" exercises, in the pejorative sense.

Perhaps, to prevent misunderstanding, I should state clearly that I am not referring or giving support to an intrusive pedagogy of divulgence. The personal pedagogy I have in mind does not require that students produce assignments in which they must share their deepest secrets, reveal their greatest fears, describe their first sexual encounters, discuss their family relationships, or other matters that invade their privacy. (Sometimes these aspects of their lives are startlingly volunteered, but that is quite a different situation from turning such disclosures into instructional fodder.) Nor am I speaking of a master-disciple relationship, in which emulous students profess the beliefs and values of the teacher and dutifully adopt the master's ways.

The achievement of high quality in any endeavor requires care; it doesn't require efficiency. In liberal education, quality requires care, not just about the subject, but also about the student. In setting the possibility of a flourishing life as its highest purpose, it ultimately values persons over knowledge—or any other subsidiary goal. At its best, being a part of an interactive learning community exemplifies a form of flourishing.

Places are loci of meaning; they have a history, gain character, and shape the quality of experience and figure in the life narratives of individuals who dwell in them. We orient ourselves and navigate in the world in relation to places. These are not new insights: even the classical-era Athenian schools were carefully sited outside the city walls, in groves or other memorable settings. Over the centuries, great attention has been given to the architecture of schools and the design of campuses. The tradition of liberal education has long involved the need for students to leave their homes and travel to a special educational place where a community of scholars could gather and learn together. Place has been necessary for community.

Place can also be a hindrance. The disruption of and distance from other aspects of life required to spend years in a residential learning community is too much of a commitment for many individuals. Recently, technology has offered us the chance to be free of residency, to be free of place constraints—and even of time-specific commitments. One doesn't need to reside on campus or commit to a full-time student status; one can, in fact, access one's course and lessons at whatever time is convenient from anywhere in the world with Internet access.

For me, the optimal conditions of liberal education require a pedagogy of the personal, a vibrant learning community, and a strong sense of place. Residential colleges offer dimensions of the learning experience that cannot be experienced in the same way through other formats. However, in both residential and non-residential formats, we can emphasize the use of new technology to create and enhance learning communities and to facilitate personal interaction (not just instructor–student e-mails). The issue of place is more intractable, I think. For the commuter, place is simply the parking lot and the room where the class meets; perhaps the instructor can make it a special place. Distance learning probably, perhaps inevitably, must relinquish a sense of place for its other gains.

The Celebration of Ignorance

There is yet one more recent development to mark as a threat to liberal education, the final one for consideration here. It is best understood within a longer historical context.

One of the hallmarks of the Enlightenment is the distinction between role and reason as the authority for truth. Intellectuals challenged the stifling assumption that special roles (pope, priest, king, ancient philosopher) carried privileged access to the truth and therefore epistemological and moral authority. Instead, the human capacity of reason, properly applied, gave all normal adults access to the inner light of truth; authority was derived from knowledge (truth) obtained by reasoning upon individual experience, which could, at least in principle, be justified to others. It led to a democratized epistemology and a widespread sense of individual autonomy, both in belief and in moral conduct. The normative vision was that belief and action should be grounded in the truth; experts retained authority, but only because of their superior knowledge and only in matters for which that knowledge was salient. This vision suited and encouraged liberal democracy, but—to avoid social disruption and dissolution—it required that individuals be capable of the rational pursuit of truth and well informed.

Today, this vision has faded. The United States, especially, has had a strong and persistent anti-intellectual populism, but this threat springs from deeper sources. In the postmodern era, we seem to have lost a grip on the value of truth, or perhaps even on the possibility of truth. Truth has become subjective, which is to say that in certain respects, it is no longer the truth. Without an anchoring concept of truth, the will has largely replaced the role of reason. Belief responds to will, not to evidence or the search for evidence; the ethics of belief seem to be reduced to one's right to believe—despite facts or expert opinion. Therefore, authority and expertise are widely suspect or disregarded—why should one take seriously the views of experts on climate change, or movie reviews, or the impact of a specific educational policy? An education that claims to be guided by the authority of the truth is therefore suspect as well. There is no basis for dialogue, no curiosity about other viewpoints; the will of others is not to be persuaded by the truth or by argument, but by non-rational means. Ignorance is not a plight, not an embarrassment or a source of shame; ignorance is normal wear, even worn proudly, a source of amusement and even celebration.[8]

To the extent that this account of contemporary society is valid—and it is certainly not the whole picture—there is both a threat to and a task for liberal education. The values and presuppositions of liberal education, as well as the intended outcomes described for each of the paradigms, are antagonistic to this trend.

Rolling back such a wave of social consciousness is not easy and
will not be accomplished quickly nor by one method. I believe,
however, there is no more promising approach than the spread of
effective liberal education. Unfortunately, when combined with
economic pressures, the chorus of those advocating that students
bypass liberal education is getting more strident.

Notes

1   One might interpret the practice of granting tenure as a granting of
    security in return for the socially beneficial, but individually costly and
    precarious, achievement of specialization. It is an interesting argument
    for tenure, especially applicable to esoteric specialties, but it works less
    well for fields which are highly marketable in the larger economy.

2   See the discussion of Plato's principle in chapter 4.

3   President Charles William Eliot of Harvard University introduced
    the "elective" system of courses in 1885. See his speech, "How
    to Transform a College with One Uniform Curriculum into a
    University," at http://www.higher-ed.org/resources/Charles_Eliot.htm
    (accessed July 2011).

4   My favorite rebuttal to the inflated importance of the choice of a
    major is to recite the backgrounds of alumni I once met in a reception
    line, beginning as follows: the first, a zoo director who had majored
    in mathematics and music; the second a cinematographer who had
    majored political science; the third a philosophy major who was a
    commercial airline pilot; and so on.

5   Anthony T. Kronman, *Education's End.*

6   It may be that one Athenian, Socrates, did in fact foresee this threat.
    One might interpret his dispute with the Sophists as a charge that they
    tried to turn education (and wisdom or truth) into a commodity to
    be sold for a price. For a masterful presentation of this interpretation,
    see Marcel Hénaff, *The Price of Truth: Gift, Money, and Philosophy*,
    trans. Jean-Louis Morhange (Palo Alto, CA: Stanford University
    Press, 2010). In the second century CE, Lucian wrote his satire, "The
    Sale of Philosophers," in which philosophical specimens (famous
    philosophers, not even thinly disguised) are auctioned off for whatever
    price they can bring—amid biting comments about their worth and
    appearance. See *Lucian: Selected Works*, trans. Bryan P. Reardon
    (Indianapolis, IN: Bobbs-Merrill, 1965).

7 In the United Kingdom, the usage differs: the term "course" commonly applies to a "course of study," within or for which one enrolls in "classes."

8 For a forceful presentation of this analysis, see Susan Jacoby, *The Age of American Unreason* (New York: Pantheon Books, 2008).

13

Promise and Prospects

If there is a single term to describe the education that can spark a lifelong love of learning, it is the term liberal education.

A. BARTLETT GIAMATTI, *A FREE AND ORDERED SPACE*

In 1492, the Italian humanist philosopher, Marsilio Ficino, wrote ebulliently to Paul of Middleburg, a Flemish scientist and cleric:

> If we are to call any age golden, it is beyond doubt that age which brings forth golden talents in different places. That such is true of this our age [no one] will hardly doubt. For this century, like a golden age, has restored to light the liberal arts, which were almost extinct: grammar, poetry, rhetoric, painting, sculpture, architecture, music ... and all this in Florence. Achieving what had been honored among the ancients, but almost forgotten since, the age has joined wisdom with eloquence, and prudence with the military art ... This century appears to have perfected astronomy, in Florence it has recalled the Platonic teaching from darkness into light ... and in Germany ... [there] have been invented the instruments for printing books.[1]

The Renaissance was in full flower—a flourishing of culture—and Ficino's delight and excitement simply overflow. Can we today comprehend this shining vision or empathize with this ebullience? Does it now, in our more complex age, seem quaint or naïve to seek cultural florescence and social progress in the stature and hope of the liberal arts and sciences?

In this final chapter, I want to return to one of the questions about liberal education posed at the outset: *What are its place, its value, and its prospects in the contemporary world?* Because elements of the answers to those questions are implied in the work of previous chapters, a distillation of conclusions would be to the point. Of course, these conclusions must be laid against relevant aspects of "the contemporary world." (Some of those aspects have already been discussed as "threats" in the last chapter.) Finally, we can address the place and value of liberal education both for contemporary society and for individual students. With that, our philosophical exploration of liberal education will come to a close.

Liberal Education: A Distillation

Liberal education is a venerable, vital tradition of educational theory and practice that responds to social, intellectual, and technological developments and in turn shapes them. Though it is continuously evolving, it is identified by its supreme aim: the formation and cultivation of a flourishing life. From this ultimate and partly moral concern, five paradigms have devolved, each of which comprehends more specific theories of curriculum and pedagogy and particular institutionalized forms. Though they represent distinct approaches, these paradigms are mutually implicative and complementary; they offer nuanced interpretations of key values, such as freedom and autonomy.

Although this account imputes a deeply moral concern to liberal education, and although it claims a special role in moral education and the value of "educated goodness," it nonetheless embraces a wider range of values in a flourishing life than the moral. It remains, however, committed to the concept and experience of intrinsic value, whether it is found in activities, states of being, or relationships; it therefore rejects attempts to reduce education or human life to purely instrumental values, whether individual or social.

The flourishing life at which liberal education aims derives in part from human universals, yet it is also responsive to cultural and individual determinants; indeed, with the democratization and globalization of education, it is likely that the conception of "the flourishing life" will be pluralistic. In any event, the tasks of envisioning and cultivating such a life are life-long and responsive to life's passages.

In the course of this analysis, I have made numerous recommendations regarding the practice of liberal education, and it may be helpful to recall here at least the major ones. One theme of these recommendations is holism. Here is a list of conclusions that reflect that theme:

- The object of liberal education is one's life as a whole.

- Liberal learning requires us to connect our experiences and may be undermined by fragmented, specialized, and packaged learning; the compartmentalization of life's spheres of activity, the segmentation and commodification of education oppose such a holistic approach.

- As illuminating as the five paradigms are individually, we need to understand their complementarity and to find ways to draw upon them all in a sound liberal education.

- Adequate theories of liberal education must incorporate all domains of practice, incorporating not merely the content of classroom instruction, but the whole educational experience, including the co-curriculum and the institutional setting.

- A sense of place is important to learning; educational technology is best used to create and enhance genuine learning communities.

- Learning must be seen as a part of living, a continuous endeavor that is not bounded by formal schooling.

- Finally, there is a holistic quality to the experience of intrinsic value, in which one delights in something for its own sake.

While these holistic affirmations imply the worthiness of efforts to unify, they do not imply unity. Neither one's life nor one's learning is presumed to be fully unified and integrated; on the contrary, the need for continual unification efforts implies that they are not. Nevertheless, these affirmations do entail that we comprehend an integrated view of the person, involving not only rationality but emotionality; not only a rich inner life of intellectual cultivation, but a life with others in our shared world. It is an education for wholeness.

To bolster a holistic approach, I have made several proposals. While learning to flourish can rarely be installed as an educational objective, stated as an intended learning outcome on a course syllabus, without serious distortion; it should nevertheless be a felt presence in the practice of liberal education. No worthy curriculum or pedagogy can be completely disconnected from the supreme aim. A specific tactic toward such a purpose would be for baccalaureate degree programs to treat the completion of a major as a general education requirement (study in depth), rather than as the focal point.

I have affirmed liberal education as a public good, indeed as a critical need in a democracy, but I have rejected the blanket priority of social aims over liberal education. Education may well contribute to economic growth, innovation, and competitiveness—in addition to social renewal, cultural critique, and effective policy making—but the promise of social benefits should not lead to treating students as human capital, training them for specific occupational slots, simply "educating for economic participation."[2] Liberal learning is of individuals, by individuals, and—at least proximately—for individuals.

But hold, please! Do not misunderstand this as a narcissistic view: learning is best accomplished in community. Nor is it an egoistic view: on the contrary, pursuing a flourishing life entails engagement with the world of work and the public sphere as well as the personal and private; it entails forming caring relationships and participating in a thriving community. Neither do I mean to suggest that each student should first and last be concerned with her own flourishing, only slowly coming to recognize that the flourishing of others is necessarily instrumental to her own. My point here is about the focus of *educators*. Educators must remember that learning happens in the minds of individuals; that liberal education is a person-centered and personal process; and that their efforts are devoted to the achievement of a good life that is distinctively each individual student's life. After all, the process of liberal education aspires not only to enable and deepen individual autonomy, but also to transform the agent as an agent. An individual with such an education will take her place in the social and economic order; the influence of many such individuals will generate the social benefits that are the hope of governmental and economic planners; and they will also critique and seek to reform that social and economic order in ways no one may anticipate in advance.

Our World

Our world is, everyone agrees, globalized—though the interpretations of "globalization" vary and the responses to it are divergent. We may debate whether an emerging cosmopolitan culture is a fact (and a shame), or whether we simply have enabled greater economic and cultural interactions on a global scale. It is clear that many of the world's problems—climate change and other environmental issues, the distribution of water and food, immigration, epidemic diseases—are transnational; indeed, they problematize the nation state. Virtually everyone now understands that local and global economies are interconnected. Just at the time when many of the world's oppressed peoples reach for democracy, citizens of developed Western democracies are, in great numbers, disillusioned with their governments, which seem unable to address vital issues intelligently and effectively. New media have made the pluralism of the world more vivid, yet also created bridges of human understanding. Centralized authority is, in many domains, being overtaken by the diffused authority of networks. To say the obvious: our world is increasingly complex.

Flourishing in our world requires the understanding of other cultures, not only for global citizenship and international policy-making, but even for the workplace and in our neighborhoods. Sorting out the competing claims of cultural identity and cosmopolitan consciousness is an insistent task for everyone. As we drown in information and manipulative advertising, the need for critical reasoning and data-informed judgment is vital both to individual plans and to public policy. Environmental problems have led us gradually to replace a posture of dominion over the earth with one of stewardship of the natural world. An ecologically sound and sustainable stewardship requires both knowledge (scientific, economic, and political) as well as shared moral commitments. A similar combination of knowledge and values is needed to cope with the burgeoning possibilities of therapeutic and creative biology— genetic alterations and other forms of human enhancement. As the sense of globalization increases, so does the realization of economic disparity and its consequences—a profound issue of social justice that clouds the human prospect.

Such a world is not the place for simplistic solutions; now is not the time for simple-mindedness. Yet many people, in coping with such issues, grasping for common sense, searching for anchoring, find them attractive. Some act as though ethical commitment requires closed-mindedness: ignorance, willful and proud, is celebrated. (Unreflective deontologists are even more dangerous than unreconstructed Utilitarians.) Technological advances and sophisticated consumer information tracking have made it possible for people to stay comfortably cocooned in their prejudices, encountering only the preferred (which is to say the familiar and self-reinforcing) music and entertainment, products, and even news. What is needed is an education for complexity, for globalization, for autonomy, for self-reflection and continuing self-development, for dialogue with other viewpoints, for critical reason and informed judgment, for wholeness and integrity. What is needed is an education that opens us to the possible as well as the actual and the necessary. What is needed is liberal education.

A Contemporary Liberal Education

Throughout our postmodern world, faculties—especially in higher education—engage in the collective dialogue intended to sculpt programs of liberal education that express both traditional values and yet address the world in which their studies will live. Most of these discussions focus on the curriculum, especially the required curriculum. The outcomes are divergent and may individually be adaptive or idealistic, conservative or innovative, clear or confused in conception. They may devolve from a considered and persuasive theoretical vision (less likely) or be muddled by the pestle of academic politics (more likely). The result is, in any case, an institutionalized conception of liberal education, the penultimate level in the "cascade of specificity." (The ground-level interactive experience for the student is the ground level, of course.)

No doubt, many of these debates are fractious and result only in rearranging labels and updating rhetoric. (I am painfully aware that "flourishing" can also refer to "brandishing," "making an ostentatious display," or "embellishing.") But some of these efforts alter the curriculum substantively and subtly shift methods of teaching. They are commendable endeavors in my book when they meet the conditions described above, and I endorse the resulting diverse experiments as advancing the tradition. The best of these conceptions not only reflect the continuities and values of the liberal education tradition, but do so in ways that address the world in which we live.

What are the features of a liberal arts curriculum that speak especially to our world? In previous chapters, I have endorsed many ideas for curricular form, from greater attention to personal roles and relationships to consideration of the social impact of science and technology. Here, I will sketch just a few other elements that seem distinctive and contemporary.

Clearly, our era is preoccupied by issues of identity and difference. The proliferation of studies on such topics is stunning, from women's studies and sexuality studies to disability studies; from critical race theory to Queer theory; from Africana Studies to Latino Studies (to cite just a few). They begin as beachheads in the course schedule or curricular islands; most require a continuing programmatic locus in order to develop further and survive. In a forward-looking curriculum, however, their influence becomes pervasive across the curriculum. Many other fields have learned much, some have been transformed, by these recent interests.

The "globalization of the curriculum" is now a popular academic slogan, and here too the movement is toward pervasiveness. The first level is, of course, to offer courses that focus on other regions of the globe—in area studies, languages, and texts. A second level is the inclusion of these "non-Western" elements in more general courses. For example, in a course on theories of human nature, one might include *The Four Beginnings*, by the ancient Chinese philosopher, Mencius; in a course on the sociology of medicine, one might include comparison studies from cultures on three continents. There is yet a third level, which might be defined as teaching with global consciousness—whatever the subject. Even courses that are devoted to American figures can have such a consciousness. For example, a seminar on Faulkner brings in the wider world when reference is made to the admiration and support of Faulkner by the French, and to his influence on Latin American writers. A course on the American Civil War gains a global dimension when the watchful responses of the rest of the world to this test of democracy are included.

Several times I have mentioned the greater place for learning by direct experience being given in liberal education: service learning, study abroad, internships, and many other forms. A truly contemporary curriculum not only blends aspects of the five paradigms, but also employs a range of methods of learning, including not only didacticism, but dialectic, rhetorical performance, training, master–apprentice relationships, aesthetic experience, empirical inquiry, experiential learning, and collaborative learning. This blend can help strengthen the ties between the curriculum and the co-curriculum. No doubt this alters the role of faculty: the authority of expertise is less dominant, and the facilitation of learning is more so. But it is crucial that the flow of energy be from the curriculum outward, not from the co-curriculum inward. A residential college is a place of learning, not a spa with intellectual diversions.

Many institutions of liberal learning have welcomed "non-traditional" students, accommodating their needs in various ways, such as evening or online classes, special advising and counseling, and different approaches to co-curricular activities. More rarely, however, is the content of courses affected. During this last half-century, we have learned much about such topics as adult development and cultural displacement. In relevant contexts, it would be educationally powerful to use those insights about life's passages and immigrants' lives to help structure the curriculum.

For a final thought on the contemporary curriculum, I want to revisit a point made in discussing one of the skills of learning: information literacy.[3] It is a goal of most current curricula, sometimes stated explicitly. (On the whole, it is good, I think, that we are all getting used to articulating educational goals—so long as we don't engage in distorting reductionism.) I said that one skill of learning, crucial for today, is the skill of determining what *not* to learn. Let me expand that idea. What is becoming essential for educators and for students of liberal education—keeping in mind the cultivation of a flourishing life—is what I will call "knowledge studies." I do not refer to epistemology or to the sociology of knowledge—though the insights of both are relevant. I mean rather a meta-study of learning and knowledge, in which both descriptive and normative issues are considered.[4] Certainly, it would include information literacy; that is, the skills of locating, evaluating, and effectively utilizing information. It would also include comparative media studies (necessarily involving the studies of technology), which would help students understand the capabilities, liabilities, and limitations of oral, written, and visual modes; of scrolls, books, and eReaders; of various virtual technologies; of libraries and networks. It would also address the complex and life-long issue of deciding what is not worth learning and what learning to pursue (and how deeply to pursue it)—issues that involve the autonomous agent's self-transformation. It would lead the student to effective strategies for learning and the "management" of knowledge.

Flourishing Together

We need liberal education, I said. But of course, we already have liberal education. At the outset, I described the positive discourse about the liberal arts and the thriving pockets of practice in liberal education. Nevertheless, the negative discourse persists; study in the liberal arts claims an alarmingly dwindling portion of all student studies; and liberal education is clearly under siege, not only from the threats and performance gaps discussed in previous chapters, but also from the severe economic, political, and social pressures now bearing down on all educational institutions. "Educate the public about liberal education" seems the obvious answer, and I have indeed spent many hours piously trying to do just that, as have countless others. Still, the public that does not understand the term "liberal arts," that does not discriminate among types of schools, keeps growing. I have been generally disappointed, however, in large-scale efforts to inform the public that become "campaigns" and shift in mode from education to sales. The world shapes us even as we try to shape the world.

Increasingly in the West, especially in the United States, education is seen as a "special interest," one among others clamoring for influence and money. And there is a sense, an institutionalized, establishmentarian sense, in which that is undeniable. But education comprises, in a larger sense, the most general of interests: it is that public good that helps to identify and secure other public goods. What could be more important to a society or to an individual than learning to flourish?

Even the best of a liberal education will not, as I have cautioned, guarantee a good person or a good life. But it is the most purposeful, most percipient, and most effective means of understanding those ideals and pursuing them. If we do not possess, perhaps we do not need, Ficino's sweeping enthusiasm for the impact of education. The simple joy in learning can become the love of learning. Flourishing, like all flowering, begins with a small seed carefully nurtured.

Notes

1 Marsilio Ficino to Paul of Middleburg, 1492. *The Letters of Marsilio Ficino*, Vol. 1, trans. Language Department of the School of Economic Science (London: Shepheard-Walwyn, 1975), 130. The clause, "the age has joined wisdom with eloquence," refers to Martianus Capella's elaborate allegory of the liberal arts, *De nuptiis Philologiae et Mercurii*—the marriage of wisdom and eloquence—written a millennium earlier. See chapter 1 and n. 26.

2 The phrase is the title of the second chapter in Brighouse, *On Education*.

3 See chapter 7.

4 Cf. Shapiro and Hughes, "Information Literacy as a Liberal Art."

BIBLIOGRAPHY

Adler, Mortimer J. *Aristotle for Everybody: Difficult Thought Made Easy*. New York: Touchstone Books, 1997.

—"The Great Ideas." *Center for the Study of the Great Ideas*. n.d. http://www.thegreatideas.org/index.html (accessed May 2011).

—*How to Think About the Great Ideas: From the Great Books of Western Civilization*. Chicago: Open Court, 2000.

—*The Paideia Proposal: An Educational Manifesto*. New York: Macmillan, 1982.

Adorno, Theodor W. "Education After Auschwitz." In *Critical Models: Interventions and Catchwords*. Translated by Henry. W. Pickford. New York: Columbia University Press, 1998.

Agrippa von Nettesheim, Henricus Cornelius. "On the Uncertainty of Our Knowledge." In *Renaissance Philosophy*, Vol. 2: *The Transalpine Thinkers*. Edited and translated by Herman Shapiro and Arturo B. Fallico. New York: The Modern Library, 1969.

Ahmed, Sara. *The Promise of Happiness*. Durham, NC: Duke University Press, 2010.

Alverno College. *Alverno College*. n.d. www.alverno.edu (accessed September 2011).

Amherst College. "The Mission of Amherst College." *Amherst College*. n.d. https://www.amherst.edu/aboutamherst/mission (accessed September 2011).

The Annapolis Group. "About the Annapolis Group." http://collegenews.org/about-the-annapolis-group (accessed July 2011).

—"About Liberal Arts Colleges." *College News*. 2011. http://collegenews.org/about-liberal-arts-colleges (accessed August 2011).

Annas, Julia. *Intelligent Virtue*. Oxford: Oxford University Press, 2011.

Appiah, Kwame Anthony. *The Ethics of Identity*. Princeton, NJ: Princeton University Press, 2005.

Ariely, Dan. *Predictably Irrational: The Hidden Forces That Shape Our Decisions*. New York: HarperCollins, 2008.

Aristotle. *The Complete Works of Aristotle*. Edited by Jonathan Barnes. 2 vols. Princeton, NJ: Princeton University Press, 1984.

Association of American Colleges & Universities, Board of Directors. "Statement on Liberal Learning." *AAC&U*. October 1998. http://www.aacu.org/about/statements/liberal_learning.cfm (accessed March 2011).

Atwill, Janet M. *Rhetoric Reclaimed: Aristotle and the Liberal Arts Tradition*. Ithaca, NY: Cornell University Press, 1998.

Baddeley, Alan, Michael W. Eysenck, and Michael C. Anderson. *Memory*. New York: Taylor & Francis, 2009.

Bailey, Charles. *Beyond the Present and Particular: A Theory of Liberal Education*. London: Routledge & Kegan Paul, 1984; Routledge, 2010.

Bereiter, Carl. "Liberal Education in a Knowledge Society." In *Liberal Education in a Knowledge Society*. Edited by Barry Smith. Chicago: Open Court, 2002.

Bloom, Allan. *The Closing of the American Mind: How Higher Education Has Failed Democracy and Impoverished the Souls of Today's Students*. New York: Simon & Schuster, 1987.

Bloom, Harold. *The Western Canon: The Books and School of the Ages*. New York: Riverhead Books, 1995.

Bok, Derek. *Universities in the Marketplace: The Commercialization of Higher Education*. Princeton, NJ: Princeton University Press, 2003.

Bok, Sissela. *Exploring Happiness: From Aristotle to Brain Science*. New Haven, CT: Yale University Press, 2010.

Bowdoin College. "Purpose: A Liberal Education at Bowdoin College." *Bowdoin College*. n.d. http://www.bowdoin.edu/about/purpose/index.shtml (accessed July 2011).

Bowker. "Bowker Reports Traditional U.S. Book Production Flat in 2009." *Bowker.com*. 2011. http://bowker.com/index.php/press-releases/616-bowker-reports-traditional-us-book-production-flat-in-2009 (accessed November 2011).

Bowyer, John W. *Three Views of Continuity and Change at the University of Chicago*. Chicago: University of Chicago Press, 1999.

Brighouse, Harry. *On Education*. London: Routledge, 2006.

Brown, Donald E. *Human Universals*. Philadelphia: Temple University Press, 1991.

Bruckner, Pascal. *Perpetual Euphoria: On the Duty to Be Happy* . Princeton, NJ: Princeton University Press, 2010.

Bryn Mawr College, Board of Trustees. "Bryn Mawr College Mission Statement." *Bryn Mawr*. 1998. http://www.brynmawr.edu/about/mission.shtml (accessed September 2011).

Burbules, Nicholas C. "The Tragic Sense of Education." *Teachers College Record* 91 (1990).

Burtchaell, James Tunstead. *The Dying of the Light: The Disengagement of Colleges and Universities from Their Christian Churches.* Grand Rapids, MI: Eerdmans Publishing, 1998.

Capella, Martianus, William Harris Stahl, Richard Johnson, and E. L. Burge. *Martianus Capella and the Seven Liberal Arts*, 2 vols. Records of Civilization: Sources and Studies 84. New York: Columbia University Press, 1971–7.

Chew, Kristina. "Don't Know Much About Anthropology: Rick Scott Censures the Liberal Arts." *Care2 Make a Difference.* 2011. http://www.care2.com/causes/dont-know-much-about-anthropology-rick-scott-criticizes-the-liberal-arts.html (accessed November 2011).

Cordner, Christopher. *Ethical Encounter: The Depth of Moral Meaning.* London: Palgrave, 2002.

—"Literature, Morality and the Individual in the Shadows of Postmodernism." *Literature and Aesthetics: Journal of the Sydney Society of Literature and Aesthetics*, 1998.

Crane, Ronald. Ronald Crane to Henry Boucher, 1931. Cited in John W. Boyer, *Three Views of Continuity and Change at the University of Chicago* (Chicago: The University of Chicago, 1999).

Cromley, Jennifer. *Learning to Learn: What the Science of Thinking and Learning Has to Offer Adult Education.* Washington, DC: The National Institute for Literacy, 2000. http://literacynet.org/lincs/resources/cromley_report.pdf (accessed September 2011).

Csikszentmihalyi, Mihaly. *Flow: The Psychology of Optimal Experience.* New York: Harper, 1991.

Curthoys, Jean. "Understanding Others." *Australian Book Review*, 2003: 47.

DeNicola, Daniel R. "The Emergence of the New American College." *Perspectives: Journal of the Association for General and Liberal Studies*, Fall–Spring, 1994: 63–78.

—"Friends, Foes, and Nel Noddings on Liberal Education." In *Philosophy of Education 2011.* Edited by Rob Kunzman. Carbondale, IL: Philosophy of Education Society, 2012.

—"Liberal Education and Moral Education." In *Character and Moral Education: A Reader.* Edited by Joseph L. DeVitis and Tianlong Yu, 179–92. New York: Peter Lang Publishing, 2011.

—"Paradigms and Paraphernalia: On the Relationship of Theory and Technology in Science." In *New Directions in the Philosophy of Technology.* Edited by Joseph C. Pitt. Dordrecht: Kluwer Publishers, 1995.

—"The Philosopher, the Teacher, and the Quest for Clarity." In *Philosophical Reflections on Society and Education.* Edited by Creighton Peden and Donald Chipman. Washington, DC: Rowman & Littlefield, 1978.

Dewey, John. "Aims and Ideals of Education." In *The Encyclopaedia and Dictionary of Education*. Edited by Foster Watson. London: Sir Isaac Pitman & Sons, 1921.

—*Art as Experience*. New York: Capricorn Books, 1958.

—*The Collected Works of John Dewey: 1882–1953*. Edited by Jo Ann Boydston. 38 vols. Carbondale, IL: Southern Illinois University Press, 1972–2008.

—*The Quest for Certainty*, in *John Dewey: The Later Works, 1925–53*, Vol. 4: 1929. Edited by Jo Ann Boydston. Carbondale, IL: Southern Illinois University Press, 1984.

—"Statements to the Conference on Curriculum for the College of Liberal Arts." In *The Later Works of John Dewey, Vol. 6: 1925–1953*. Edited by Jo Ann Boydston and Sidney Ratner. Carbondale, IL: Southern Illinois University Press, 1985.

Donoghue, Frank. *The Last Professors: The Corporate University and the Fate of the Humanities*. 3rd edn. New York: Fordham University Press, 2008.

Downie, R. S., Eileen M. Loudfoot, and Elizabeth Telfer. *Education and Personal Relationships: A Philosophical Study*. London: Methuen, 1974.

Eliot, Charles William. "How to Transform a College with One Uniform Curriculum into a University." *Higher Education Resource Hub!* 1885. http://www.higher-ed.org/resources/Charles_Eliot.htm (accessed July 2011).

Eliot, T. S. "Choruses from *The Rock*." In *T. S. Eliot: Complete Poems and Plays, 1909–1950*. New York: Houghton Mifflin Harcourt, 1971.

Epictetus. *The Discourses*. Edited and translated by George Long. The Internet Classics Archive. 2004-09. http://classics.mit.edu/Epictetus/discourses.html (accessed November 2011).

European College of Liberal Arts. *European College of Liberal Arts (ECLA)*. 2011. http://www.ecla.de/ (accessed August 2011).

Ferrall, Jr., Victor E. *Liberal Arts at the Brink*. Cambridge, MA: Harvard University Press, 2011.

Ficino, Marsilio. Marsilio Ficino to Paul of Middleburg, 1492. *The Letters of Marsilio Ficino*. Translated by the Language Department of the School of Economic Science. 8 vols. London: Shepheard-Walwyn, 1975–2010.

Fish, Stanley E. *Save the World on Your Own Time*. Oxford: Oxford University Press, 2008.

Foucault, Michel. *Discipline and Punish: The Birth of the Prison*. Translated by Alan Sheridan. 2nd edn. New York: Vintage Books, 1995.

Frankfurt, Harry G. "Freedom of the Will and the Concept of a Person." In *The Importance of What We Care About*. Cambridge: Cambridge University Press, 1988.

Freire, Paolo. *Education for Critical Consciousness*. New York: Seabury Press, 1973.

—*Pedagogy of the Oppressed*. New York: Continuum, 1970.

Gallie, Walter Bryce. "Essentially Contested Concepts." *Proceedings of the Aristotelian Society* 56 (1956): 167–98.

Gettysburg College Board of Trustees. "Gettysburg College Mission Statement." *Gettysburg College*. 2003. http://www.gettysburg.edu/about/college_history/mission_statement.dot (accessed September 2011).

Giamatti, A. Bartlett. *A Free and Ordered Space: The Real World of the University*. New York: W. W. Norton, 1988.

Gillespie, Susan. "Opening Minds: The International Liberal Education Movement." *World Policy Journal* (Winter 2001–2): 79–89.

Graff, Gerald. *Professing Literature: An Institutional History*. 20th anniv. edn. Chicago: University of Chicago Press, 2007.

Graubard, Stephen and Steven Koblik, eds. *Distinctively American: The Residential Liberal Arts Colleges*. New Brunswick, NJ: Transaction Publishers, 2000.

Greco, John. *Achieving Knowledge: A Virtue-Theoretic Account of Epistemic Normativity*. Cambridge: Cambridge University Press, 2010.

Griffin, James. *Well-Being: Its Meaning, Measurement, and Moral Importance*. Oxford: Clarendon Press, 1986.

Hansen, Elaine Tuttle. "President's Welcome." *Bates College*. n.d. http://home.bates.edu/about/welcome/ (accessed September 2011).

Harris, W. T. "Editor's Preface." In *The Education of Man*, by Friedrich Froebel. Translated by W. N. Hailmann. New York: D. Appleton, 1891.

Hart, H. L. A. *The Concept of Law*. Oxford: Oxford University Press, 1961.

Haverford College. "Course Catalogue: Statement of Purpose." *Haverford College*. n.d. http://www.haverford.edu/catalog/statement_of_purpose.php (accessed September 2011).

Heidegger, Martin. *Being and Time (Sein und Zeit)*. Translated by John Macquarrie and Edward Robinson. New York: Harper & Bros., 1962.

Hénaff, Marcel. *The Price of Truth: Gift, Money, and* Philosophy. Translated by Jean-Louis Morhange. Palo Alto, CA: Stanford University Press, 2010.

Hirsch, Jr., E. D. *Cultural Literacy: What Every American Needs to Know*. New York: Vintage Books, 1988.

Hirst, Paul H. *Knowledge and the Curriculum*. London: Routledge & Kegan Paul, 1974.

—"Liberal Education and the Nature of Knowledge." In *Philosophical Analysis and Education*. Edited by Reginald D. Archambault. London: Routledge & Kegan Paul, 1965.

Hutchins, Robert M. *The Higher Learning in America*. New Haven, CT: Yale University Press, 1936.

Huxley, T. H. "A Liberal Education and Where To Find It." In *T. H. Huxley on Education: A Selection from His Writings*. Edited by Cyril Bibby. Cambridge: Cambridge University Press, 2010.

The International Listening Association. *International Listening Association*. 2011. http://www.listen.org/ (accessed September 2011).

Israel, John. "The Idea of Liberal Education in China." In *The Limits of Reform in China*. Edited by R. A. Morse. Boulder, CO: Westview Press, 1983.

Jacoby, Susan. *The Age of American Unreason*. New York: Pantheon Books, 2008.

Jarvis, Peter. *Towards a Comprehensive Theory of Human Learning*. London: Routledge, 2006.

Kazepides, Tasos. *Education as Dialogue: Its Prerequisites and Its Enemies*. Montreal-Kingston, QC: McGill-Queen's University Press, 2010.

Keene, Suzanne. *Empathy and the Novel*. Oxford: Oxford University Press, 2010.

Kekes, John. *The Enlargement of Life: Moral Imagination at Work*. Ithaca, NY: Cornell University Press, 2006.

Kimball, Bruce A. "The Condition of American Liberal Education." In *The Condition of American Liberal Education: Pragmatism and a Changing Tradition*. Edited by Robert Orrill. New York: The College Board, 1995.

—"A Historical Perspective." In *Rethinking Liberal Education*. Edited by Nicholas H. Farnham and Adam Yarmolinsky. New York: Oxford University Press, 1996.

—*Orators & Philosophers: A History of the Idea of Liberal Education*. New York: Teachers College Press, 1986.

Kraut, Richard. *Aristotle on the Human Good*. Princeton, NJ: Princeton University Press, 1989.

—*What Is Good and Why: The Ethics of Well-Being*. Cambridge, MA: Harvard University Press, 2007.

Kronman, A. T. *Education's End: Why Our Colleges and Universities Have Given Up on the Meaning of Life*. New Haven, CT: Yale University Press, 2007.

Kuhn, Thomas S. *The Structure of Scientific Revolutions*. Chicago: University of Chicago Press, 1971.

Kvanig, Jonathan L. *The Value of Knowledge and the Pursuit of Understanding*. Cambridge: Cambridge University Press, 2003.

Lear, Jonathan. *Radical Hope: Ethics in the Face of Cultural Devastation.* Cambridge, MA: Harvard University Press, 2008.

Letwin, Oliver. *Ethics, Emotion and the Unity of the Self.* London: Croom Helm, 1987.

Levinson, Meira. *The Demands of Liberal Education.* Oxford: Oxford University Press, 1999.

Lewis, Harry R. *Excellence Without a Soul.* New York: Public Affairs, 2006.

Lieberman, David. *Human Learning and Memory.* Cambridge: Cambridge University Press, 2012.

Lucian. "The Sale of Philosophers." In *Lucian: Selected Works.* Translated by Bryan P. Reardon. Indianapolis, IN: Bobbs-Merrill, 1965.

Lyotard, Jean-François. *The Postmodern Condition: A Report on Knowledge.* Translated by Geoff Bennington and Brian Massumi. Minneapolis, MN: University of Minnesota Press, 1984.

MacIntyre, Alasdair. *After Virtue: A Study in Moral Theory.* 2nd. edn. Notre Dame, IN: Notre Dame University Press, 1984.

Martin, Jane Roland. *Changing the Educational Landscape: Philosophy, Women, and Curriculum.* New York: Routledge, 1994.

—*Coming of Age in Academe: Rekindling Women's Hopes and Reforming the Academy.* New York: Routledge, 2000.

—*Cultural Miseducation: In Search of a Democratic Solution.* New York: Teachers College Press, 2002.

—*Education Reconfigured: Culture, Encounter, and Change.* New York: Routledge, 2011.

—*Educational Metamorphoses: Philosophical Reflections on Identity and Culture.* Lanham, MD: Rowman and Littlefield, 2007.

—*Reclaiming a Conversation: The Ideal of the Educated Woman.* New Haven, CT: Yale University Press, 1985.

Marx, Karl. *Economic and Philosophic Manuscripts of 1844.* Translated by Martin Milligan. Amherst, NY: Prometheus Books, 1988.

Mautner, Thomas. *The Penguin Dictionary of Philosophy.* 2nd. edn. London: Penguin Books, 2005.

Mayer-Shönberger, Viktor. *Delete: The Virtue of Forgetting in the Digital Age.* Princeton, NJ: Princeton University Press, 2011.

McMahon, Darrin M. *Happiness: A History.* New York: Grove Press, 2006.

Menand, Louis. *The Marketplace of Ideas: Resistance and Reform in the American University.* New York: W. W. Norton, 2010.

Mill, John Stuart. *Autobiography.* In *The Collected Works of John Stuart Mill,* Vol. 1. Edited by Jack Stillinger and John M. Robson. Toronto: University of Toronto Press, 1967.

—*Inaugural Address at St. Andrews*. London: Longmans, Green, Reader, and Dyer, 1867.

—*Utilitarianism*. London: Parker, Son, and Bourn, 1863.

Milton, John. *Tractate of Education*. Edited by Edward E. Morris. London: Macmillan, 1895.

Montessori, Maria. *Education for a New World*. Oxford: Clio Press, 1989; Montessori Teachers Collective, http://www.moteaco.com/abcclio/world.html (accessed July 2011).

Mulcahy, D. G. *The Educated Person: Toward a New Paradigm for Liberal Education*. Lanham, MD: Rowman and Littlefield, 2008.

Nagel, Thomas. "What Is It Like to Be a Bat?" *Philosophical Review* 82, no. 4 (1974): 435–50.

National Center for Education Statistics. "Baccalaurate Degrees Awarded by Field." *NCES*. 2011. http://nces.ed.gov/programs/coe/2010/section5/indicator41.asp (accessed 2011).

Newman, John Henry. *The Idea of a University*. London: Longmans Green & Co, 1898; New York: Doubleday, 1959.

Noddings, Nel. *The Challenge to Care in Schools: An Alternative Approach to Education*. New York: Teachers College Press, 2005.

—"Conversation as Moral Education." In *Educating Moral People*. New York: Teachers College Press, 2002.

—*Educating Moral People: a Caring Alternative to Character Education*. New York: Teachers College Press, 2002.

—*Happiness and Education*. Cambridge: Cambridge University Press, 2004.

—"Is Teaching a Practice?" *Journal of Philosophy of Education* 36 (2003).

Norton, David L. *Personal Destinies: A Philosophy of Ethical Individualism*. Princeton, NJ: Princeton University Press, 1976.

Nussbaum, Martha C. *Cultivating Humanity: A Classical Defense of Reform in Liberal Education*. Cambridge, MA: Harvard University Press, 1997.

—*Not for Profit: Why Democracy Needs the Humanities*. Princeton, NJ: Princeton University Press, 2010.

—*Women and Moral Development: The Capabilities Approach*. Cambridge: Cambridge University Press, 2001.

Oakeshott, Michael J. *The Voice of Liberal Learning: Michael Oakeshott on Education*. Edited by Timothy Fuller. New Haven, CT: Yale University Press, 1989.

—"The Voice of Poetry in the Conversation of Mankind." In *Rationalism in Politics and Other Essays*. London: Methuen, 1962.

Oakley, Francis. "Against Nostalgia: Reflections on Our Present Discontents in American Higher Education." In *The Politics of*

Liberal Education. Edited by Darryl J. Gless and Barbara Herrnstein Smith. Durham, NC: Duke University Press, 1992.

Ovid. *Epistolae ex Ponto (Letters from Pontus).* Translated by A. L. Wheeler. Cambridge, MA: Loeb Library, 1924.

The Partnership for 21st Century Skills. *About Us / Our Mission.* 2004. http://www.p21.org (accessed September 2011).

Paul, Ellen Frankel, Fred D. Miller, Jr., and Jeffrey Paul. *Human Flourishing.* Cambridge: Cambridge University Press, 1999.

Peters, R. S. "Aims of Education—A Conceptual Inquiry." In *The Philosophy of Education.* Edited by R. S. Peters. Oxford: Oxford University Press, 1973.

—"Education as Initiation." In *Philosophical Analysis and Education.* Edited by Reginald D. Archambault. London: Routledge & Kegan Paul, 1965.

—*Ethics and Education.* Chicago: Scott, Foresman, 1967.

—"Must an Educator Have an Aim?" In *Authority, Responsibility and Education.* Edited by R. S. Peters. London: George Allen & Unwin Ltd., 1963.

Phenix, Philip H. *Realms of Meaning: A Philosophy of the Curriculum for General Education.* New York: McGraw-Hill, 1964.

Pico della Mirandola, Giovanni. "Oration on the Dignity of Man." In *Renaissance Philosophy,* Vol. 1: *The Italian Philosophers.* Edited and translated by Arturo B. Fallico and Herman Shapiro. New York: Modern Library, 1967.

Pieper, Josef. *Leisure: The Basis of Culture.* Translated by Gerald Malsbary. South Bend, IN: St. Augustine's Press, 1998 (1948).

Pirsig, Robert M. *Zen and the Art of Motorcycle Maintenance: An Inquiry into Values.* New York: William Morrow, 1974.

Plato. *Philebus.* Translated by Benjamin Jowett. The Internet Classics Archive. http://classics.mit.edu/Plato/philebus.html (accessed November 2011).

—*Republic.* Translated by G. M. A. Grube, revised by C. D. C. Reeve. Indianapolis, IN: Hackett Publishing, 1992.

Polanyi, Michael. *Personal Knowledge: Towards a Post-Critical Philosophy.* Chicago: University of Chicago Press, 1958.

Popper, Karl. *Objective Knowledge: An Evolutionary Approach.* Rev. edn. Oxford: Oxford University Press, 1979.

Poulakos, Takis. *Speaking for the Polis: Isocrates' Rhetorical Education.* Columbia, SC: University of South Carolina Press, 1997.

Putnam, Hilary. *The Collapse of the Fact/Value Dichotomy and Other Essays.* Cambridge, MA: Harvard University Press, 2004.

Rawls, John. *A Theory of Justice.* Cambridge, MA: Harvard University Press, 1971.

Rodriguez, Richard. *Hunger of Memory: The Education of Richard Rodriguez.* Boston: David R. Godine, 1982.

Roland, Jane. "On Knowing How and Knowing That." *Philosophical Review* 67, no. 3 (July 1958): 379–88.

Rollins College. *Report of the College Planning Committee, October 1980.* Winter Park, FL: Rollins College, 1980 (unpublished). Copies available in Rollins College Archives.

Rorty, Richard. "Education as Socialization and Individualization." In *Philosophy and Social Hope.* London: Penguin Books, 1999.

—Interview. In *American Philosopher*, produced and directed by Phillip McReynolds. 2011. http://vimeo.com/21268165 (accessed July 2011).

—"Universality and Truth." In *Rorty and His Critics.* Edited by Robert B. Brandom. Cambridge: Blackwell, 2001.

Rorty, Richard, and Eduardo Mendieta. *Take Care of Freedom and Truth Will Take Care of Itself: Interviews with Richard Rorty.* Palo Alto, CA: Stanford University Press, 2005.

Rousseau, Jean-Jacques. *Emile: Or, On Education.* Translated by Allan Bloom. New York: Basic Books, 1979.

Russell, Willy. *Educating Rita.* Essex: Longman Group, 1985.

Ryle, Gilbert. *The Concept of Mind.* New York: Barnes & Noble, 1949.

Sassoon, Siegfried. "Grandeur of Ghosts." In *Collected Poems, 1908-56.* London: Faber & Faber, 1986.

Scanlon, T. M. *What We Owe Each Other.* Cambridge, MA: Harvard University Press, 1998.

Scheffler, Israel. *Conditions of Knowledge: An Introduction to Epistemology and Education.* Glenview, IL: Scott, Foresman, 1965.

—"Moral Education and the Democratic Ideal." In *Reason and Teaching.* Indianapolis, IN: Bobbs-Merrill, 1973.

Schneps, M. H. and P. M. Sadler, producers and directors. *A Private Universe.* Pyramid Films. 1988.

Scriven, Michael, and Richard W. Paul. "Defining Critical Thinking: Critical Thinking as Defined by the National Council for Excellence in Critical Thinking, 1987." *The Critical Thinking Community (The Foundation for Critical Thinking).* 1987. http://www.criticalthinking. org/aboutCT/define_critical_thinking.cfm (accessed September 2011).

Scruton, Roger. *I Drink Therefore I Am.* London: Continuum, 2009.

Searle, John. "The Storm Over the University." *The New York Review of Books*, December 6, 1990.

Seligman, Martin E. P. *Flourish: A Visionary New Understanding of Happiness and Well-being.* New York: Simon & Schuster, 2011.

Sen, Amartya. *Commodities and Capabilities.* Oxford: Oxford University Press, 1985.

Shapiro, Jeremy J., and Shelly K. Hughes. "Information Literacy as a Liberal Art: Enlightenment Proposals for a New Curriculum." *Educom Review.* March/April 1996. http://net.educause.edu/apps/er/review/reviewarticles/31231.html (accessed September 2011).

Shuman, Samuel. *Small Colleges in Twenty-First Century America.* Baltimore: Johns Hopkins University Press, 2008.

Sosa, Ernest. *Knowledge in Perspective: Selected Essays in Epistemology.* Cambridge: Cambridge University Press, 1991.

——"The Raft and the Pyramid: Coherence versus Foundations in the Theory of Knowledge." *Midwest Studies in Philosophy* 5, no. 1 (September 1980): 3–26.

St. John's College. *St. John's College.* 2011. http://www.sjca.edu/ (accessed August 2011).

Straddon, J. E. R. *Adaptive Behavior and Learning.* Cambridge: Cambridge University Press, 1983.

Taylor, Mark C. *Crisis on Campus: A Bold Plan for Reforming Our Colleges and Universities.* New York: Knopf, 2010.

Thorley, John. *Athenian Democracy.* 2nd edn. London: Routledge, 2004.

Unger, Peter K. *Ignorance: A Case for Scepticism.* Oxford: Clarendon Press, 1979.

Useem, Michael. *Liberal Education and the Corporation: The Hiring and Advancement of College Graduates.* New York: de Gruyter, 1989.

Vergerio, Pier Paolo. "The Character and Studies Befitting a Free-born Youth." In *Humanist Educational Treatises.* Translated by Craig W. Kallendorf. Cambridge, MA: I Tatti Renaissance Library, Harvard University Press, 2002.

Washington & Lee University. "Mission Statement." *Washington & Lee University.* n.d. http://www.wlu.edu/x52661.xml (accessed September 2011).

Weber, Max. *The Protestant Ethic and the Spirit of Capitalism.* Translated by Talcott Parsons. New York: Scribners' Sons, 1958.

Wesleyan University. "Mission Statement." Wesleyan University. n.d. http://www.wesleyan.edu/about/mission.html (accessed September 2011).

Whewell, William. *On the Principles of English University Education.* 2nd edn. London: John W. Parker, 1838.

White, John. *The Aims of Education Restated.* London: Routledge & Kegan Paul, 1982.

White, Nicholas. *A Brief History of Happiness.* Malden, MA: Wiley-Blackwell, 2006.

Williams College, Board of Trustees. "Mission and Purposes." *Williams College.* April 14, 2007. http://archives.williams.edu/mission-and-purposes-2007.php (accessed March 2011).

Wilson, Eric G. *Against Happiness: In Praise of Melancholy*. New York: Farrar, Straus, and Giroux, 2008.

Wilson, Woodrow. "Princeton in the Nation's Service." In *The Papers of Woodrow Wilson*, Vol. 10, 1896–8. Edited by Arthur S. Link. Princeton, NJ: Princeton University Press, 1971.

Zagzebski, Linda Trinkhaus. *Virtues of the Mind: An Inquiry into the Nature of Virtue and the Ethical Foundations of Knowledge*. Cambridge: Cambridge University Press, 1996.

INDEX OF NAMES

INDEX OF TERMS